KU-431-156

Thomas H. Cook was born in Fort Payne, Alabama. He has been a college English teacher and a book review editor, but is best known as a hugely popular crime writer. He is the winner of the Edgar Award for *The Chatham School Affair* and has been shortlisted for the CWA Duncan Lawrie Dagger and the Anthony Award. He lives in New York and Los Angeles. *Tragic Shores* is his first non-fiction book.

Also by Thomas H. Cook

Thomas H. Cook

TRAGIC SHORES

A Memoir of Dark Travel

Quercus

First published in Great Britain in 2017 by Quercus
This paperback edition published in 2018 by

Quercus Editions Ltd
Carmelite House
50 Victoria Embankment
London EC4Y 0DZ

An Hachette UK company

A CIP catalogue record for this book is available
from the British Library

PB ISBN 978 1 78206 503 6

10 9 8 7 6 5 4 3 2 1

Typeset by CC Book Production

Printed and bound in Great Britain by Clays Ltd, St Ives plc

For Susan Terner and Justine Cook,
my most wonderful companions in darkness, and
for Sean Melwing and Terner Thomas Cook-Melwing
for whom I wish all the light of this world.

Tourists take their world with them. Travellers go into the world.

Justine Cook

Table of Contents

By Way of the Alcázar

I have come to thank dark places for the light they bring to life.

First lines are important. They set the tone of a book, and in a work like this one, focused as it is on travelling to some of the saddest places on earth, it is necessary to state at the outset that what follows is less sad than revelatory and appreciative. This book is about the power of dark places to add a grave beauty, like that of Hardy's Egdon Heath, so 'oversadly tinged', to our lives. Dark places demand nothing of you. In speaking of them one need not make a great show of deep thought or erudition. In fact, all such pretence should be cast aside in order to receive whatever gifts, often unexpected and sometimes profoundly intimate, dark places offer to those who visit them. 'To know the dark,' as Wendell Berry says, one must 'go without sight and find that dark, too, blossoms and sings.'

In fact, dark places do just that, but always on their own terms, never to be prodded into profundity, or diminished by inflated expectations, or urged to move us in any particular way or teach us any particular lesson. Dark places do not moralize, nor offer Delphic pronouncements. Nor do they promise a sudden enlightenment. At best, we stand like children before them, quiet, listening, taking from them what we can.

I was only nineteen when I first heard the call of dark places. I was living in Atlanta, Georgia, at the time, and had recently taken a job with a film distributor. One of my duties was to retrieve the company's film at the end of the movie's run. On this particular night I'd come to the city's only art house, a theatre that ran foreign films and documentaries almost no one came to see, and thus, in that way, a rather sad place itself. I'd arrived at the theatre at around one in the morning, bleary-eyed from a full day's work followed by evening classes at an inexpensive state college. Mine was a charmless, night-school life, financially stretched and without leisure.

So it was a bone-tired and somewhat aggrieved young man who arrived at Film Forum that night, not at all pleased to hear that the film I'd come for had somehow been mislaid. They were looking for it, the owner assured me, and in the meantime, he invited me to watch the film currently being screened.

The film was called *To Die in Madrid*. It was a documentary about the Spanish Civil War. The history it told was very stark, and I have always remembered bedraggled soldiers and weary refugees struggling along perilous mountain trails. What struck me most powerfully, however, was that in the midst of a film that chronicled such generalized suffering, the film-maker had paused to relate a very personal tragedy that had occurred in the Alcázar, the fortress that has commanded the heights of Toledo since Roman times, and which figures very prominently in El Greco's famous rendering of the town.

On 23 July 1936, the phone rang in the office of the Alcázar's commanding officer, Colonel José Moscardó. He was told that Republican forces had captured his sixteen-year-old son, Luis, and that if he did not surrender the fortress, Luis would be executed. The colonel asked to speak to his son, presumably to verify his capture. The boy was brought to the phone, and for a few extraordinarily anguished moments, Colonel Moscardó talked to Luis. At the end of that brief conversation, and in a tone that could only have been fraught with sorrow, Colonel Moscardó uttered a few words whose solemn meaning would be seared into the memory of Spain. In effect, Moscardó said, 'Prepare to die, my son.'

Accounts vary as to what happened next. Some say Luis was shot immediately. Others say that his execution occurred a month later. But die he did, and by all accounts, he did so bravely. The Alcázar, though frightfully damaged in the ensuing bombardment, never fell.

From the moment I saw that scene in *To Die in Madrid*, I felt a very powerful need to visit the Alcázar, to enter the room where that terrible exchange had taken place, and, if possible, even to see the very phone Colonel Moscardó had held that day in 1936. This need was inexplicable. I had no idea from where it came.

Nearly twenty years passed before I had the means to answer the call of the Alcázar. By then I was married and a father, and so my wife Susan and my daughter Justine were both with me on the short bus ride from Madrid to Toledo. Even so, I felt curiously alone. It was as if something was gathering around me, sealing me off, drawing me in. Susan later said that I 'behaved like a deep-sea diver', alone in the depths, and this was an apt description of the solitude and vaguely perilous anticipation that came over me that morning as I closed in upon Toledo.

The Alcázar is very large, with many rooms, and the crowds that day were thick and slow-moving. They oozed from room to room, pausing at this display cabinet or that one, some filled with uniforms, some with weapons, for by then the Alcázar had been converted into a military museum.

At last I entered a large, rectangular room that was in terrible disrepair, as if a small bomb had gone off inside it. The walls were pocked with holes and there were large chips in the plaster and the woodwork. It was divided roughly in half by a red cord visitors were not allowed to cross. This was Colonel Moscardó's office, reverently preserved in its exact state on the day he left the Alcázar. His portrait hung from one wall, the fifty-eight-year-old Moscardó very solemn in his uniform, a firm grasp on his sabre. There was also a portrait of Luis, very much a young man, casually dressed in civilian trousers and a billowy white shirt. A large desk remained in place behind the red cord. It was about halfway into the room, and beside it sat a small table upon which rested a phone protectively encased in glass.

It looked no different from any other phone of the period. It was black and made of Bakelite. But this phone was *that* phone, the one over which Colonel Moscardó and Luis had spoken on that tragic day, a phone that now rested in sacred silence as lines of tourists filed by.

Most of these visitors did not pause for very long as they moved through the room. But I had travelled so far, and the phone now before me had come to occupy so mythic a place in my mind, that I lingered for a time, trying to imagine how charged with sorrow the air must have been on the day it rang into history. For a while, I simply stood and stared at it in a nearly hypnotic way, as one might stare at a religious relic. At last, I thought, I had answered that strange call. Then, with the crowd pressing around me, I strolled out onto one of the wide ramparts of the Alcázar, looked down at the graceful terraces of Toledo, and to my immense surprise, recalled not some aspect of Spanish history but, of all things, my father. With that recollection, I suddenly realized that the inexplicable compulsion I'd felt so many years before at the Film Forum, one so strong it had never dissipated, and which had brought me thousands of miles, across a wide ocean, into a foreign country, and finally to the Alcázar, had begun with him.

In terms of foreign travel, my father had done it only once, as a soldier during the Second World War. He rarely spoke of any of the places he had been, either in Europe or North Africa, and I never heard him express the slightest desire to return to any of them. In one of the few vaguely 'tourist' photographs

I have of my father during this period, he sits astride a camel, dressed in his army fatigues, sporting a devilish grin. He sent this picture to my mother in 1945, and years later, when I asked him where it was taken, he said, 'Somewhere in Africa,' and left it at that.

My father was, to say the least, not a man of letters. In fact, the only thing he ever said to me with regard to reading was that it caused headaches. He also suffered so severely from what is now called Attention Deficit Disorder that he could barely sit still long enough to watch a television programme, unless it was the *Friday Night Fights*, and even then only the featherweights moved fast enough to hold his interest. But he was an immensely kind man, who worked hard, and I had nothing but respect for him. Still, it must be said that we had nothing whatsoever in common. In fact, in fundamental ways, we were rather like the devout and doubting priests in *The Devils of Loudun*; we sat in the same room, but not in the same universe.

So it was quite astonishing to me that I'd thought of him after seeing Colonel Moscardó's phone. It was even more surprising that I'd suddenly recalled his voice quite vividly, as if he'd miraculously materialized beside me.

Tommy, wanna see something?

I always had, and so off we'd go to flooded fields, exploded barns or some other scene of natural destruction. I remember speeding over a bridge whose actual roadway was under water, so that we'd seemed to plunge into the creek itself, great curls of brown foam arcing up and over the truck's mud-caked fenders as we surged recklessly and heedlessly across it. It was said of Lorca that it was the green he loved. For my father, it was the white. Ice storms mesmerized him. The fact that weight, accumulated one frozen droplet at a time, could bring down enormous trees, crack heavy limbs, snap thick electrical cables, held a genuine fascination for him. He would sometimes approach a bush encased in ice, strike it with his gloved hand so that it shattered in a crystalline spray, then shake his head at the magnificent peculiarity of it all.

Though I could not have voiced it as a boy, I know now that my father's attraction was to the bizarre disarrangement of familiar objects, to all that is topsy-turvy or in some form contrary to the normal shape of things. Lured to travel solely by the urge to see such sights, he sought out barns unroofed by storms, trucks and tractors that had been taken up by tornadoes then deposited in fantastical poses, upside down or standing straight up in the middle of a field. These surreal scenes were my father's Magritte or Dalí, paintings done by nature and hung in the only museum he knew or cared to know.

But of all the bizarre and freakish things my father and I saw together, the one I most powerfully recalled as I stood at the Alcázar, still locked in memories of him, was the scene that had provoked him to utter the only philosophical statement I ever heard him make.

The drownings had occurred at night, the two little boats lost in blackness as they'd drifted in the treacherous currents of the Tennessee River. Earlier in the day, a family of eight had rowed out to one of the many islands that dot the river. They'd planned to return to shore well before sunset, but had delayed and delayed, until they'd finally set off in the dark. During the trip back to shore, the boats had collided and overturned, and all but the father had drowned.

Under normal circumstances, my father would have skimmed the local paper's account of these drownings and thought nothing more of it. The difference in this case was that all the bodies had been sent to a funeral parlour in the nearby town of Rainsville, Alabama, *where they were on display*!

Tommy, wanna see something?

The tiny funeral parlour in Rainsville looked like a crowded picnic ground by the time my father and I arrived. Large numbers of people milled about or stood in little knots of conversation among the parked cars. A long line of visitors also snaked from the front door of the parlour and wound out onto the front lawn.

My father had little patience for such lines, but some mental calculation led him to decide that here was a sight worth waiting for, and so we joined the line. It moved slowly – at least so it would have seemed to my father's itchy internal clock – but eventually we ascended the cement stairs and passed into the little mortuary where, at a still-tender age, I confronted the terrible consequences that may arise from even the most innocent of miscalculations.

The coffins had been placed end to end along the walls of the room, beginning with the largest, for the overweight grandmother, and ending with the smallest, for her infant grandchild. All the caskets were open, the people inside flat on their backs, of course, hands folded together, their skin truly waxen beneath the fluorescent lights. Their hair was neatly combed, and their faces were rouged and powdered to look as natural as possible. Only their lips suggested that something terrible had happened to them. They were swollen and faintly blue, and ever after, these chilling characteristics would represent death by drowning to me; a body filling with suffocating streams of water that rushed into gasping mouths until even the lips bulged with an anguished urge to expel it.

Outside, the lone survivor of this tragedy stood with a few other men, from time to time wiping his moist, red-rimmed eyes with the sleeve of his shirt. To my surprise, my father approached this small gathering. After a moment, one of the men in this group turned to him and said, 'It's a terrible thing, ain't it, Shorty, them kids dying like that?' To this my father replied, 'Yeah, but you know, dying at that age, there's many a bad thing them kids'll never have to see.'

This was the only comment on human life my father had ever made within my hearing, and its grim message could not have been more stark: life was filled with tragedies, some so deep and fraught with pain that to die young, before experiencing *this*, surely would be a blessing. It was the darkest thing I had ever heard, or would ever hear, and from that moment on, it never left me.

I was living in New York City many years later when I learned

9

that he was dying. I returned to Alabama and stayed with him for the next six weeks. He looked tired and faded and was now almost entirely deaf. Even the bold newspaper headlines couldn't hold his attention, so he spent most of his time sitting in a rocking chair on our deck. He rarely spoke, but once he came out of a long silence and said, 'You can't be jolly all the time.' Then, quite suddenly, he began to weep.

'Papa,' I asked, 'wanna see something?'

He did, and so we made one last journey together, this time into the mountains that surround our town. It was summer, with warm air and blue skies, so there was nothing unusual to see, nothing disordered, nothing touched by the dark wonder of our old pursuits. We were back home within an hour.

He died two weeks later.

I poured his ashes into an urn, and placed my favourite picture of him in front of it. There he remains to this day, 'somewhere in Africa', still in his army fatigues, sitting astride a camel, that devilish grin eternally on his lips.

Since his death, I'd thought of him many times, of course. Susan had always called him 'a good person', her highest compliment, and that he'd surely been. But for all that, my father had essentially remained the man who'd advised me not to read, a father with whom I'd had nothing in common, and such would he have been to me for ever were it not for the light that came to me from the darkness of the Alcázar. For as I'd stood on its ramparts that day, I'd suddenly realized that it was my father who had first opened my mind to darkness by taking me to places that held the tragic essence of all literature and art: accident, folly, the utter indifference of nature. He'd introduced me to the weird and the frightful, the arbitrary, the unfair, the inexplicable. In doing so, he'd created a need to see places yet darker and more tragic than any we'd ever seen. In effect, he'd given me a thirst, but he'd also shown me the well.

Since that first revelation, and over a lifetime of travel, I've learned that other sites of dark renown are no less generous to those who take the trouble to visit them. At such places, our thoughts can become unmoored and free to roam, allowing us to experience our most intimate relationship with the past. In a sense, they generously provide a crossroads where two histories meet, our own and humanity's, and the result can be an astonishingly loving embrace of the present by the past. One thing is clear: there is much to be gained where much has been lost, and we deny ourselves that bounty at the peril of our souls.

For this reason, a memoir of dark travel need not be dark at all. It need not be a book of sorrows, nor one long slog through history's abattoir. Rather, it can be, as this one is, a grateful celebration of the mysterious power of dark places to overcome their own darkness, touch us with unexpected feeling, bestow unexpected insights, some of them quite restorative to the heart. They can reintroduce us to ourselves, to those we love, and to all humanity, and by that means offer to each of us, in a different way, an entirely different light.

Lourdes

'Well, God sure didn't make it easy to get to,' Susan said in her sardonic non-believer's tone as we closed in upon Lourdes.

It was late in August 1991, and we were negotiating the narrow mountain road that leads to this most renowned of holy sites. We had been driving for several hours by then, and the oppressive heat now added an extra dollop of discomfort to the journey. Susan was exhausted, as was Justine, but as usual we hadn't booked ahead, and so, in hopes of reaching our destination early enough to find a vacant hotel room, we pressed on along the winding road that led, at last, to Lourdes.

Susan released a long sigh when we finally reached it. 'Cross yourselves,' she said.

What spread out before us was a compact jumble of a town that seemed painfully squeezed into a narrow valley, a place that was not at all picturesque in the way of the many Pyrenean villages we'd seen by then. Unlike those largely sedate mountain settlements, this one, perhaps because of what we already knew about it, seemed to vibrate with the flutter of banknotes.

But I also knew that from the very beginning of its religious notoriety Lourdes had defied expectations. What I didn't know as we wound our way into the town was that it was going to do so again.

At the time of the first apparition, Lourdes was barely French, save that it was situated within that country's borders. Certainly the lives of the Lourdais, as the people of Lourdes called themselves, could hardly have been more different from or more utterly ignored by the great salons of Paris. Lourdes, by almost any definition, was a remote mountain backwater, and the Lourdais were the hayseeds of France.

By the late nineteenth century, however, Zola could describe Lourdes this way:

> *Coming from all parts, trains were rushing across that land of France at the same hour, all directing their course yonder towards the holy Grotto, bringing thirty thousand patients and pilgrims to the Virgin's feet. And he reflected that other days of the year witnessed a like rush of human beings, that not a week went by without Lourdes beholding the arrival of some pilgrimage; that it was not merely France which set out on the march, but all Europe, the whole world; that in certain years of great religious fervour there had been three hundred thousand, and even five hundred thousand, pilgrims and patients streaming to the spot. (Lourdes: Of the Three Cities)*

Even now, the Pyrenees are daunting. Riding on horseback through its mountain passes, as we had done only a few days before we visited Lourdes, is an oddly confining experience. The grey walls of the mountains both tower over and press in upon you. The precipices are high and the ravines are deep. As one narrow canyon slithers around to reveal another, you realize that if you were not with a seasoned guide, you would very likely soon find yourself wandering aimlessly through a maze of grey stone.

The isolation imposed by the Pyrenees is one of its most salient features, and Lourdes was one of the more isolated of Pyrenean villages. Susan had been quite right. It had surely not been chosen in accordance with the old real-estate dictum of location, location, location.

As a matter of fact, before the railway, it had taken a full thirty-two hours to go from Bordeaux to Bagnères de Bigorre at the entrance to the Adour valley, and from there, the traveller had to endure another twenty-five kilometres before reaching Lourdes, the entire journey made by a coach so violently jostled that one such traveller later recommended it as a fitting conveyance through Dante's inferno.

In addition to geographical isolation and Parisian indifference, Lourdes had also suffered from the fact that its people had few means of support. There were no spa waters at Lourdes, so it had not prospered as had certain of its neighbouring towns, and its few industries, such as metallurgy and textiles, were so primitive that by the mid-nineteenth century, they had all but been replaced by more technically advanced processes and people.

The poverty that resulted was grinding, indeed, and there were few families in and around Lourdes who did not live hardscrabble lives. They grew wheat, rye, potatoes and the like, and common fields allowed them to raise cattle and sheep and pigs, but there was little truly arable land and the money needed to feed their animals was scarce. For these people, the wolf was always at the door, along with a host of respiratory and gastrointestinal diseases. To these afflictions were added chronic malnutrition and the occasional scourge of cholera. In every way, Lourdes might have been expected to drift idly into the future, unheralded and unknown, a poor mountain village whose poverty was unlikely ever to be noticed, much less relieved.

Among the unfortunate of Lourdes, there was perhaps no family more unfortunate than that of François Soubirous. He had once dreamed of owning a mill, but a series of troubles overtook him, so that by the 1850s he had been reduced to a common labourer. But even the lowest labour was hard to come by in Lourdes, so that in the end François, along with his wife and five children, eventually found himself homeless. A relative allowed them to live in his dreaded *cachot*, a single room with two beds. Outside there was an open privy, so that the interior of the room continually stank.

It was from this dark, unheated room that François's eldest daughter, fourteen-year-old Bernadette, proceeded on the morning of 11 February 1858. Her task was to scavenge for firewood in an area known as Massabielle, a sandy outcrop overlooked by a stony grotto that lay a little way outside the village.

Massabielle, like Lourdes, had little to recommend it. It was overrun by pigs, and filled with their waste, a stinking recess within a jagged wall of Pyrenean stone. But it was common land, and so it could be foraged without fear of trespass or its consequent penalty, and so it was a small hand, however filthy, that remained open to the poor.

On that morning, Bernadette had come with two other young women, neither of whom saw anything save Bernadette herself, suddenly frozen in place and staring fixedly into the grotto.

Like Lourdes, neither the grotto nor the girl nor the apparitions she claimed to see were particularly impressive. Bernadette was by all accounts a very ignorant girl. She spoke no French, could barely read, and knew almost nothing of Catholic doctrine save the rosary. Early interrogators thought her slow-witted. Whatever cunning she possessed, according to the nuns at her school, was certainly low. For these reasons, it is perhaps not surprising that when Bernadette returned home that day and told of her apparition, her mother first slapped her, then threatened to beat her should she have any more such crazy visions.

But she did have more visions, and not a single one within their number was what might have been expected from such a girl as she, nor did they suggest the spectacular transformation of poor, unnoticed Lourdes that would be their fantastically unanticipated result.

First of all, modest little Bernadette never claimed to have seen the Virgin Mary, though the apparition did finally identify itself as 'the Immaculate Conception', a designation, according to Bernadette's teachers, she could not have heard. Whether this is so, or not, one thing is clear: Bernadette's description of the figure she saw did not remotely resemble any vision of Mary yet known. In fact, she did not see a woman at all. Rather, her bafflingly odd apparition was of a quite happy female child, clothed in white, and smiling, with yellow roses at its feet. Bernadette called it 'Aquero', which in her patois of Gascon-Occitan means simply 'that one'. It did not speak, but it held a rosary and made the sign of the cross. No one else saw anything, and so this first apparition was not timed, though it could not have lasted for more than a few seconds, after which Bernadette returned home to be slapped and threatened and forbidden to return to the grotto, since clearly she could not go there and retain her reason.

But she did return, and this, too, was surprising, given not only that Bernadette was young and by nature passive and obedient, but also that she was asthmatic, stricken with a stomach disorder, and probably already suffering from the tuberculosis that would kill her in a few short years, and thus, for all those reasons, a young girl with very limited strength. And yet, despite a constellation of afflictions that should certainly have weakened the will of a girl who'd never shown much will in the first place, Bernadette not only returned to the grotto a scant three days later, but did so with a dozen witnesses at her side, a fourfold increase in attendance that presaged a changing fate both for Bernadette and for Lourdes.

Once again 'Aquero' did not speak, but neither did it flinch when Bernadette threw the holy water she'd brought with her in order to determine if the apparition came from God or the Devil. After that, she seems to have gone into a trance that lasted long enough to create alarm, so that some of the children returned to Lourdes and summoned their parents for help. This latter group included Bernadette's mother, who wanted to beat her recalcitrant daughter but was restrained by the crowd.

Visions now came apace, particularly after Aquero finally spoke, in the Lourdais dialect, of course, since he/she/it seemed not to know a word of French. On this occasion, Aquero requested that Bernadette 'have the goodness' to attend him/her/it at the grotto fifteen more times. Bernadette agreed, and by that time her mother was powerless to stop her. After the sixth apparition, however, the gimlet eyes of local authority at last took notice, and Bernadette was hauled before the local constable, who, after questioning her, promptly deemed the whole hallucinatory business a girlish prank.

And yet while under this interrogation, Bernadette had remained firm and never changed her story. Oddly, however, this very steadfastness seems to have loosened Aquero's tongue, so that during the next few apparitions the mission of Lourdes as a place of penitence and prayer began to take shape. Bernadette also became more animated during these latter occasions. At the ninth apparition she fell to the ground and began to dig. She eventually found water and drank it, then pulled up wild plants and ate them, an alarming performance that so infuriated her aunt that she was seen to slap her niece as they made their way back home. But behind them, as they walked away, the people who'd remained at the grotto began to cup their hands and drink the water Bernadette had found. The busy, bustling, miracle-working Lourdes we would later find tucked inside the eternally unmoving Pyrenees had begun.

The waters of Lourdes contain chlorides of soda, lime and magnesia, various bicarbonates and silicates, iron oxide, sodium sulphate, phosphate and various organic matter. Since Bernadette's first drink, twenty-seven thousand gallons a week have flowed from the spring she discovered. By believers they are thought to be healing, or at least medicinal, and vast quantities are bottled up and taken home by the six million pilgrims who now visit Lourdes each year.

It is these crowds that now seem most to represent the thoroughly unexpected development of Lourdes after Bernadette, and which have caused it to gain an undisguised disdain among those who visit it, as we did, for something other than a cure. Secular tourists often flee the place as quickly as possible, usually shaking their heads at the vulgar spectacle the town incontestably presents. No less a literary light than Emile Zola came here in 1892, and so despised the place that he later wrote an entire novel – his most successful – in order to debunk it. Since Zola, countless other travellers have come to Lourdes only to see the 'miracle show' he described, and to decry it.

Admittedly, there is much to decry, for upon first observation Lourdes gives the appearance of an enormous carnival sideshow, which is more or less what Flaubert, along with scores of other literary sceptics, called it. Hotels crowd the town, and there is the sort of bustle in their lobbies that you more often experience in theme park accommodations, save that in the hotels of Lourdes, the lobbies bristle with wheelchairs. At our hotel, they were folded up and parked in long columns that spread across the lobby, so many of them that the sunlight on their chrome frames continually flashed as we passed by, which gave us the impression of being incessantly photographed by waves of small cameras.

It was high summer when we came to Lourdes, a prime season for pilgrimages, and the town had the feel of a busy village on market day. In hundreds of French towns, the atmosphere would have been essentially the same. What made Lourdes different was its goods. In other towns of this size, you would have seen the products of nearby fields: tomatoes, peppers, sunflowers, lavender. But in Lourdes, you saw manufactured goods, most of them no doubt made in factories far from town, yet almost all of them connected to the shrine. The variety of offerings was impressive: every manner of representation of Christ and the Virgin Mary, along with countless renderings of Bernadette in a beatific pose, usually on her knees, hands folded before her, eyes cast towards something in the distance. There were entire walls of rosaries, entire counters of prayer books and prayer cards. There were racks of postcards bearing photographs of the shrine, the grotto, a view of Lourdes shot from somewhere overhead, and scores of different pictures of the procession. There were key chains bearing the image of Bernadette and plates bearing the image of the shrine and shopping bags and canteens bearing the image of the grotto. Floating willy-nilly in this welter of religious tchotchkes were odd secular goods: a porcelain Porky Pig and a plastic Daffy Duck, along with an assortment of horses and rabbits.

I don't know why, but amid this sea of religious and non-religious kitsch, I noticed clear plastic figures in the shape of the Virgin Mary. Images of the Virgin Mary were everywhere in Lourdes, of course, but the odd thing about this particular representation was that she wore a large blue crown that could be unscrewed, thus turning the sacred effigy into a water container.

'That's what we should bring back from Lourdes,' Susan said.

I had no doubt why she had chosen this particular souvenir. It was cheap and clearly mass produced, and for all of us at that instant, it represented a hardly imaginable vulgarization of something that was surely meant to hold, both for Bernadette and for the faithful who still came here, some sense of the sacred. In that way nothing could be more appropriate to represent the commercialization of Lourdes than these figures. We bought eight of the smallest, stuffed them into our backpacks and continued on our stroll through the town.

Lourdes by then had proved itself exactly what its worse detractors had always claimed it to be – a religious honky-tonk, filled with gaudy merchandise that catered to the most pedestrian taste. There was nothing serene about it, and certainly nothing sombre. The shopkeepers were almost frenzied in the way they aggressively stuffed their windows and outside displays. Lourdes, in that way, seemed in a hurry to sell you what it could and send you on your way. It was like a restaurant perpetually over-booked, so that it was easy to feel harassed and hurried. Every shop seemed to say: *Buy something and get the hell out of here. We have another group coming in.*

During that crowded, noisy walk through the town, it struck me that Lourdes could only meet expectations that were low. There was too much neon, often of the same light blue that adorned the Virgin Mary's flowing robes. There was too much for sale, most of it absurdly expensive, like buying food in an airport, vendible only in a trap. There was too much bad taste. I thought of the little stall I'd seen years before on the path up towards Mont Saint-Michel. It had been stocked with plastic machine guns, and I'd thought it wildly inappropriate. But now, compared to the spirit-numbing vulgarity of Lourdes, that little stall seemed merely a momentary lapse of judgement.

In fact, the atmosphere of Lourdes was so like a perverse carnival, and the weather so gruellingly hot, that we might have gone directly back to our hotel and left as early as possible the next morning. But something in Susan, perhaps her often displayed intuition that even here something could be salvaged, bid us pause, think things through, give hustling, vulgar Lourdes just one more chance.

'Let's wait and watch the procession,' she said.

This was typical of Susan as a traveller, her intense desire to take from each place she visited all that could be taken from it, to experience it fully and by means of all the available senses, to hear, to see, to taste, to feel. And so, yes, we would stay for the procession.

Those who'd made the journey to be healed had already begun to gather in the lobby of our hotel by the time we returned. It was only late afternoon, but they were spilling into the streets, gathering in their assigned groups, and in general preparing themselves for the nightly procession to the Basilica of the Rosary. There were a great many people sitting in wheelchairs or lying face up on gurneys, attended by a retinue of friends, relatives, nurses and nuns, along with the volunteers who show up at Lourdes each day to lend whatever assistance they can. The commercialism of Lourdes, the town, now gave way to a great preparatory bustle as people scurried about organizing this particular assemblage, or drawing together that one, so that those who'd come to Lourdes together would remain with their group during the procession. It was the sort of dashing about that reminded me of teachers working to keep schoolchildren in line, except that in this case the number of people in their charge stretched into the infinite distance, with more and more coming, so that by the time the sun began to set over the distant basilica, it was no longer possible to tell where the throng finally ended.

By then, I'd felt myself quite resistant even to this sort of scene, and thus unable to feel the sympathy it might otherwise have evoked. The crass nature of the town, the rapacity of the shops, along with the overpriced junk sold in them, had effectively numbed that part of me that might normally have been

23

moved by the hundreds of people gathered around me in their wheelchairs and hospital beds.

Mercifully, night at last began to fall and as the air cooled, a kind of whisper settled over the vast throng that had gathered to share this one moment in their lives. Soon candles were lit, and the hush deepened, and at a signal I did not see, the procession began to move quite slowly, as if to a beat wholly different from the town's frenzied commercial rhythms. There was no hurry in the forward progress, no rushing ahead. The handicapped and the lame, the blind and the deaf, the wounded and the mortally ill, along with those who cared for them, moved behind banners bearing the names of the towns and villages from which they'd come. Many had dressed, or been dressed, for the occasion, in suits and dresses that were often threadbare, a suggestion that this journey to Lourdes was, perhaps, the first they had ever made. Clearly, these were people who were done with the business of buying and selling, so that it was entirely fitting that the pace of Lourdes respectfully slowed in order to accommodate the solemn momentum of their gently rolling beds and chairs, the soft beat of their crutches and their canes. Ahead and behind each unhurriedly marching column, hundreds, perhaps thousands, of candles now flickered in the darkness, a river of light that stretched as far as I could see. They were singing their Marian hymns or repeating the rosary, while at the distant basilica, an ever-changing voice – a little girl, a woman, an old man – recited the rosary in the innumerable languages of global Catholicism. In those tender, plangent voices, vulgarity dissolved into reverence, and that which had been a market became a church, and thus occurred, to an unbeliever like myself, the only true miracle of Lourdes.

Such is the solemn lesson, I thought, that substance ever teaches show.

On that thought I glanced at Susan and saw that a great well of feeling had risen in her in response to this slowly moving caravan of frailty and infirmity, and thus the degree to which Lourdes had suddenly defied her own earlier expectations. There was nothing cheap now, nothing shallow. Here was humanity as a vast tableau of woundedness and need, of life in all its terrible unfairness, the hobbling old and the stricken young, the feeble and the pale, Lourdes seen no longer as a greedy bazaar of religious trifles, but as the Mount of Olives, a place briefly set aside for the meek who gathered here, and who, by all available evidence, had inherited not the earth, but only its myriad afflictions.

She looked at me, then down at Justine, who stood at her side, motionless and silent, all her youthful agitation stilled, her attention utterly fixed on this stricken cavalcade.

Then Susan drew her gaze back to me and smiled that inexpressibly knowing smile of hers.

'Beautiful,' she whispered.

And despite all that Lourdes had done to make itself ugly, beautiful it truly was.

Auschwitz

When Susan and I left Madrid on that bright morning in late May, Justine huddled sleepily in the back seat of the little Peugeot we'd rented, our route was already set. We would drive eastward across Spain, turn abruptly north at Barcelona, then move further north into France. At some point beyond Grenoble, we would again head eastward into Switzerland, then to Austria, and from there into Hungary, where we would make another northern turn, this time towards Poland, with Auschwitz as our destination.

On the last leg of that journey, we left Budapest with what we thought was plenty of time to make it to Kraków by late in the afternoon. But this was 1992, and the roads of Eastern Europe were badly maintained, and often blocked by one obstacle or another, and in addition to all that, we'd run into a terrible rainstorm in the Carpathian Mountains, so that it was well past midnight when we'd finally approached the Polish border.

The small, concrete border station we encountered there was right out of a Cold War spy novel, isolated and charmless, and anything but welcoming.

We were utterly exhausted, and had hopes of quickly making it to Kraków for a long sleep, but the guards at the border, who'd probably been snoozing at the time we arrived, were in no hurry to let us pass. There were three of them, and when I got out of the car, they quickly surrounded me. It was then I noticed that each of them appeared to be wearing only part of a shared uniform. One wore an ill-fitting cap, another an ill-fitting jacket, the third a pair of equally ill-fitting trousers. The oldest of the guards kept asking questions in Polish, questions which the youngest guard repeated much more slowly and loudly and which he seemed to consider a form of translation. I had no idea what I was being asked, of course, but I didn't want to say either yes or no to every question, and so I nodded and shook my head alternately, indicating yes to one question, no to the next. The border guards got more and more perplexed, of course. I could only imagine what they were saying and hearing:

'You are travelling with your family?'

A nod, yes.

'This is your wife and daughter?'

A shake of the head, no.

This went on for several minutes, during which the guards seemed more and more at a loss as to what they should do. I never felt in danger, but I dreaded the possibility that at some point the guards would simply give up and refuse us entry into

Poland. It was their country, after all, and they were officials with a duty to perform. They had no reason simply to let us pass, and they certainly had a right to be suspicious of an American family driving a French car with a Spanish licence plate that suddenly turned up at a remote border station in the Carpathian Mountains at two in the morning.

But quite unaccountably, they continued to question me, and I continued to answer yes and no alternately. Not surprisingly, no headway was made, and everyone got more and more frustrated, and it all seemed quite hopeless until a voice suddenly came from behind me. 'May I be of assistance, sir?'

When I turned, I fully expected to see an angel complete with silver wings. Instead, I saw a short, well-dressed man in his late forties.

'My name is Ziggy,' he said. 'You're American?'

'Yes.'

'I lived in New York for many years,' he told me, 'but my wife missed her family in Kraków, and so we have returned. I will help you with the guards.'

It turned out that the border guards wanted only one thing: proof that the car we were driving was insured. I had no such proof, save that it was a car I'd rented using American Express, and thus, it was automatically insured.

'Do you have a piece of green paper?' Ziggy asked.

'I don't know,' I answered. 'I could look for one.'

'Please do,' Ziggy said, with a quick glance at the guards. 'That is what they want.'

'Any green piece of paper?' I asked.

Ziggy kept a smile rigidly in place. 'Any piece will do.'

I dug through the mass of junk in the glove compartment of the Peugeot and, sure enough, found a single sheet of vaguely green paper. It was a Hungarian receipt of some sort, probably for petrol.

'Will this do?' I asked when I handed it to Ziggy.

He didn't bother to look at it. 'Absolutely,' he said, then strode up to the oldest of the guards and presented my proof of car insurance.

A huge smile broke over the guard's face. He said something in Polish and the other guards almost fainted with relief, as if they'd narrowly averted an international incident.

'You may pass the border now,' Ziggy said when he came back to me. 'You can follow me to Kraków.'

The barricade lifted and Susan eased our car into Poland. As we passed, I glanced into the stationhouse in time to see the older guard pull out a file drawer from which bulged hundreds of scraps of green paper. He stuffed mine in with the others, then, as we passed, gave us a friendly wave.

For the next hour or so we followed Ziggy to Kraków, and from there to a small motel. Before he left us, I asked if I might take him and his family to dinner in Kraków the next night. He said he would love to, but couldn't because of certain medical tests he'd scheduled for the next day. With that we said goodbye and one of those strangers in whose kindness every traveller must trust disappeared into the night.

At the hotel desk, I asked the clerk to indicate the way to Auschwitz, but he said it was too complicated for his English to explain and suggested that I hire a taxi driver to take us to the road that led directly to the camp. He said he could have a car ready for us the next day.

The driver showed up very punctually the following morning. He was a small, shrivelled man who looked to be in his late sixties, though in Eastern Europe at that time people often appeared a good deal older than their age. He smiled as he came towards me, thrust out his hand and spoke to me in German, the only language he thought we both might understand.

'*Guten Tag, mein Herr*,' he said.

Hearing that language in this place was all my mind required to ask the inevitable questions: What had this man done during the war? What had he seen? How had he survived? These questions were asked with an undercurrent of dreadful suspicion. Most Poles don't speak German. Why did he? Such is the tainted air that surrounds Auschwitz: anyone of a certain age might have done anything.

He spoke again in German. I heard '*wollen Sie*' and '*gehen*' and then 'Auschwitz' and from those snatched words, I gathered that he was confirming that we wanted to go to the camp.

In my very broken German, I answered that we did.

In response, the old man pointed to his car, and this time I made out a '*Sie*', a '*können*' and a '*folgen*'. Added to the wave of his hand, I understood that we were to follow him.

I thanked him and indicated our car.

He smiled, and this time I noticed that his teeth were yellow and broken, the result of long years of neglect. '*Gut*,' he said quietly, and very respectfully, in the way I couldn't help but imagine him speaking to some stereotypically haughty German officer.

We got into our intrepid little Peugeot and pulled in behind the taxi. For a moment, the taxi didn't move. Then quite suddenly it spouted a grimy plume from its rusty tailpipe and, like a creature already weary from hard labour, it inched forward and out onto the main road.

We followed the cab all the way out of Kraków. The old man was very careful not to lose us, always pulling over and waiting patiently when we fell behind. Finally, at some point on the outskirts of town, he brought his car to a stop. We pulled in behind him, and I got out.

He was smoking an unfiltered cigarette, and I noticed that his fingers were yellow from years of doing the same. In the bright sunlight he seemed more ragged than earlier, with wiry white hair that shot out from his head, his brown suit a size too big, with very wide lapels, a relic of the forties.

He said something that sounded like, '*Alles gut?*'

I nodded as if I fully understood.

With a broad gesture he pointed down a very ordinary road, one that might have led to the most innocent of towns. 'Oświęcim,' he said. The Polish word for Auschwitz.

I looked down the road and felt a certain incontestable inner quaking, for of all the dark places I'd visited, or ever considered visiting, this was surely the darkest.

'*Fahren Sie immer direkt*,' the old man told me. Drive straight ahead.

We had not negotiated a fee for his services, so I simply started peeling off bills of Polish money until he seemed genuinely surprised and happy, at which point I stopped.

'*Danke*,' I said, and from the sheer Germanness of it, the weight of my destination grew a little heavier, the 'unicum', as Primo Levi had called it, the *anus mundi*, the place people had most often selected as the darkest place on earth.

The drive to Auschwitz took us through a rural part of Poland that seemed unchanged since the end of the war. The fields were tilled by ancient tractors and threshers, all of them spouting black, oily smoke. Much of the labour appeared to be still done by hand, wheat piled onto creaking wooden lorries and borne to market – or to somewhere – by animals.

We reached Oświęcim in a little over half an hour. Like parts of Kraków, it seemed to slump beneath a coating of grey dust, though in fact there was no dust at all, so I knew that this greyness came more from my sense of the inner world of Poland at that time, rather than its present-day streets and towns. Everything seemed cheerless and oppressed, a world sapped of energy, where people worked because it was expected of them, but without the slightest spark of hope that through their labour they might enhance their lives. *Arbeit* had no more made Poles *frei* under Communism than it had freed the forced labourers of Auschwitz. The impenetrable cloud of Sovietism had hung over their heads for nearly fifty years by then, and though things were certainly falling apart in Moscow at that time, I wondered if Russia's crumbling might strike the people of Poland as some distant opera of bungling power and bottomless corruption that would, in the end, only replace one oppression with another, as the Russians had replaced the Germans. For oppression, as the colourless, enervated streets of Oświęcim seemed to suggest, was all the Poles had ever known.

Auschwitz was only a little way out of town, and my first impression was of how large it was, how far it extended, a city in itself, with row upon row of one-storey wooden buildings, along with considerably higher ones made of brick. I'd seen the usual films of Auschwitz from the air, but even these had made it seem smaller and more geographically concentrated than it was. Auschwitz was not a camp. Auschwitz was a world.

Like any other such historic site, it had a visitors' centre. Large, air-conditioned tour buses were parked outside the building, and for a moment I feared that there might actually be Auschwitz T-shirts on sale inside, or shelves of little Auschwitz snow-globes. That was not the case, however. In fact, the interior of the visitors' centre was sombre in itself, with a striking sculpture as its centrepiece, a human body twisted into the shape of a swastika, and which quite effectively suggested mankind broken on the wheel of Nazism.

It made for a solemn introduction to what lay ahead, but just in case anyone had the idea that Auschwitz was a theme park, a sign had been erected at the entrance to the camp. In several languages, it alerted entering visitors that here was a place of profound suffering, and that they should behave in such a way as to give due respect to that suffering. You could take pictures, it seemed to say, but without the cheesy smiles. There should be no horseplay at Auschwitz, no swinging on doors or climbing fences. Auschwitz was not an attraction. It was a memorial to unimaginable suffering.

I was quite surprised that this sign appeared actually to have a chilling effect on the small group of visitors now moving further into the camp. Several parents took their smaller children's hands. Others, whose children were old enough to read, stopped before the sign, waited as they read it, and only then moved on.

The *Arbeit Macht Frei* gate loomed just ahead. Though it does not tower over anything, and its ironwork expanse is only a few metres, it is probably the most recognizable symbol of the twenty thousand death camps that dotted Europe under Nazism, and it was here, as I passed beneath it, that the heaviness of Auschwitz began to fall over me. I thought of Turgenev's description of the 'timorous alarm' he'd noticed in Jews and which he'd seemed to think the product of some peculiar racial paranoia. Surely Auschwitz had been proof enough that their dread had been real, though perhaps not even the timorous Jew of Turgenev's short story could have imagined the demonic sweep of Auschwitz, the German staff of 7,000 needed to maintain the base camp and its forty-five sub camps, the 1.1 million Jewish prisoners who died here, along with 150,000 Poles, 23,000 gypsies, 15,000 Soviet POWs, 400 Jehovah's Witnesses, and to whose astonishing sum must be added unknown numbers of homosexuals, political prisoners of every stripe, and people who for one reason or another had simply run foul of Nazi rule.

I knew that it had been the Jews of Hamburg who'd first passed beneath this gate, a small segment of a Jewish population that was the most assimilated in Europe. One third of all German Jews living in Germany in 1932 had married non-Jews, and on the day the first of the Hamburg trains left the city, some had worn the German uniform in which they'd fought during World War I. Of all the Jews of Europe, the Jews of Germany would have had the least reason to be 'timorous', and yet it was they who had first taken the path I now took beneath this iconic gate and into the bowels of the camp.

With every step I took from then on, the weightiness of Auschwitz grew weightier. It accumulated incrementally at each stop along the way. At the gravel pit behind Block 11, I paused to look at the rectangular field in which Polish political prisoners and Russian prisoners of war had been forced to toil, no matter what the weather. It was clothed in summer green now, and might have passed for a well-manicured English lawn. The grass was short and the ground was uniformly flat. As the scene of a garden party, it would have been perfect for a pleasant game of croquet. In 1944, it had been bordered by a grassy lip, and it was from this squat eyrie that SS officers had kept watch on the prisoners who toiled beneath them. One witness later remembered an SS officer randomly firing into this pit as he strolled leisurely along its slightly raised, rectangular rim. He'd done it whenever the mood struck him, hitting no one in particular.

At Auschwitz, murder for the most part had been carried out methodically, but it had also been done with unspeakable casualness, a matter of mood, a game of sport. The people in this pit had not been allowed to glance up from their labour, so that they'd simply heard the shots, then glimpsed the bustle as the body was removed, through it all waiting for the next shot to be fired.

I stepped away, now just that much heavier, and walked into one of the barracks. Enclosed behind a Plexiglas wall, I saw, then felt, the weight of shoes in great piles, of eyeglasses and various artificial limbs in great piles, of mounds of human hair, the weight of suitcases that swelled towards the ceiling.

This steadily accumulating weight is the true 'thereness' of Auschwitz. Despite the ubiquitous once-electrified barbed wire, it is open and expansive enough to give little sense of actual imprisonment. The grasses of Auschwitz are green and the trees that shade the SS barracks are tall, and if you peered out over the camp from the top of its administrative building, it would not appear significantly different from a children's summer camp. For that reason, the weight you feel is not the heaviness of enclosure, for there is nothing claustrophobic about Auschwitz. It is the sheer weight of suffering and the utterly fiendish ways in which it was inflicted that bear down upon you as you walk the wide streets of the camp. Here cruelty, hopelessness, and suffering congealed in a form, by a means, and to an extent that resulted in the birth of something genuinely new.

One element of that dark star has been much mentioned,

the fact that at Auschwitz the most modern of methods met the most primitive of impulses as the many achievements of the industrial age were made to manufacture death. Concrete though this idea is, it remains somewhat abstract until you confront its stark reality at Auschwitz. For here you actually see the greatest discoveries of the modern age put to the primitive purpose of ethnic annihilation. You see lines and lines of electrified wire, all of it meticulously strung. You see the railway, and note how efficiently it bore the cattle cars and their cargo practically to the doors of the equally efficient underground gas chambers. Just outside those chambers, you see the industrial ovens that reduced that cargo to ash.

Another weight is added in seeing all this, for even the briefest visit to Auschwitz makes it clear that so extensive a killing machine could not have been built and operated without the application of considerable skill. Auschwitz was not a killing field; it was a killing factory. There is sophisticated design here that could only have been provided by highly trained engineers. There are structures at Auschwitz that could only have been built by skilled craftsmen. There are medical buildings where doctors worked and administrative buildings whose functions were carried out by bureaucrats and office workers of considerable ability. At Auschwitz, you wonder who hewed the wood, fired the glass, moulded the steel, stitched the flag that hangs in one of the barracks, all the thousand thousand hands that were applied to the task of building it, a labour only a small portion of which could have been done by the prisoners themselves. And this leaves out the enormous labour involved in the deportations, a pan-European enterprise that encompassed every region the Germans occupied or over which they spread their influence, from Scandinavia in the north, to the Channel Islands in the west, to the Ukraine in the east, to Greece in the south. The terrible truth that descends upon you at Auschwitz is that this was a world that only the larger world beyond it could have created and sustained, and this fact adds the weight of a universal stain.

It is a weight that finally imposes a strange silence, so that as I made my way deeper into the camp, I found that I had absolutely nothing to say either to Susan or Justine. By then revenge had taken the place of pity, and I could feel only the need to know absolutely that someone had been punished for all this.

At least one man had been, of course, Rudolf Höss, the camp commandant, and it was with some relief that I reached the spot where he'd been hanged in 1947. I knew that he'd shouted 'Heil Hitler' before being executed, a strange outburst since in his memoir, he'd claimed not to be anti-Semitic, nor even much of a Nazi. But if this were true, why that final 'Heil Hitler'? It was not a question I could answer, save that at base perhaps Höss had been a characteristically stubborn male who, like a man who won't ask directions, simply could not admit that he'd spectacularly misjudged the trajectory of history, allied himself to the wrong side, and in that way proved himself to be not nearly so clever as he'd supposed.

The gas chambers of Auschwitz had been blown up, one by prisoners, the others by the Germans themselves in a delusional moment, both crazed and terrified no doubt by the spectre of defeat, when they seemed actually to have believed that murder on so massive a scale would not finally out. The chambers had been reconstructed, and when I entered the first of them, an old man stood at the door of one of the ovens. He wore a yarmulke and a tallith was draped over his shoulders. He was saying Kaddish, the Jewish prayer for the dead, while his family, a grown son and grandchildren, looked on. They were stone-faced as they watched him, but when I glanced at Susan, I saw that she was very moved. Her eyes were glistening, and her features bore a grief that seemed immediate, as if a loved one had just died. She was Jewish, but she was a secular Jew, so I don't think her sorrow was simply for 'her own'. Rather, it was for everyone, that sense of pity, goodness of heart and sympathy for all mankind that in Yiddish is called *rachmunis*.

Hers were the only tears I saw in Auschwitz that day, and my reaction was to lead Susan out of the crematorium, where she regained her composure.

'Do you want to leave now?' I asked.

She shook her head and looked at Justine, who stood, staring at her with obvious concern. 'No,' she said. She had brought her daughter hundreds of miles to see this place, and she would not be driven from it, even by her own emotions.

And so we continued, moving among the barracks first of Auschwitz, then of Birkenau, and finally back to our last stop of that day, the infamous Block 11.

Block 11 was the first administrative building at Auschwitz

and where the first test of Zyklon B had been carried out on Russian prisoners. But it was also a prison within a prison, where Auschwitz inmates were taken to be punished, and in that sense, it was arguably the most feared place in the camp.

A visit to Auschwitz, as I had learned by then, was a kind of descent in which the visitor goes from horror to horror, and in that process, and almost without knowing it, begins to seek a bottom.

At Auschwitz, Block 11, by many accounts, had provided that bottom because, quite simply, there was nothing that could not be done to a human being that was not done in the grey, unlit chambers of its cellar.

Nothing about the exterior of Block 11 declares it purpose, or how that purpose was achieved. It is almost identical to the camp's other administrative buildings. It is made of plain red brick, with a short span of concrete steps. There is a courtyard behind it, and a wall where scores of executions were carried out. Someone had placed flowers at this site, but no one had lingered there.

A small group of visitors moved in and out of the building, and downstairs, in its dreaded cellar, I found a few teenagers strolling nonchalantly among the rooms, looking as teenagers always look, vaguely out of sorts with wherever they happen to find themselves. The adults, on the other hand, struck me as quite uncertain of how they should behave in such a place. Their faces were inexpressive, and when you met them eye to eye, they glanced away, as if uneasy as to why you were looking at them. *Do you think us German? And if you think us Poles, do you blame us, too?*

Save for Jews, Auschwitz is a minefield of blame. Everyone lies within the cross-hairs of an accusation. Why did the Austrians vote for Hitler in the Anschluss? Why did the French turn over their Jewish citizens so easily? Why did residents of country after country participate in the deportations? Why didn't the British and Americans intervene more quickly by bombing the camp?

Everyone knows there can be no real answer to these questions, but everyone also knows that they will never stop being asked.

At last I reached the infamous standing cells of Block 11. If Auschwitz had a bottom, it was here. There were four such cells, and each was less than a square metre. As many as four prisoners would be stuffed into this space, and so they were not really cells at all. They were coffins for the living that were entered by a tiny door at the base. Prisoners slithered into the cell, then stood up. After that, they would never sit again because there is no room to sit. Once entombed within this space, they could not bend their knees or lower their heads. There was no light, no ventilation, and often there was no food, so that the standing cells were also starving cells in which prisoners stood until they died.

The process sometimes took days, and I found myself wondering what a human being would think when he could literally do nothing else. Under such prolonged and horrendous circumstances, would thought itself become indistinguishable from physical pain, each memory an ache?

It was also in Block 11, in this case in Cell 27, that the first experiment in mass killing by gas was begun on 3 September 1941, a full three months before Eichmann, Heydrich and others met at Wannsee, a suburb of Berlin, to plan the Final Solution. During the next three days, 600 Russian POWs and around 250 prisoners deemed too sick to work met their deaths, a 'success' that served to convince Wannsee's extermination elite that Zyklon B, an insecticide, would provide the most efficient method for eliminating the 'vermin' of Europe.

I left Block 11 silently, like the others, glancing away from them just as they'd glanced away from me. The opaque walls and dark cells in the basement had worked like a mirror upon me, and it had been impossible to like what I saw in that glass. For the truth was stark: I could not with any confidence say that I would have behaved differently than the nameless people who will forever stand accused of Auschwitz, the people who went to their jobs in Paris and Amsterdam, Budapest and Vienna, the ordinary men and women who put bread on the table and a roof over their heads, and who, as they ate dinner one evening, glanced out the window as a truck pulled up to the house across the way. Like them, I would probably have watched in terrible silence as my neighbours were brought down the stairs, well-dressed as the Hamburg Jews had been, carrying their neatly packed suitcases in their hands and with their bewildered children in their arms. Like them, I would probably have reduced my moral responsibility to the tight circle of my own family obligations.

Such is the final weight of Auschwitz, the burden of an unflattering self-recognition, of accepting what might have been your own cowardice in a dark time, the fact that in the faces of those who'd watched the round-ups from the Channel Islands to the Ukraine, in the faces of those who'd looked down from their urban balconies or out their village windows, in the faces of those who'd lined the many roads of deportation, or watched as the cattle cars rumbled by, you can see your own face, too.

We had nearly reached the gate that now mocked any assurance I might have had in my own heroism. The old man we'd seen at the ovens was now leaving the camp as well. He recognized us from our earlier meeting, no doubt struck by Susan's tears, a stranger's tears, when his own family had shed none.

'My wife and I met here in the camp,' he said to Susan in a heavily accented English. 'But she didn't want to come back with me. It was . . . too hard.'

We talked on for a time, the son and grandchildren looking on with a sense of uneasiness, as if they feared the old man might embarrass them. Or perhaps they simply couldn't find a way to react to all this horror that would satisfy their grandfather's purpose in bringing them here, and so had chosen to tamp down any reaction at all.

A few minutes later, we passed beneath the *Arbeit Macht Frei* gate, then back through the welcome centre and finally to our car for the return drive to Kraków.

An incontestable relief swept over me. I was glad to be leaving. For the truth is, Auschwitz had squeezed something out of me that left me shrunken and deflated, with some earlier faith in myself no longer quite intact. It is a damage that flows outwards, like a stain, and that touches all humanity, so that I left the camp feeling older and weaker and more morally destitute, looking for renewal.

Ultimately, what I found was Ziggy, and each time I've thought of him – and I've done so many times since my journey to Auschwitz – he has emerged like a small crack in the dreadful wall of the camp. I think of him, and I am once again at that lonely border station, bereft of language, custom, direction, everything. *May I be of assistance, sir?*

Ziggy's offer does not offset Auschwitz's grim lesson that we can have no confidence in the moral steadfastness of ourselves, nor in our courage, nor in our capacity for self-sacrifice. We can believe only that when other forces do not misshape us, we will not of our own accord take the shape of a swastika nor bend others to that shape. When not forced to betray ourselves or others, or to torture or kill another human being, most of us will not do so. Had I been a 'timorous' Jew at a Polish border crossing in 1944, and had those three partially uniformed guards been crisply uniformed SS, then I have little doubt that Ziggy would have offered no assistance. He was a man with a job, a family, and fear was the order of the day. But that night in 1992, he could let the better angels of his nature assert themselves, and that is what he did. This is cold comfort, but it is the only comfort available in the wake of Auschwitz. It is stark and simple, with nothing at all beyond its plain declaration that if no malignant force imposes its will upon him, a man will probably help a stranger find his way.

Snapshot: Cosenza

One of Susan's characteristics as a traveller was that she could stop the car after driving for six or seven hours, close her eyes for ten minutes, then awaken with all the energy of one who'd just had a full night's sleep.

Justine and I, on the other hand, were not good nappers. For that reason, we would generally leave Susan to her deep snooze, and either play a few hands of rummy or simply take a stroll. On this particular day, the choice was a stroll, and so, after going only a few yards beyond our car, we found ourselves standing on a dusty precipice, staring down at a quite unimpressive river.

Justine is twelve years old on this day in 1992, our second summer of being on the road in Europe. Below us, the Busento River makes its timeless journey through Calabria towards the Ionian Sea. It is a short river, only around ninety-five kilometres, and in every way physically undistinguished. It is also without fame. One can gaze on the Danube, the Tiber, the Thames, the

Seine, the Mississippi, the Mekong, and know that here is a stream that has flowed through great events, that eminent men and women have strolled along its banks. The Busento has only its narrow, turgid self to recommend it, and Justine is clearly not impressed.

It has been a long day of travel, with many stops at what Justine has come to call 'broken pot museums'. We have been several weeks on the road, beginning in Madrid, where we have been living for the last fourteen months, then up along the north-eastern coast of Spain, across the south of France, down the western coast of Italy to where, on this quite hot day, poor little Cosenza offers its modest shade.

There is a small rustle of air to drive away the long day's heat, both of which contribute to the drowsiness of the moment, along with the sense of a twilight exhaustion settling in. A twelve-year-old can only take so many examples of ancient pottery before interest cracks as surely as the pots, and it is clear to me that Justine's attention is now at its ebb. But she is a patient traveller, and so she peers out over the river without complaint. Even so, I know that her mind has essentially emptied, that she is no longer able to absorb the scene, nor have any reason to remember it. Nor can I think of any way to make this short pause in our travels less boring than it is. Then, without warning, I recall a little historical fact probably picked up from one of the guide books I'd brought with us on this trip.

And so I say, 'You know, Alaric died here in Cosenza.'

I don't tell Justine who Alaric was. I know she will ask.

'Who was Alaric?' Justine asks.

'He was an emperor of Rome,' I answer nonchalantly, as if it is an inconsequential matter, nothing to dwell upon. But I know at that instant that I am in the midst of testing a theory. 'He was the last pagan one.'

Justine shrugs, as anyone would who has little notion of what a pagan is, and only enough knowledge of history to gather that Rome had once been a very important place.

I let a few seconds pass, let Justine's weariness settle over her again.

Then I say, 'They buried him in a river.'

'They buried him in a river?' Justine asks unbelievingly.

'Yes, they buried him in this one,' I tell her. 'The Busento. The one we're looking at.'

I see a spark reappear in her otherwise road-weary eyes. 'How do you bury someone in a river?'

'Well, you can't. Unless you reroute it.'

'How do you do that?'

'You have people dig a whole new channel for the water,' I answer. 'Then, with all that water flowing in another channel, you bury the person in the riverbed where the river once flowed.' I nod towards the muddy little stream before us. 'That's what they did with the Busento.'

Justine looks towards the river, and I see another spark, this one a trifle more sustained, like a fuse lit and weakly burning.

'Hundreds of slaves must have been at work,' I continue.

She has now turned to me, listening.

'And when they had rerouted the river, they buried Alaric along with his treasure, then they returned the river to its original course.'

She is listening closely now.

'And in order to keep his burial place secret,' I tell her, 'they slaughtered all the slaves who'd worked to reroute the river and lay Alaric to rest.' I see a dark hint of surprise in her eyes that the story has taken so murderous a turn.

'So that now, no one knows for sure where Alaric is buried,' I add in conclusion, then nod towards the turgidly flowing Busento. 'Save that it is somewhere in this river.'

With that, Justine turns to face the river once again, her expression much changed from its earlier listlessness. It may be awe at the task of rerouting the river, or it may be revulsion at the slaughter that followed it. It may even be a sense of the absurdity of the enterprise itself, the squandering of so much life and labour for so vain a purpose. But whatever it is that has deepened the features of my daughter, one thing is clear: darkness has done its magic work, and so for this brief moment, as she peers out over the embankment, the lowly Busento is no longer simply another little river without character or consequence, boring and forgettable. In this little girl, for this brief moment, it has carved out a place for itself in the tragic narrative of human life, that other, larger river we all share.

Kalaupapa

'It seemed to me there was contamination everywhere,' Ernie Pyle wrote of the leper colony at Kalaupapa when he came here in 1937. 'In the air, in everything I touched, in mere sight and thought. Not uncleanness, not foulness, not even danger – but an invisible and innocent evil everywhere.'

Because it was thought to have been brought to the islands by Chinese immigrants in the 1830s, the Hawaiian natives called it 'ma'i Pake', the Chinese disease, and in an early report, a certain Dr William Hillebrand noted that it was a 'genuine Oriental leprosy'. In that same report, Hillebrand, who believed the disease to be highly infectious, warned of an epidemic that could only be prevented by the 'isolation' of those afflicted by it. In the years to come, isolation would become imprisonment, always for life, and for that reason, Hansen's disease (so named after the discoverer of the bacterium that causes it) became known by those later isolated for having contracted it as the 'the disease that is also a crime'.

Hillebrand had suggested a box canyon, where people at various stages of the disease could be isolated from the rest of society. This proved impractical, however. What was needed was a Devil's Island for lepers, a place so inaccessible that it could be reached only with great difficulty and could not be escaped at all. Various sites were considered, but in the end the powers that be chose a bleak, wind-tossed peninsula about the size and shape of Manhattan. It was formed of volcanic rock and swept out from the northern coast of Molokai. Best of all, a gigantic cliff, at points over three thousand feet tall, thus the highest sea cliffs on earth, towered over the one portion of the peninsula that was not wracked by brutal surf. To those charged with isolating the lepers of Hawaii, nature seemed miraculously to have provided a perfect place, quite literally a 'prison fortified by nature', as Robert Louis Stevenson later called it. It was known as Kalaupapa, and in the years that followed the disastrous arrival of the first of Hawaii's lepers, it was destined to become what one observer called 'the most infamous place on earth'.

The Hawaiian Islands are the most isolated landforms in the world, and Kalaupapa, which means 'flat leaf' or 'flat plain' in Hawaiian, is arguably the most isolated place in Hawaii. Most people have seen it only once, and even then very distantly, without knowing what they saw. In the opening scene of *Jurassic Park* it is called Isla Sorna, and is said to lie 207 miles off the western coast of Costa Rica. The camera is careful to show only the conical formation at the base of the North Shore Cliffs and a panoramic view of the sea cliffs, thus avoiding the actual site of the leper colony that was created there in January of 1866. The colony still exists today, though few lepers live there, none of them by force, but simply because at the closing of the colony, they had no place to go, and thus, at the urging of the entertainer Don Ho and others, were permitted to remain in what is now officially designated as a national park.

But national park or no, few people make the journey to Kalaupapa. In August of 2007, when Susan and I went there, we were joined by a scant dozen others, all of us atop the mules whose hard task it was to bear us first down, then back up the sea cliffs, a very treacherous trail, hard on the body as well as the nerves, since there are twenty-six switchbacks along the route, not one of which appeared wide enough to accommodate a canary, let alone a mule and rider. It was for that reason, no doubt, that before the journey began, riders were made to sign a paper that read like a death warrant, and which relieved the guides of all responsibility should you by chance experience an unexpectedly hasty trip to the bottom. In the early provisioning of the colony, cows had experienced just that, losing their footing and plunging towards the rocks below at a terminal speed of 135 miles per hour, where they burst like gigantic watermelons on the unforgiving stones, a surreal scene observed in dark wonder by the residents at the base.

Perhaps to relieve the ever-building anxiety of the riders, the proprietor of the Kalaupapa mule ride played a ukulele and crooned light-hearted songs as we saddled up. He wore a flow-ered shirt and straw hat, and flashed a smile I found not one bit comforting. Then, with a wave of the hand, he motioned us in the direction of the cliffs, where, when we reached them, I noticed several of my fellow riders avert their eyes from the aerial view of the sea below, as if to confront the journey towards it would prevent them from making it.

I could see that for Susan, this tactic wasn't working. This was a woman who did not like reins as a medium of control. A donkey had once gotten away from her in the Pyrenees, and it had taken an enormous effort on her part finally to bring it to heel. Justine and I had watched this process with fear and trembling, because the donkey, with its precious cargo, had many times skirted the edge of a ravine so precipitous that, had it gone over it, no subsequent sure footing would have saved the day. That this same woman was now mounted on a mule whose destination rested three thousand feet below struck fear in my heart.

'Are you okay?' I asked as I and my mule came up beside her.

Susan patted the muscular neck of the mule she was riding. 'He's so sweet,' she said delightedly.

I did not share in this delight. 'I hope he stays that way.'

The descent to Kalaupapa takes about two hours. There are no places to stop on the trail, and the switchbacks are at such hair turns that it truly seems impossible to negotiate them without scraping knees, legs and shoulders against the jagged stone from which they are carved. The mules know better, however, and move relentlessly forward, the steady thud of their hooves practically the only sound because you are so high above the shore that you cannot hear what below, as you will eventually discover, is the nearly deafening roar of the surf as it pounds the lava stone of the peninsula. The ride is often at a deeply descending angle, and for that reason you must clasp your legs very tightly around the mule's sweating flanks then curl your spine backward at a radical angle. A failure to do this will send you somersaulting over the mule's always stubbornly lowered head, either to land in the brush or plunge through it into free fall. The mules move in what appears to be a haze of tedium, their attention diverted only by the occasional attempt to eat the riotous plant life that is forever threatening to overrun the trail. Here and there, they loll their heads right or left to grab a stray leaf. Any effort to prevent this will fail. Several times I used all my strength to keep the mule's head up, a force the mule seemed hardly to notice, so that I thought of the monument to the war animals I'd seen in Park Lane in London, these same mules, carved in stone, hauling cannons and lorries heaped with ammunition. Theirs was a strength, a capacity for arduous labour, that I admired, and several times during the ride to and from Kalaupapa, I found myself in awe of these mules, and felt for them, if it can be said without smarmy sentiment, a kind of love.

From a distance, the shores of Kalaupapa look pretty much like any other rugged beach. It is a brown spur of land edged in volcanic stone and scattered with scrub brush, 'sunburnt and dust-colored, blackened at the edges', as Charles Warren

Stoddard once described it. But had you looked out across the white-capped bay on 6 January 1866, you would have seen the barely seaworthy schooner *Eliza Warwick* at anchor in the unforgiving harbour.

Several days before, the first of those chosen to inhabit Kalaupapa had made a slow, anguished walk to the harbour in Honolulu. A procession of friends and relatives accompanied them. An observer described this procession as 'a funeral in which the dead themselves walked'.

The first to board was J.D. Kahauliko, duly recorded as 'Exile Number 1'. He was followed by eight men and three women, all of them taken from their families for the crime of having Hansen's disease. Once on Kalaupapa, not one of them would ever leave its forbidding shore.

On the day they came here, these first prisoners of Kalaupapa were taken ashore by a whaling boat. They disembarked and stared about, no doubt wondering where the houses were, the hospital. They saw nothing of the kind, for nothing had been prepared for them. One can only imagine with what impossible dread they must have looked back to see the whaling boat that had deposited them in this bleak, inhospitable place now hurriedly on its way back to the *Eliza Warwick*.

With that ship's departure, the first residents of Kalaupapa were alone in a place they had never seen. Even worse, they found themselves horribly exposed, the wind billowing out their shirts and dresses and playing havoc with their hair. They had all been splashed by the sea, their clothes at first soaking wet, then covered with the dust that blew up all around them, so that within a few minutes they were caked with it. By then, night had begun to fall, and so they were no doubt relieved when a man on horseback arrived, an irascible Frenchman named Louis Lepart, who spoke little English and no Hawaiian. He supplied a few tools, then led them towards the storm-devastated huts where they would spend this first night of the rest of their lives.

Such was the beginning of Kalaupapa, a peninsula so ill-prepared to receive the people who'd landed on its shores that a more cruel arrival could hardly have been imagined than the one you would have witnessed had you been there on that long-ago January day.

And yet, over the next few months, far more cruel arrivals did, in fact, occur. Whale boats would overturn in the roiling surf, spewing out their human cargo, men, women and children who, at that point, would either drown or be swept towards the lava rocks and battered to death. Often no landing could be made at all, and so the hired captains of supply boats simply tossed their crates overboard, returned to Honolulu, and claimed payment for deliveries that were never made save to the bottom of the sea. If the more dire tales are true, these same hard-bitten seamen sometimes tossed their human cargo into the sea as well, salt water pouring into open wounds as this most despised of all Hawaii's population struggled in the heaving waters or sank beneath them.

Had you remained witness to the story of Kalaupapa for the next seven years, you would have seen nothing change. The boats would have come and gone. Those who survived the arrival would have staggered onto shore, then been marched to the settlement to eke out an existence in little hardscrabble gardens and to live in huts constructed of whatever poor supplies could be found for shelter.

Thus was Kalaupapa, beside which, according to Father Damien, the Belgian missionary who arrived here in 1873, there was no sadder place on earth.

His modest church rests on a dusty lot in what might be called central Kalaupapa, a spare gathering of small houses, mostly made of concrete and aluminium siding, with a few rust-streaked Quonset huts. The windows of these houses are shuttered during the carefully scheduled intervals outsiders are allowed in the village. There is no strolling about Kalaupapa, no idling on the beach, no splashing in the waves, no windsurfing, no snorkelling, no open-pit barbecues, no thatch-roofed seaside bars dispensing drinks served in coconut shells and crowned with paper umbrellas. No one is allowed to stay overnight and each stop is planned ahead. Venturing beyond those designated spots is not permitted.

And so, once you have reached the base of the sea cliffs, you drop heavily from your mule, sore and thirsty, and with your mind still trying to recover from the nervous exhaustion caused by the narrow, cliff-side trail. You have a brief lunch, then board an ancient bus oddly designated 'Damien Tours'. Ours also sported a bumper sticker that read: *DO NOT WASH. This vehicle is undergoing a scientific dirt test.* This levity at first struck me as wildly inappropriate, despite the fact that I knew there'd always been jokes at Kalaupapa. Once, Damien had scolded a boy for not 'toeing the mark', this said lightly to a boy who had no toes, a joke that had prompted one writer to observe that on Kalaupapa all humour was black.

Still, what followed our boarding of this bus was anything but funny. For the next hour or so, it rattled through a village that appeared in almost every way entirely abandoned. There were no people on the street nor lounging on the porches of the houses we passed. There was no one out hanging laundry, or strolling to the post office, or sitting on the steps of the theatre. At Fuesaina's Bar, where small snacks were available, there were no customers save the dozen or so people who'd come with us down the sea cliffs.

And so, despite the fact that Hansen's disease is now curable – in fact, it was never especially contagious – it seemed clear that the ravages of the disease, the collapse of the nose, the falling away of ears and fingers and toes, its many facial disfigurements, has created an exile of its own. These last survivors of Kalaupapa had managed to weather the terrible adversities of the place itself, the biting dust and lashing winds, but in the end the affliction had succeeded in its relentless effort to exclude them from the larger community of mankind. As the town's small museum demonstrated, they had ingeniously fashioned shoes held in place by tape rather than strings, shaped knives and forks and spoons that could be held by fingerless hands, and even cut slits in the church floor which allowed the drool from their ravaged mouths to fall to the ground beneath it. But in the struggle to isolate them from the rest of us, to leave its mark upon them, and deliver them into exile, the disease at last had won, a victory easily glimpsed in these deserted streets, and which, until the last of its victims no longer sits in shuttered rooms and waits for the rest of us to leave, will continue to render Kalaupapa a sad and desolate place.

And sad and desolate it truly is; a spit of land that seems still to lie beneath the pall of the disease that made it infamous. Everything about Kalaupapa remains strikingly bleak and curiously still, despite the relentlessly whipping winds. The guides hardly ever speak save to point out this cemetery or that workshed as the bus rumbles past them. The museum cashier had nothing to say, but sat, head down, idly flipping through a magazine. Even the vendors at Fuesaina's Bar spoke only enough to reveal a price or count out change. None of these people actually had Hansen's disease, and yet they seemed in some way stricken by it, as if the mood of Kalaupapa, the grim nature of its history, was itself an affliction.

But then, how could it be otherwise? Kalaupapa has nothing but its history, and the darkness of that history is everywhere on display. Photographs of ravaged faces, hands, feet, as might be expected to demonstrate the actual nature of the disease, but also pictures of Father Damien, none of them showing a priest in the vigour of his youth, but only the dark visage of a man prematurely old and wracked by disease. Other photographs are yet more grim, Damien actually on his deathbed, hollow-eyed and wrapped in blankets, staring up sorrowfully, so that he appears at last to have regretted the martyrdom he chose. In these pictures, sainthood seems far away, and we sense not the glory of Damien's moral achievement, but the suffering that was its price. For that reason, the photographs of him that festoon the public places of Kalaupapa tell a somewhat false story. For in fact, Damien was nothing if not devoted to his mission, nor did he ever utter a single sentence to suggest anything but a full acceptance of the life he felt himself ordained to live.

By all accounts – and to say this as generously as possible – he was not a complicated man. In fact, his religious faith was so fundamental it often seemed childlike. Though by no means sufficiently nuanced to be a mystic, Damien had sometimes heard 'inner voices', once felt that he'd been instructed to build a church by John the Baptist himself, and had at other times believed himself divinely guided to the specific place where some ailing person lay abed. Martyrdom is often the product of spiritual ambition, and so it seems to have been with Damien. As a young man he'd committed himself to self-mortification, a devotion certain of his fellow villagers thought a consequence of his being a little 'thick'. Even so, he'd been repulsed by his first experience of the lepers with whom he would spend the rest of his life. He had hated the look of them and later took up tobacco in order to mask their repellent smell. And yet, in the end, he had placed the communion wafer in a thousand rotting mouths, nursed and sheltered monstrously afflicted bodies, and worked, often in the dictatorial style of an exasperated father, to save souls of whose immortality he had not the slightest doubt. At forty-nine, he had welcomed the final onslaught of disease because, as he said, it would rid him of all earthly affection, and prepare his way to God.

His grave was fittingly the last stop on Damien's Tours. It is a modest affair and, in fact, only Damien's right hand is buried here, the remainder of his body having been claimed by his native Belgium. The grave rests beside St Philomena's Church, beneath the very pandanus tree under which Damien had spent his first night at Kalaupapa. The grave itself is enclosed by a short wrought-iron fence. A large black cross rises from a base that bears Damien's name. On the day we visited, an assortment of leis, some plastic, some made of fresh flowers, hung from this fence, along with a few rosaries. Father Joseph Dutton is buried just behind Damien, but since second place is never a position of renown, no one seemed to notice the equally selfless priest who'd succeeded Damien, and in many ways accomplished more for the residents of Kalaupapa than had Damien himself. So much more, as a matter of fact, that by 1908, when Jack London came here expecting to find 'the most cursed place on earth', he found 'happy' lepers racing horses and donkeys, singing and dancing, and on one surreal occasion, in full celebration of the Fourth of July.

Others have seen Kalaupapa in similarly pleasing ways, particularly as the harshness of its history has passed through the rose-coloured lenses of Damien's self-sacrifice, a martyrdom that has been portrayed quite lavishly in books and films. Saintliness can sweeten even the bitterest of breads, and the heroic deeds of this Belgian priest have loomed so large in the history of Kalaupapa that the actual lepers of Molokai have all but disappeared behind the blinding curtain of his tattered cassock. People like their saints without warts, as the late Christopher Hitchens discovered when he cast too unblinking an eye on Mother Teresa. It is hard not to feel that Damien's labours, fine and arduous though they were, have bestowed upon Kalaupapa the same divine light Malcolm Muggeridge claimed to find in the death house overseen by Mother Teresa, and whose radiance obscured the grim realities of the place. Damien's beatification, the saint as celebrity, has worked a similar magic on Kalaupapa, his grave now the central attraction of the island, its protective iron railing hung with worshipful leis and rosaries, while the graves of those who anonymously died here remain starkly unadorned, their squat stones lashed by the same violent winds that tore at their clothes and drove sand into their wounds.

The fact that the dread history of Kalaupapa has faded as Damien's halo has brightened struck me as the saddest aspect of the place. It was no doubt for that reason that, as we boarded the bus again and were on our way back towards the far end of the promontory, back along the dusty road, past cemetery after cemetery, the bus scourged by the same untiring wind, the cliffs towering above us, and to our right, the imprisoning sea, I thought of Kathryn Hulme.

Nearly fifty years before, Ms Hulme, the celebrated author of *The Nun's Story*, had made this same journey, and found Kalaupapa not unlike a New England village save for its tropical vegetation, the jasmine and oleander she recorded, along with the ever-swaying coconut palms. At journey's end, she had found the peninsula 'a bright finger of land where martyrs live forever' beside a deep, delphinium blue. It was a description that spoke fully to the fact that more often than not what we see is that which is already in our eyes. I had moved over the same terrain and found no charm in Kalaupapa, nothing to lift it from its tragic history, no tale of moral triumph to be sung that could in any way ameliorate the colony's long and numerous horrors. In that sea, scores had drowned. On those rocks, others had been bashed to death. In these cemeteries were buried hundreds of unheralded men, women and children whose only crime had been to contract the 'invisible and innocent evil' of a dread bacterium. No act of martyrdom on the part of someone else, saint or otherwise, could restore their blasted lives nor make beautiful the natural prison to which they had been sentenced and in which they had been doomed to die. Notwithstanding Ms Hulme's Pollyannic portrait, Kalaupapa was not and had never been a New England village. It had always been a leper colony. And it still was.

The mules were waiting for us when we returned to the dusty little picnic ground where we'd left them to rest up for the ascent, also made without a stop, and far more gruelling, at least for the mules. With each step up the trail, Kalaupapa grew smaller and smaller until it was once again indistinguishable from any other coastal village.

Once back at the barn from which we'd left, we fortunate day-trippers to Kalaupapa dismounted so that the weary mules could quickly be fed and watered. Most of our fellow riders immediately headed for their cars and were quickly away. But Susan wanted to walk back down the trail to the edge of the cliffs. It was quite a distance, but she thought it necessary in order 'to stretch my bones'. I knew that this was only an excuse. There was something in Susan that was always reluctant to leave a place. For her, each departure seemed final, even at those times when we'd left London or Paris or Madrid with plans already made to return. It was an end-of-voyage melancholy she had exhibited even at the end of our first trip, when she was only twenty-five, and which our French taxi driver had noticed as he'd driven us along the Seine in early morning fog, headed for the airport. He'd glanced back, taken in Susan's curiously sorrowful expression, and said quite sadly and softly and in sweetly accented English, 'Goodbye, Paris.'

I knew that this was but another occasion of her dark nostalgia, but by then I had gotten used to it. It was, and would forever be, I thought, an aspect of our travel. At each departure, she would fear that there would never be enough time or enough money, or perhaps simply enough luck for her within the scheme of things, to bring her back again.

'Now is the time to be in Kalaupapa,' I said as she stared out in the general direction of the village. 'When the people who live there come outside and can be themselves.'

'But they couldn't be themselves if we were there now,'

Susan said. 'They'd have to stay in their houses, behind those shutters.'

But we were gone now, and so I could imagine the residents of Kalaupapa emerging into the open air, gathering on their porches. There they would no doubt talk of the day's events, I thought, of television shows or whatever movie was playing at their cinema. In small groups, they would exchange neighbourhood gossip, discuss the latest news from the wide world beyond them. Perhaps, from time to time, someone would engage in the black humour of Kalaupapa and a burst of laughter would ripple through the twilight. Now, as night fell, they could freely come out, as Susan had said, from behind those shutters.

But how had they felt earlier in the day? I asked myself suddenly. How had they felt as they'd sat in their closed houses, behind their shuttered windows, listening as our tourist bus rumbled by? Would they have felt even more imprisoned, even more isolated and set apart? During our visit, had their dungeon walls narrowed, the light dimmed? Had our presence among them, however brief, imposed an added sentence to those afflicted by the disease that was also a crime?

Surely it had, I decided, for how could it have not?

'We shouldn't have gone there, Susan,' I said.

She nodded. 'I was just thinking that.'

With that shared conclusion, even gazing towards the colony from a great height now seemed an unjustifiable voyeurism, Kalaupapa's true message the unavoidable one that there are certain dark places where, because people still remain captive within them, you simply should not go. Of all the dark places we had visited or would ever visit, it was the only one whose darkness had not retreated into history, where the evils of the past remained in the present, where toes and fingers still fell away and drool still strained through slits in the church floor, where people remained in place simply because they had no other place to go. Down there, three thousand feet below, that which had once happened was happening still, and this, it seemed to me, made Kalaupapa somehow inviolate, a tragic shore not to be visited again until that tragedy, and all those who still suffered it, had at last secured their sacred privacy behind the tightly closed shutters of time.

Verdun

'How ironic,' Susan said after we'd noticed perhaps the fourth large billboard.

What she'd said was certainly true, for the one presence that relentlessly proclaims itself to anyone heading out of Paris towards Verdun is Disneyland. There are colourful billboards featuring Mickey Mouse all along the highway. They mark the route in rhythmic succession, and it is easy to imagine the ever-building excitement they are intended to generate. We are getting nearer and nearer, they seem to say, to the ultimate good time.

Fair enough. Such amusements have their place and no one is the worse for visiting them. I have many times visited and enjoyed such places. But the case for darkness reminds us that there are other places, too, that down this same road lies Verdun, and that it also has much to offer: the beauty of the softly flowing Meuse, for one, and the lovely forests of the Ardennes, but in addition to these, the possibility of a moving exchange, a conversation with yourself, or your wife or husband, or, perhaps most usefully, with your children. The parents of those who perished at Verdun never had that opportunity.

Before the bloodletting of trench warfare, and most particularly the 'meat-grinder' of Verdun, battle still held a glow and a glory, every wound wrapped in a flag.

> *We few, we happy few, we band of brothers.*
> *For he today that sheds his blood with me*
> *Shall be my brother; be he ne'er so vile,*
> *This day shall gentle his condition.*
> *And gentlemen in England now abed*
> *Shall think themselves accursed they were not here,*
> *And hold their manhoods cheap whiles any speaks*
> *That fought with us upon Saint Crispin's day.*

So declares Henry V in an address to his troops before the battle of Agincourt in the fourth act of Shakespeare's *Henry V.* It is a speech that might easily have been made anywhere in Europe prior to 1914. Indeed, before the fighting began, French and German parents had wildly cheered their departing sons, most fully expecting them to return. 'We were showered with presents at every station,' Paul Hub, a twenty-three-year-old German law clerk, wrote to his fiancée as he marched off to war in 1914. As his earliest letters show, Hub had experienced the same romantic exhilaration no doubt shared by almost every one of the nearly 68,000,000 men called up by the Allied and

Central powers during the course of the war. In due course, he would also come to share their profound sorrow and soul-numbing disillusionment.

In the run-up to armed conflict, even one on so vast a scale, few envision a long struggle, or heart-breaking casualties, or anything but victory. These blinders were certainly in place as Europe let slip the dogs of war, and the guns of August at last released their fire.

The First World War's subsequent carnage so bloodied war's romantic imagery, however, that by the time it ended on 11 November 1918, few could recall with anything but tragic irony the glory days of its beginning. In the years following the war, even patriotism would come under relentless scrutiny, along with capitalism, socialism and any other belief in human advancement. In the mournful, smouldering aftermath of that war, the intellectual and artistic worlds had said, to use Robert Graves' telling phrase, 'goodbye to all that'.

As if to torture us with the very irony Susan had earlier noticed, the route from Paris to Disneyland is the same that had rushed the flower of French youth, those who would have been the great-great-grandfathers of the carloads of children who now whiz towards France's number one family-friendly attraction, to Verdun during the early months of 1916. Young men had been crammed into every imaginable conveyance – wagons, cars, trucks, buses – and had arrived in numbers that would have staggered the imagination of anyone familiar with the history of warfare up until that time. Between 24 February and 6 March alone, for example, some 3,500 trucks brought 190,000 men from the railway station at Bar-le-Duc. And this was only the first wave in a sea of young men whose task it would be to defend the forty forts that dotted the valley of the Meuse.

The small, badly maintained road that once led from Bar-le-Duc to Verdun is now called the Voie Sacrée, Sacred Road, and it is only when you leave the highway and turn onto it that you get a sense that Disneyland is at last very far behind you. The Voie Sacrée is now just a road, but in 1916 it was a vein that pumped men and supplies into the longest battle in human history, a ten-month struggle that was fought over an area little more than ten miles square. In that tiny corner of the world a quarter of a million men would die, a toll greater than both sides suffered during the four bloody years of the American Civil War, which was itself an unprecedented struggle that had produced eleven epic battles, each the size of Waterloo.

We arrived at night in a steady rain, older travellers now, both in our fifties. The Hostellerie Coq Hardi was not accessible by car, so we parked a few blocks distant, then made our way through the nearly deserted streets. The hotel was in the usual style of Lorraine, with an old-fashioned dining room, hung with luxurious red drapes, the tables adorned with large silver candelabra. Unfortunately, the tables were mostly empty. When I commented upon the paucity of guests, the night clerk simply shrugged and said, 'No one comes here any more.' This was confirmed by the purely local traffic on the road we'd taken that same evening, where I'd noticed the generally empty parking lots of the town's roadside hotels. Verdun, so it seemed, had been waylaid by time, a town, and an event, that were now sinking from human memory.

Verdun had not sunk alone into this well of forgetfulness. Over the years, Britain, too, had become less rigorously observant of the 'two minutes of silence' the nation had inaugurated on 11 November 1919, when at the stroke of eleven a.m. the entire country fell silent in remembrance of those lost to the Great War. True, the Queen still attended services at the Cenotaph on the Sunday closest to 11 November, and in various places the fallen were honoured in solemn silence. These observances were a far cry, however, from that earliest and most profound commemoration when, according to newspaper accounts, a reverential silence was so solemnly and universally observed that not one phone call was made in London. It was a silence that was 'almost pain', according to the *Manchester Guardian*, a brief moment in time when the 'spirit of memory brooded over all'.

Without doubt, however, France had tried to keep its lost sons alive. For example, between 1920 and 1925, it erected thirty thousand war memorials. As Geoff Dyer pointed out, this amounted to fifty a day. And as late as 1930, a hundred thousand people had signed the guest book at the Menin Gate in just three months.

This passion to remember was no longer visible, however, so that entering the town that evening, it seemed to me that even here, at the fiery core of the Great War, solemn remembrance had been abandoned, leaving in its wake poor, forgotten Verdun.

71

The rain had ended by the next morning, so that Susan and I could stroll up the short pedestrian walkway that rises towards the Victory monument. The monument is imposing in that it is set within the town walls and surrounded by small buildings. In Paris it would be barely noticed, but in Verdun it appears massive. Two parallel sets of stairs separated by greenery and small fountains rise towards a column about thirty metres high. A statue of Charlemagne sits atop this column, his arms resting on a gigantic sword. A single word, *Verdun*, is carved near the top of the column, but there are no battle reliefs or military statues to suggest how or at what cost the victory commemorated by this monument was achieved. As a monument, it is singularly bland, but at the top of the stairs, you can look out over the Meuse to a low rise of hills beyond which, as I knew, stretched the battlefield itself. Had one been standing here in 1916, it would have been possible to see the actual glow of the battle, a hellish red tint created by perpetually exploding armaments and which had given the distant battlefield the look of a continually stoked furnace.

In places like Verdun, it is hard not to notice those who would most likely have been touched by the events that marked it. On this particular morning, we had taken a table in a small café not far from the Victory monument and ordered the standard *petit déjeuner*. The croissant, butter, jam and coffee arrived on a tray carried by a young woman who smiled brightly as she served us. I noticed that she wore a wedding band, and because of that, it struck me that a woman of her age, living in Verdun in 1916, might well have watched her husband march into the hills that awaited him just across the river. If so, it would have been unlikely for her ever to have seen him again, for Verdun was an insatiable devourer of young men. For that reason, at its end, this smiling young woman in all probability would have been one of the 650,000 war widows left to mourn their husbands in the France of 1919, part of those 'rings of sorrow', as T.E. Lawrence called them, that spread out to engulf the family and friends of the fallen and thus extend the destructive effects of war into the unforeseeable future. With that in mind, it was hard to see how the Victory monument could celebrate anything but the god of carnage.

After breakfast we returned to our car, passed under Porte Chaussée, the town's fifteenth-century gate, then crossed the Meuse and headed up into the hills, towards a memorial that could hardly have been more different from the Victory monument.

The Douaumont ossuary is very stark, and unlike the Victory monument, it is not about what was won at Verdun. It is about what was lost here. The central tower of the ossuary rises forty-two metres and looks down on the largest First World War cemetery in France. Lines of crosses stand before the ossuary like soldiers at attention. There are over sixteen thousand of them, a fraction of the 250,000 men who died on the adjoining battlefields of Verdun. On either side of the tower, there are two great archways. They are covered floor-to-ceiling with plaques bearing the names of French soldiers killed. The plaques are pale white, almost the colour of ivory, but the interiors of the archways are lit in such a way as to give the air a reddish tint. There are numerous alcoves, and through their small windows it is possible to see the actual bones of the fallen. Other than the plaques, which were purchased by friends and relatives, there is no pretence to bestowing any form of individuality upon the dead. It cannot even be claimed with any certainty that all the bones are French. It is as if the ossuary's pinkish air is designed to deny that individuality for the simple reason that an exploding shell does exactly the same; that is, turns a human being into a ghastly pink spray.

The scale of killing at Verdun was simply unimaginable, and the ossuary, despite its piles and piles of bones, and the rows and rows of crosses that flank it, can offer only a sampling of the destruction that rained down upon living human beings for a full three hundred days. It was a destruction that was entirely intended. Verdun was, from its inception, conceived as a slaughterhouse. The strategist of this hell was Erich von Falkenhayn, German chief of staff. In order to break the stalemate on the Western Front, Falkenhayn advised, in his Christmas Day letter to Kaiser Wilhelm, that the French army had to be 'bled white'. Verdun was considered the best choice because it was so dear to the French heart, and could not be lost without doing serious damage to French morale. Falkenhayn believed that the French would pay any price to hold Verdun, and so he set about making that price as high as possible, prompting the forbidding code name for the Verdun campaign: *Operation 'Gericht'* which generally means 'Judgement', but which can also be translated as 'Execution'.

What happened next created a battlefield with the highest density of death ever recorded by historians or suffered by men in arms. To the usual armoury of rifle and bayonet were added flame-throwers and poison gas that charred and blistered the skin on contact. Some German soldiers were so blackened by such burns that their comrades sometimes fired on them, thinking them French Senegalese.

Worst still was the fact that 70 per cent of those who died at Verdun did so as a result of artillery fire, a peculiarly gruesome form of human destruction that immensely added to the psychological hellishness of the battle – soldiers as the mincemeat of the Meuse; war, quite literally, as meat-grinder. At Verdun, as one soldier wrote, men sank beneath 'the stuff of blackest nightmare'.

After leaving the ossuary to tour the actual battlefield, it became clear that the landscape created by the torrent of shells that rained down upon Verdun remains one of the most torturous on earth. Witnesses to the battle had variously described that landscape as 'flayed' or 'murdered'. Some had described the land as grey, some as yellow, some as black. One airman had noted 'red-roofed Verdun' below his plane. To another it had appeared as 'the humid skin of a monstrous toad'. To James McConnell it seemed 'to belong to another world. Every sign of humanity has been swept away. The woods and roads have vanished like chalk wiped from a blackboard; of the villages nothing remains but gray smears.'

By the end of the battle, the fields of Verdun had been

essentially stripped of life, its vegetation either burnt or uprooted by explosion.

Battlefields scar the land, to be sure, but the odd thing about Verdun, as I found that day, was that this scarring had been so deep the landscape had been unable to recover. This was not true of Normandy, nor even of the Somme. But at Verdun, the endless bombardment that marked the battle had created a surreal world of bulges and depressions that was the very opposite of what might be called 'rolling hills'. The land does not undulate at Verdun, it seethes. Even from the roadside, the earth appears oddly distorted, as if some principle of gravity is being ignored, so that the earth bucks up and dips in strange contortions. Walking these same fields provides an immediate explanation. At Verdun, a combination of shell craters gouged out in countless explosions and mounds of earth that were lifted skyward in those same explosions has created a landscape bulbous with green tumours. Just as strangely, the tree line rises jaggedly because some trees have grown out of the bottom of the craters while others have sprouted on the mounds. This has given the forests of Verdun a sense of movement, but a movement that is halting, uneven, woodlands that, like wounded soldiers, seem to limp. It is as if the land has steadfastly refused to forget what was done to it, and in that act of enforced remembrance, is determined to display its scars.

All of those scars were man-made, of course, and a little further on, we found the ones that have remained most emblematic of World War I, the trenches. Often they ran for a few metres, then stopped abruptly where some shell had hit dead-on and in the explosion collapsed the walls. They were sometimes quite shallow, the deeper ruts having been filled in by the explosions that had fallen on either side, lifting great gobs of earth that had then cascaded in curtains of mud and debris back into the trenches, so that they continually had to be dug out and reinforced. The physical labour of removing with pick and shovel so much unforgiving ground had to have been monumental. For that reason it is possible to view the immense network of trenches that criss-cross Verdun as one might stare at a vast stretch of railroad or at a great bridge, and simply, silently, consider the labour of so enormous an enterprise. Add the conditions under which that labour was carried out and the nightmare of life at Verdun deepens and grows unbearable, the foot soldiers who lived it so doomed they would ultimately be called 'wastage' by their own high command.

Fort Douaumont is the central fortress of Verdun, the cornerstone, as General Pétain himself had called it, to the whole defence of the region. It was also unquestionably the strongest fort in the world, which made the comic opera of its capture all the more humiliating to the French. For Douaumont fell not to a fierce assault or to the relentless battering of German artillery, but absurdly to a certain Sergeant Kunze, who simply bumbled into a breach, crawled inside the fort, stumbled upon the kitchen larder, where he took a leisurely lunch break, then, with rifle in hand, proceeded to take the fort more or less single-handedly. By all accounts Kunze was a sturdy peasant who, according to

Alistair Horne, possessed that particular brand of courage that flows from a very limited imagination. That the strongest fort in the world, the cornerstone of the Verdun defence, should fall to such a man stung the French, and provided, at least for the Germans, a moment of supreme comic relief.

Farcical as this episode was, any sense of combat buffoonery quickly vanishes as you enter the fort itself. There is a cold darkness to Douaumont, a sense of being buried alive, which must have been vastly amplified to those entombed here during endless nights and days of bombardment. Douaumont is largely a buried fortress, all its many rooms sunk deep beneath the ground. It is dark and dank, and has the vampirish feel of a crypt, which made the continual peals of laughter that breached the sombreness of Douaumont on the day Susan and I walked its gloomy corridors all the more jarring.

A large group of German high school students had entered Douaumont just ahead of us, and at no time during the next few minutes did the stark reality of the fort impinge upon their playful mood. They skipped along the hallways and darted in and out of rooms, almost always giggling, as if Douaumont were a theme park. Large metal plates had been strategically placed on the floors of the corridors by the fort's staff, and we'd been shown how to lift them, then let them fall with a deafening concussion. The resulting sound, which was painfully loud, was said to be practically muted compared to what the soldiers inside Douaumont had endured twenty-four hours a day as thousands of shells rained down upon them. This demonstration fascinated these students no end, so that at each heavy metal plate they laughingly made as much noise as possible, repeatedly lifting, then crashing down the plates so that the cavernous depths of Douaumont shuddered with these internal explosions.

The noise was so loud, so at once abrupt and sustained, that after a few minutes I found myself locked in a kind of mental crouch. With each concussion, my teeth clenched, my eyes blinked, my head jerked, my muscles tightened. Soon my nerves began to fray, and although I am a patient man, slow to anger, I finally became fiercely irritated with these mindless kids.

'This is unbearable,' I said to Susan, and suddenly realized that within only a few minutes, I had begun to exhibit in very mild form the classic signs of shell shock. We were standing in one of the dormitories of Douaumont, its walls lined with the metal frames of the beds these men had used, and upon which they had tossed, no doubt night after night finding no possibility of sleep. 'This is unbearable,' I'd said seconds before. Now I could only wonder at what the soldiers housed in the many less impregnable fortresses of Verdun had borne, along with those yet more frightfully exposed, the thousands of men who'd squatted in the open trenches I'd just walked. Being shelled, rather than actually fighting, was, as Louis Simpson wrote, the true job of the infantrymen.

The bones of as many as 130,000 of those men are encased in the glass-walled ossuary, and after leaving Douaumont, we returned there to see a film on Verdun. The theatre was small, and very quiet, which was a welcome relief from the hideous din of earlier. For a time, it appeared that we would have the place to ourselves. Then, just before the film began, the same students who'd plagued us at the fort bustled in, joking and laughing and kidding with each other as they spread out across the theatre. They had the loose-limbed casualness of youth, and once seated, they flung their arms and legs over the backs of the seats, still chattering loudly even as the film began.

For the next thirty minutes, a series of stark, black-and-white images flickered on the screen. There in all its photographic detail was the story of Verdun, the endless line of trucks that had moved up the Voie Sacrée, carrying their loads of men and munitions, then those same men later digging trenches or storming out of them, plunging through smoke, fire, rain, snow, men loading shells or carrying stretchers, or simply limping along, held up by crutches or other soldiers, men at last buried in mud or hanging from concertina wire or blown into fragments carried in curtains of glistening red, their bones now gathered in this place, where they would remain forever, as unindividualized as plankton.

When the film ended, Susan and I sat solemnly in the wake of what we'd just seen, and watched as the students instantly leaped to their feet, resumed their chatter, and rushed in an unruly mass towards the gift shop that adjoined the theatre. They were still there when we came out the same entrance, and their youthful frenzy had not abated. They dashed from one counter to the next, asking to see this, to try that. At one point several of them gathered around a rotating display of leather bracelets that bore various names. They were looking for their own, of course, eagerly spinning the display until Hans or Fritz appeared, then snatching it from the display and rushing to the nearest cashier.

Above us, along the walls of the great arches of the ossuary, other names had been engraved, for here at Verdun there had surely been a Jules and a Philippe, a boy not much older than these German boys, but for whom history had prepared a more tragic fate.

The students were quickly gone, and on the way out, I could see them climbing onto the bus that would return them safely to wherever they were staying. They'd had an amusing lark on an old battlefield, made lots of noise in an old fort, bought a little trinket as a souvenir, and tonight they would give Verdun not another thought.

The bus pulled away, and some of the students waved to us. They were smiling as if to say, *What a good time we all had, eh?* I waved back, as anyone would, but I had never felt the utterly impenetrable nature of youth more wrenchingly than at that moment. Nothing of Verdun's horror had pierced them despite the terrible fact that it is youth that pays the high price of war, and to the extent that the young cannot be made to hate it, those who are young will more likely be doomed to suffer it. The failure of even so fruitless and sanguinary a battlefield as Verdun to impress this inconvenient truth upon those most likely later to endure the scourge of war added immensely to the sadness that was natural to the place.

'Those kids didn't learn a thing from coming here,' I said regretfully. 'All they did was horse around.'

This was a gloomy speculation, but fortunately, it was not my final one upon experiencing Verdun. For when I glanced back towards the ossuary, I thought of Paul Hub, that German office clerk who'd marched off to war with such unrestrained enthusiasm in 1914. He had fought at Verdun two years later, and in one of his last letters to his fiancée, he'd written in a voice much changed from his earlier letters, a voice much deepened by the reality of war: 'We had on us the stench of dead bodies. The bread we ate, the stagnant water we drank; everything we touched had a rotten smell . . . the earth around us was literally stuffed with corpses.' This was no exaggeration, for in fact, fourteen million shells had rained down upon the youth of Verdun, two hundred for each casualty. Hub himself had died at Maricourt on 26 August 1918. Thinking of him as I faced the ossuary, I wondered what he might have thought had he lived to be an old man, with children and grandchildren, lived to return here to Verdun. Might he have been less severe in his judgement of these German high school students? Might he have seen their playfulness in a wholly different light?

I couldn't say, of course. But I do know this much: like Paul Hub, the dead in that looming tower had also been very young, and so, it is possible that they would have forgiven these school-trip kids, perhaps even deeply envied their many future occasions for youthful frivolity, for 'horsing around', for doing those heedless, youthful things they, themselves, these dead so very young, had been cruelly denied. Gazing down from the ossuary, those ghostly young men who had perished at Verdun might well have dreamed of nothing so much as once again being able to laugh and make fun, as young people do, to leap about and jostle each other, to fling their arms over theatre seats, buy bracelets with their names on them, and in some solemn, reverent place, like the young everywhere, do some frivolous and irreverent thing.

Snapshot: Nadi, Fiji

It was late at night when Susan and I arrived in Fiji after a three-and-a-half-hour flight from Brisbane that had been preceded by another three-hour flight from Cairns. These are not long flights, of course, but the dead of night has never been my favourite arrival time. Predictably the terminal at Nadi was deserted, the shops shut tight, so that once the passengers from our plane had dispersed towards various exits, then vanished into the night, we were left alone to find our hotel transport.

From our first trip together, which had been to London, where we had arrived with no reservations, carrying nothing but our bags, Susan and I had agreed that part of the thrill of travel was the possibility of suddenly finding ourselves in the position of having no idea what to do next. In continued search of that thrill, Susan had repeatedly cautioned against what she thought of as the cowardliness of following a set itinerary. 'Only pussies,' she once said, 'book ahead.'

Following that precarious philosophy of the road, we had repeatedly set off to parts unknown with no notion of where we might stay on any particular night save the vague idea that it would be in a particular place . . . providing we had actually made it there by end of day. Some years before we had set off from Madrid with no plan whatsoever except that the furthest eastern destination would be Kraków and our furthest northern destination would be Amsterdam, both of which we would reach at some point before returning to Madrid in what we estimated to be approximately two months. The following summer we had done pretty much the same thing, only with our sights set on southern, rather than northern Europe, the final destination, as Susan characteristically stated it, 'somewhere in Sicily'.

Despite the fact that this particular leg of our current journey had been arranged and fully paid for by the Adelaide Book Festival, our arrival in the dead of night in Nadi, Fiji, briefly reminded us of our earlier, unscripted adventures, and we liked that very much. I could almost hear Susan's unspoken, 'Perfect.'

And so it was two quite happy, somewhat nostalgic, and decidedly middle-aged travellers who'd wandered out of the airport terminal that night, relishing the fact that for the moment we were very much at sea with regard to our next move. Unfortunately, as all people learn, nothing lasts forever, and in this case, our feeling of displacement, of being thrown upon our own resources, lasted only a few minutes before we were spotted by a slender young man who waved us towards him, and who, as we approached, cheerfully bolted forward.

'Thomas Cook?' he asked, then turned to Susan. 'Susan Terner?'

We both nodded.

The man smiled as he strung necklaces of white flowers around each of our necks. 'Welcome to Fiji,' he said, then ushered us into a resort minivan and set off for our quarters, a long drive during which we could smell the lushness of the island, but could see not so much as a lily pad.

The next morning revealed the storybook Fiji that attracts thousands of tourists each year, a place of dazzling beaches and shimmering seas where it is possible to idle at numerous carefully manicured resorts, then, at vacation's end, be whisked back to Nadi and onto a plane, and from there rise above an idyllic island whose many beauties have been recorded in great heaps of glittering photographs.

But there is another Fiji that such travellers do not know, but which is easy to discover if one is willing, however briefly, to step out of the perfectly coiffed world of the resort.

Save for the windshield, there are no windows on the island's local buses, as Susan and I learned the morning we headed back into Nadi. Instead, a large cloth flap is lowered over the side of the bus in the event of rain, and on this particular day, some were up and some were down, depending upon whether the bus had recently passed through a shower burst. The bus was crowded with the usual throng of uniformed resort workers, but the seat directly to my right wasn't taken.

The man who later took it was very large. I am very small, and so, as if to ease any apprehension on my part, he offered a big Fijian smile, and said, 'People don't think of island people as big. But Fijians are a big people. Like me. But nice.' He had a deep, warm voice that reminded me of James Earl Jones. 'Where are you from?'

'The States.'

'They use Fijians as bouncers in the States.'

'Really?'

'Because we are big, but nice.'

'I see.'

'I lived in London,' he told me. 'I managed a hotel.' He was dressed in a wrinkled linen suit that was quite frayed and a white shirt and narrow black tie, the mark of a professional.

We talked on for a time as the bus rumbled through the tumbledown outreaches of Nadi. On either side there were small houses with roofs of the rippling corrugated tin used in shanty towns throughout the world. Brightly coloured curtains flapped through glassless windows, and outside many homes, the revered dead had been buried beneath marble slabs that often took up quite a large part of the front lawn.

'Why tin roofs?' I asked my large Fijian acquaintance. 'It must be very hot inside.'

He shrugged. 'Tin is cheap.'

He had loved his days in London, he said, but gave no reason for returning to the island. As he talked, he seemed to become less like a professional than a man being interviewed for a job he really needed. Some strange secret purpose began to tingle in his every move.

'Where are you staying?' he asked.

I told him the name of the resort. He appeared impressed. 'What do you do?'

I told him that I was a writer and that I was writing a book about the unexpected rewards of visiting 'the saddest places on earth'.

His eyes glittered like a prospector who'd just discovered a gold nugget at the bottom of his pan. 'I think this meeting was meant to be,' he said, but gave no reason for this sudden turn towards the fated.

The bus came to a halt at the beginning of Nadi's downtown area, a low line of shops, with vendors standing outside, usually issuing quite aggressive invitations to come in.

We ended up at a small restaurant, quite nice by Nadi standards.

'For your book you maybe want to know things about Fiji,' he said after a moment. 'Maybe you want me to take some pictures for you?'

His tone had become odd, to say the least, as if I'd expressed an interest in learning Fiji's military secrets. A hint of fear shimmied up my spine. For the first time it struck me that I might be talking to a police agent. And I had already told him where I was staying.

'No, thanks,' I said quickly.

He appeared disappointed to hear this, like a man no longer sure that fate had provided me for his benefit. It was then it struck me that he'd seen me as an opportunity, an escape route, and that this fantasy had been building and becoming more elaborate as our encounter had lengthened.

After a brief silence, I asked, 'What was the worst thing that ever happened on Fiji?'

His expression became quite grave. 'The thing that maybe makes it the saddest place on earth?' he asked.

I nodded.

He turned the question over for a moment, then gave the saddest answer I ever heard.

'Independence,' he said. 'The British would never have permitted Fiji to be the way it is.'

I suddenly recalled an alarming sign that I'd noticed a day or so before. It had been on the road between Nadi and Lautoka, Fiji's second largest city. It faced the main connecting road, well placed to be seen by thousands of Fijians every day. On the sign there were two perpetually open eyes. Large letters said: YOU ARE BEING WATCHED. At the bottom of the sign, those who are watching nakedly declared themselves: POLICE CONSTABULARY.

Was it this, I wondered, that the post-colonial British would never have permitted to go on in Fiji? Yes, it was, of course, as Amnesty International's report on repression later made clear: Fiji was a paradise marred by beatings, jailings, murders, all carried out by the Fijian police.

For this reason, a Fijian had now judged national independence the saddest thing that had ever happened to his native land.

I have often thought how soul-searing it must be for a man to believe his own people incapable of self-rule, his own people fated to endure oppression and corruption, his own people forever in need of some larger power to uphold the boundaries of civil life. Ideologists can forever debate whether it was the very nature of colonial rule that made a successful decolonization impossible, but that endless and mutually contradictory debate has little to do with what I saw in the sad eyes of the man who sat across from me that day in Nadi. His was a form of dispossession I had never encountered, and it was very raw, so that he seemed even now to be reaching out for rescue, myself a lifeboat he could see drifting away from him, leaving him stranded not in a distant land, but here, in Fiji, among his own, at home.

We left the restaurant an hour or so later, and walked together down the dismal main street of Nadi. By then he knew that nothing fateful had entered his life, nothing that would miraculously change his situation. And so, he fell back to the more common way of befriending tourists, by guiding me quite aggressively into this shop or that one, always with a big smile, an activity for which he most likely received a small gratuity from each shop owner. He had probably hoped that he might be some sort of paid informer to a Western writer, and in that capacity prove himself invaluable, and by that means eventually – and by some dreamy magic that was only in his mind – work himself back to London or some other great city of the West. The death of that dream showed itself almost physically, so that this big Fijian, large enough to be a bouncer in the States, now seemed small and vaguely helpless, just another street hawker on a street filled with them.

We parted in front of the last emporium into which he'd ushered me, and in which, once again, I'd bought nothing. A light rain had begun to fall, and the candy-coloured flaps of the buses were down. People were huddled beneath the shop awnings, Fijians and Indian-Fijians pressed together within a small dry space. I offered my hand. His eyes filled with what I can only describe as the stricken look of one who had wholly misconstrued a situation, then inflated it, and was now in the painful throes of his own, brief hope's deflation. I don't recall that he even said goodbye.

Kamakura

Kamakura had once been the largest city in Japan, and it is said to have been the fourth largest city in the world in 1250 AD. Today the population is about 200,000. It is one of the most visited of Japanese cities, both by the Japanese themselves, and by foreigners, for whom its nearness to Tokyo, only about thirty kilometres, offers the advantage of convenience. Most visitors come here to see the Great Buddha, along with the Hasedera temple, renowned for its beauty and serenity, but which I had come to see because I'd been darkly, and almost guardedly, apprised of its crimes. 'Go there,' a friend had told me, 'but just be aware of what you're really seeing.'

Upon arrival, Kamakura looks very much like any other Japanese city of comparable size. The streets are narrow, and they are lined with small shops selling shoes and produce and porcelain dishes. After a few days in Tokyo, it was a welcome relief from the crowds and hurried pace of the capital. Kamakura is a very welcoming city, with an easy-going pace. There is no bustle in the streets, no great sense of everyone urgently having somewhere to go. I could smell rice being cooked in small, open-air restaurants, which further emphasized the charm of smallness when compared to Tokyo's urban sprawl.

Although Kamakura is one of Japan's temple towns, very much on the sacred circuit, it can't touch Kyoto in terms of beauty, or Nara in terms of scale. There is also the problem that a great many of Kamakura's temples were destroyed by the Great Kanto earthquake of 1923, with the result that quite a few of the city's 'ancient' temples aren't really ancient at all, but relatively new replicas, a hint of legerdemain – of things not being exactly what they seem – that would become gravely representative of the place as the day wore on and I began more and more deeply to experience it.

The Great Buddha of Kamakura is completely genuine, however. Though the temple that once housed it was destroyed, the statue itself survived the earthquake's devastation, and now fittingly sits in the open air. On the day I saw it, it was surrounded by mobs of tourists and students, mostly Japanese. Uniformed teenagers were busily taking up photo-friendly positions in front of the Buddha. Once in place, they smiled as their teacher snapped a photograph, then quickly dispersed, most of them towards the little shops and ice-cream stands that adjoin the square.

This Great Buddha of Kamakura is called the Daibutsu, and with a height of 13.35 metres and a weight of 93 tons, it is very impressive indeed. Other than at Tōdai-ji, in Nara, there is none larger in Japan. Seated in the lotus position, with hands resting palm up, the Buddha appears lost in serene meditation. And why not, for this is an Amida Buddha, the central figure of a particular sect whose hope it is to reach a 'pure land' from whose spiritual springboard its members can at last attain nirvana.

It took me only about ten minutes to walk up the hill from the Daibutsu to Hasedera. It was a path lined with the usual concentration of shops and roadside stands. I could have bought kimonos, chopsticks, soup, but the further I ascended towards the shrine the more I felt myself depart the more commercially driven life of Japan and enter one in which the pace of economic life gave way to spiritual yearning. For that reason, it would later seem to me that the sinister tentacles of Hasedera had even touched the path that rose to it.

On first impression, the Hasedera temple is a lovely complex of shrines, caves, ponds, streams, and flower gardens that wind along the hillside overlooking Kamakura and the bay that borders it. Physically, the shrine and its surrounding grounds appear little different from other such places in Japan. The landscaping is delicate, and the paths seem designed for meditative strolling. There are perfectly placed lily ponds and water gurgles out of slanted bamboo chutes. Garden sculptures rest in groves surrounded by lush vegetation. There are pools of shimmering koi and flowers everywhere. Like the temples that so grace Kyoto, it is a serene invitation to rest and meditate. So much so, that even the gigantic, gilded wooden statue of Kannon, the goddess of mercy, at nine metres high the tallest wooden image in Japan, gives off a sense of uncomplicated compassion. After all, its eleven heads, each face with a different expression, are meant to convey the goddess's openness to the great variety of human suffering.

Hasedera, however, is overwhelmingly dedicated to one kind of loss, and this is what distinguishes it, and, in that way, both darkens and to some degree corrupts it, so that it is possible to leave its immaculate pools and gardens less with a sense of one's soul having been cleansed than of its having been seeded with suspicion. For Hasedera is neither what it seems, nor what it purports to be. Sadly, perhaps profoundly so, Hasedera is a confidence trick whose setting is probably the most beautiful on earth. Had *The Picture of Dorian Gray* been about a temple, its author could have found no more fitting one than Hasedera to represent the twin poles of beauty and corruption.

There are imposing statues at Hasedera – not only of brightly gilded Kannon, but also of Amida, the Buddha who promised his followers rebirth in a pure land – but it is the smaller ones you begin to notice as you wind your way along the temple's elegantly landscaped trails. Some are larger than others, though I saw none that was more than a metre high, and most were well under it. The statues appear to be machine-made of grey concrete, though some are also made of wood. In form, they are entirely uniform, cookie-cutter images of a bald Buddhist monk, clothed in a sacramental robe, with small hands raised to chest height and clutching each other in a vaguely prayerful pose. At first, they appear scattered about rather randomly, one or two peeping out from the radiant hydrangeas, a few gathered by a pond, others along a semicircular rest area. I hardly noticed them. But as I moved deeper into the shrine's expansive grounds, their numbers steadily grew, almost like the black birds on the school playground in Hitchcock's film, until I began to feel the sinister presence of this small, silent throng. This is Jizō, the Japanese name for Ksitigarbha, a Buddhist bodhisattva, or enlightened being, generally portrayed as the guardian of children who never actually lived, the unborn, the stillborn, and the aborted. According to the beliefs for which Hasedera serves as a shrine, these children cannot cross the mythical Sanzu River, and without this crossing they cannot make their way to the afterlife for the simple reason that, having never lived, they were denied the ability to accumulate enough good deeds to attain immortality. It is Jizō's purpose to intervene on behalf of these children, which he does by piling stones on the bank of the river in an eternal act of penance for which, of course, he is to be rewarded.

The day I came to Hasedera, there were hundreds upon hundreds of Jizōs, standing in ranks, shoulder to shoulder, like little frozen soldiers. Many were adorned with bibs, shirts, sweaters, little knit caps and hats, most of which appeared woven by hand, the gifts of grieving or guilt-stricken mothers. You see mournful women throughout the grounds of Hasedera. They come to clean their personal Jizō, or to bring it new clothes. They often burn incense at its feet, so that trails of sweetly aromatic smoke rise first into the stone face of Jizō, then upward into the surrounding trees. Some fifty thousand of these statues have been purchased over the years; 'purchased' being both the operative word and the one that most burdens Hasedera with its weighty sadness.

The stigma of abortion barely exists in Japan, where studies show that 80 to 85 per cent of women approve of it, and even here, at Hasedera, the women are said to come less out of guilt than in response to the teachings of the Jizō, the cult that operates the shrine and for whose penitential acts they wish to show their gratitude. But approving of abortion and aborting your own child are two very different things, and so, within the windowless room of cultist teaching, the gratitude of these mothers makes perfect sense given that their child, by their own volition, was denied access to the afterlife. But other mothers come here, too, mothers who had no hand in the act of nature that denied their children life. This is why, according to one account, the red bibs and hats that adorn so many of the Jizō statues at Hasedera are said to represent the amniotic sack and caul, red in order to depict the mother's blood.

These Jizō statues crown the hillsides of Hasedera. They look down from rocky shelves, and it is hard to imagine that in their stony visages and dense formations there is only a 'hint' of intimidation, as some writers have suggested. For these figures, both in their form and in the way they are massed together in military columns, appear quite forbidding, and in that way reveal what Hasedera actually is: a temple devoted to spiritual bribery. Bribery because the Jizō statues cost around eighty dollars apiece, and if that is not enough, the grounds of the shrine are scattered with small shops where yet more costly gifts can be bought for these little, purchased effigies. Fresh flowers are on sale, as is incense, and there are wooden boards (also for sale) upon which grieving or guilt-ridden mothers (I saw no men involved in any of the Jizō rituals) can leave apologies to or messages and prayers for their lost children. In addition, once purchased, the Jizō statues must be given a 'home', that is, a space on the grounds of the shrine, small, of course, only a few square inches, but which must be rented from the temple. A grieving mother does not simply buy a Jizō, hang a red bib around its neck and depart with a suitably comforted heart. There is a set fee for maintaining your personal Jizō, and after a certain time, all Jizōs currently in place are plucked from their rented resting places and either destroyed or recycled back into the shrine's busy shops. In either case, the grieving mother must buy a new one.

And so, not without reason, certain commentators on the Jizō cult have noted that shrines like Hasedera have become involved in questionable practices, most of which have to do with exploiting maternal grief. Some shrines post messages warning that the souls of 'returned' children (*mizuko*) will remain in limbo should the shrine's rituals (most of which incur additional costs) not be scrupulously observed. Other offerings are also encouraged, and in some cases it has even been suggested that the failure to make an offering might result in an act of *tatari*, or retribution on the part of the angry unborn.

The odd thing is that I felt no sense of this grim exploitation while actually strolling the lovely paths of Hasedera. This was not a carnival midway, with hawkers waving people into tents. Monks padded about in their flowing orange robes or sat in booths, quietly dispensing the shrine's many goods. I only had to look out over the ranks of Jizō to calculate how many women had come this way, how carefully they had dressed their Jizōs, and it struck me that their plight, the sheer, sad dignity of their effort somehow to reach their lost child, had, against considerable odds, reclaimed some part of Hasedera for themselves. In that way, Hasedera had both charmed and blinded me to the stark extortion that is its purpose and design.

This was a tolerance and appreciation of Hasedera of which I was immediately disabused when I noticed a woman standing in front of a long line of Jizōs, some in their characteristic red bibs and matching hats, but most in miniature clothes that had been bought or sewn especially for them. She was dressed in a white blouse with black skirt and matching jacket. She looked like any other professional, a woman who might be a lawyer or an accountant, modern in every detail of hair and dress and bearing. She'd lit incense at the foot of one of the Jizōs, and she suddenly bent forward and softly fanned its twining smoke so that it drifted into the statue's motionless face. She'd also brought a few small toys which she'd placed at the statue's feet. After a moment, she knelt before the Jizō and made a deep bow of her head. She remained in this position for a long time before she finally lifted her head and gazed quite lovingly into the

Jizō's stony eyes. In that pose she looked exactly like a mother comforting a small child who'd perhaps fallen off a bicycle and scraped a knee.

I had visited the Daibutsu before I'd walked the grounds of Hasedera, of course, and in that brief encounter, I'd thoughtlessly judged it admirably serene. But as I continued to watch this woman go through the rituals no doubt demanded by Jizō, the dark undercurrent of Hasedera began to shake those formerly tranquil waters, so that I now understood why my friend had so clearly thought it among the saddest places she had ever seen.

'Go there,' she'd told me, 'but just be aware of what you're really seeing.'

So what was I seeing beyond the beauty and serenity of the temple's exquisite grounds, or even beyond the obvious fraudulence in which that same beauty and serenity played so deceptive a role? After all, various scams call to us from every corner of life, call to our avarice when we are well, and to our terror when we are sick, life itself a road strewn with schemes and quackery. Nor was it any specific aspect of the Jizō cult, nor any of the nefarious activities that are said to be routinely practised by it, that struck me as either less or more offensive than others I had seen much nearer to home and in far less lovely places. The Hasedera temple is not by any means the only place where the tree of religious chicanery had sunk its roots in hallowed ground.

No, what I saw at Hasedera, and which made it one of the saddest places on earth to me, was a woman who had come here to comfort a lifeless effigy in whom she somehow saw the image of her unborn child, and in the dark aftermath of whose loss she was seeking comfort. Perhaps she was doing this to escape the supposed anger of her lost child, or perhaps she was doing it because she'd succumbed to some other of Hasedera's many spiritual enticements. But whatever her reason, in the end she had purchased not just a small statue, but a way of not confronting the irreversibly random, pitiless and unfair nature of life, and even of some of our decisions. She had chosen to purchase a way out of folly, accident and all that is darkly fickle, a ransom somehow meant to liberate both herself and her child from the tragedy they shared.

And so, for me, the sadness of Hasedera resided in the naked way it both exposed and exploited our refusal to accept things as they truly are, and for that reason seek a false 'nirvana' that ultimately devalues the very wounds that drive us to such devices in the first place. For its call to the woman who knelt with head bowed before her Jizō was not that she should endure the loss of a child, but that she should participate in a charade whose ultimate claim is that her child was never really lost at all, but remains somewhere, out there, in need of a knit cap or a little plastic toy, and whose individual identity as a unique human being somehow resides in a squat stone effigy, rather than having long ago vanished into the undifferentiating vastness of oblivion. But no illusion can staunch the flow of a wounded reality save in the mind of whomever embraces the illusion. For that reason, to embrace Hasedera's call is to cast aside the very real loss that was this child's, its entire unlived life, in order to gain a counterfeit solace for ourselves by believing that somehow, purchase by purchase, we can build a little boat by which our unborn child can be ferried across the Santu River into the waiting arms of paradise.

Such was Hasedera's base merchandise, it seemed to me, and in selling what it sold, it was surely not alone.

I have to admit that this harsh evaluation was my final conclusion with regard to Hasedera. Nor did I expect ever to revise its severity. But some years later, when a friend of mine lost her child, my mind suddenly returned to this shrine, so beautiful, yet so corrupt that it seemed to shine and stink, in the words of a famous American insult, 'like rotten mackerel in the moonlight'. I thought once again of the women I'd seen there, but rather than lingering on the melancholy delusion to which they clung, my memory of Hasedera drew me to a very different place, the cemetery of East Finchley, where in September 1860 Thomas Huxley had stood at the grave of his three-year-old son, Noel. Huxley had subsequently written a famous, and quite beautiful, letter in which he'd once again expressed his agnosticism. He could not believe in the afterlife, he said, nor entertain any comforting notion that he would ever see his son again. Unlike the women at Hasedera, Huxley had chosen to bear his grief without the aide of spiritual chicanery.

Faced with such vastly different responses, I found myself re-evaluating my earlier condemnation of Hasedera, and with it, the women who sought solace there. In recalling the beauty of the place, and the way these grieving mothers sought to retain some impossible connection to their lost children, it stuck me simply that in the face of overwhelming loss, perhaps one should be allowed to react to it as one sees fit without garnering the contempt of those inclined to deal with it quite differently. Because of my own disbelief in the supernatural, I hoped that if confronted by such loss, I would face it as Huxley had faced Noel's death, unaided by delusion. Even so, when I thought of my friend's loss, then the mourning mothers of Hasedera, and finally of Huxley, it seemed clear that grief, itself, is all of a piece, somehow, the woman bowing before Jizō different from Huxley only in the way each had chosen to bear the unbearable. Without doubt I favoured Huxley's response, but was there anything in it that truly made it better, braver, or more noble than the prayerful women of Hasedera? Was a grief unassuaged by delusion any purer or braver or less charged with pain than one that hopefully embraced it? Was not profound loss and its attendant anguish the same for every human being who suffered it? Hamlet had declared that in the matter of death, 'the readiness is all'. After my two visits to Hasedera, the first physically, the second in memory, it seemed obvious to me that for grief readiness is very far from all, and because of that, both the grief of Huxley at East Finchley and of the woman at Hasedera must equally be granted their dark places in the world.

Machecoul

Late one afternoon, as we were driving in Brittany, I told Susan about an incident from my childhood.

My mother had always warned me never to leave school if she were not there to pick me up. Each day, I waited for her at the same place. My mother worked not far from the school, so the wait was never very long. But one day, in a driving rain, something held her up, and so I simply stood in the usual place and waited. After a time, a car pulled up and the door on the passenger's side swung open. It was the mother of one of my classmates, a woman I knew well. 'Get in, Tommy,' she said, 'your mother asked me to pick you up.' I shook my head. The woman looked quite surprised that I wouldn't get in her car. 'Come on, Tommy, get in,' she said. 'I wouldn't hurt you.' I looked her dead in the eye, according to the story she later told my mother, then replied, 'That's what they all say.'

Five hundred years before, in the region of western France

through which we were at that very moment travelling, some other little boy of about my age when I'd waited for my mother that day in the rain had no doubt strolled down one of this area's remote country roads at the end of day. Or it might have been early in the morning, or noon, or just as night fell. The time of day did not matter to those who combed the hills and valleys of Bretagne in search of boys like this one. The person who approached this child might have been a man, but it might also have been a woman. It might have been a knight. It might also have been a priest. There were perhaps as many as fourteen of these people, all of them servants of the lord who lived in the great castle at Machecoul. For some fourteen years they scoured Brittany, their eyes peeled for the figure of a young boy whose shape and countenance might please their master. Once such a boy was found, this man or woman would offer enticements either to the child, or to his peasant parents, enticements it would be hard for either to refuse. For what they offered was an undreamed of opportunity to serve Gilles de Rais, the richest lord the region had ever known, a marshal of France, a man who'd fought with Joan of Arc at Orléans, and who owned not only the castle at Machecoul, but no less opulent ones in Tiffauges, Champtocé, and Chabanais.

Such an opportunity could only have seemed heaven sent. For it would be in one of Gilles de Rais' grand chateaux the boy would live, and in which he would be taught a skill and given a livelihood. The world was uncertain, with no guarantee of bread, and by taking such an offer, this little boy would be provided daily sustenance, along with an assured place in the otherwise precarious scheme of things. Given such circumstances, it is not surprising that in the end the carriage door swung open and the little boy got in, and from there was escorted to Machecoul.

It was during a guided visit to one of the upper towers of this castle that la dame de Jarville and Thomin d'Araguin were shown a peephole, and looking through it, saw two men digging at the base of the castle watchtower. The men were removing sacks that appeared to have been long buried in the ground, a great many of them. Neither ever recorded what they saw, nor is there any evidence that they spoke of it to anyone, though by then they may well have heard the rumour of dark deeds at Machecoul, that children taken inside its walls were never seen again.

But theirs was not the only silence that concealed the crimes of Machecoul. Gilles de Rais, whom Georges Bataille called 'the most abject criminal of all time', was a married man, and his wife, Catherine of Thouars, an 'effaced shadow' according to Abbot Bourdeaut, surely must have noticed the walled-up entrance to one of the castle's towers, as she surely must also have noticed the glow of candles as her husband incessantly mounted those stairs on the many nights he did not come to her, and remained as silent as the noble visitors who'd seen the sacks. Others shared her silence. The knights who'd observed countless boys enter but never leave Machecoul reported nothing. Nor did the villagers of Bretagne who'd missed their sons, nor the priests who'd consoled those villagers, though both villager and priest must have wondered why it was that so very many of these vanished boys had last been seen with Roger de Briqueville on his great horse, or Perrine Martin in her black cowl, or some other minion of Gilles de Rais. It is this silence that still pervades Machecoul, and makes it, of all the places I've ever known, the most terrifyingly mute.

The town of Machecoul lies about forty kilometres from Nantes. It is small, with around 5,500 inhabitants. In most ways it is ordinary. There is no lovely square, as is so common in many French towns, and its atmosphere is quiet. As a place, it is as pale as the façade of its modest hôtel de ville. In every way, it quickly fades from memory, its place in French history distinguished only by the Vendée uprising, which began here in March of 1793.

But it is also here, in a large chateau, that history's first recorded serial killer carried out his deeds, crimes so monstrous in their details that they were much changed in the various books that were later written and in the films later made about what happened here. There would be far fewer victims in these accounts, and they would be older and of a different sex than the children, mostly boys, who'd died under the exquisitely conceived tortures of Machecoul.

No signs alert the motorist that Machecoul is anything but a quite typical Breton town. As a site, it is nearly invisible, even to the French. 'You are going where?' I was often asked by my French friends when I mentioned my plan to visit Machecoul. Even those very few who knew that some of Gilles de Rais' outrages had been committed in Machecoul were perplexed by my intention to go there. 'The Bluebeard people go to Tiffauges,' a Parisian friend told me. 'Machecoul is forgotten.'

And indeed, this is true. Maplandia.com lists Machecoul, but says nothing of Gilles de Rais or even of his more famous *nom de crime*, Bluebeard. Virtualglobetrotting.com provides an aerial photo of the chateau, but when one clicks on 'more information', none appears. One travel site mentions that Gilles de Rais was born in Machecoul, but says nothing of what he did there as a man. Nor does the village's most advertised hotel list the chateau as a place those who stay there might wish to visit. Something wicked this way came, but as far as the traveller to Machecoul is concerned, it came and went and left little trace except for the chateau towards which no road sign guides you.

Even so, it is there, perched upon a small rise and for the most part surrounded by trees, a ruin that is very ruined indeed, and which has an atmosphere entirely different, as I later discovered, from the far more tourist friendly Tiffauges, the village which is indeed, as my friend told me, where the 'Bluebeard people' go.

Above all, there is no sense of the theatrical at Machecoul. Unlike Tiffauges, where Gilles de Rais carried out many equally atrocious crimes, Machecoul remains sinister. It looms brokenly in the distance, two jutting columns of rubble that look out over weedy grounds and a small, turgid stream that gives off the musky odour of a swamp. Where the castle at Tiffauges has become a stage set for various productions, one of which was being filmed the day I visited it, Machecoul stands with no defined purpose, and certainly without enticements, a rough stone ruin that rises like a dry scab from the unruly vegetation, then sinks back upon itself, as weighty as its crimes. The carefully maintained grounds of Tiffauges were littered with props. A gallows. Catapults. Colourfully striped tents. Its buildings were draped in flags and bunting, and the entire area had the air of a light-hearted re-enactment. Machecoul has none of these melodramatic encrustations. While Tiffauges, with its many enticements, seems to be about the children who on any given day will gather there to see the Gilles de Rais Show, Machecoul in its unkempt gloom speaks of the children who were brought here long ago, and who, under the cruellest imaginable circumstances, met the master of the house.

The reality of that man has not departed from Machecoul. You walk the grounds he walked, and feel him around you, hovering like the low fog that everywhere suggests the sinister. There is something about a monumental psychopath that weights the air through which he moved. It is hard to express, but it is different from the weightiness of a battlefield or a death camp. It is as if you are in the company of a soul that simply could not rise, so that you walk the grounds he walked as if captured in a fetid mist.

No portrait was ever made of Gilles de Rais, so that we know only that his beard was so black it glinted blue, and thus spawned the myth of Bluebeard. At Machecoul, along with other of his many chateaux, he presided over a huge retinue of servants and retainers. He put on splendid theatrical productions and threw luxurious banquets. He liked silk, velvet, fur, as well as sumptuous foods. His library contained a collection of the most exquisite books, from Saint Augustine's *The City of God* to Suetonius's *Lives of the Caesars*, in whose salacious, semi-pornographic passages one biographer claimed to have found the locus of Gilles' crimes. He preferred gold to any baser metal, and adorned his windows with stained glass. Nothing was too rare for him to acquire, or too expensive for him to buy. He was, by all accounts, driven to the point of frenzy to display his wealth and power, riding with a royal escort and an ecclesiastical assembly, along with a herald of two hundred men-at-arms whose trumpeters announced him. In Gilles de Rais, one meets man as demon-god.

If worldly show had been enough, he might have been merely a voluptuary, a gourmand, or perhaps no more than his age's example of the Wall Street executive with the jewel-encrusted shower curtain, a bloated, supercilious, foolish man, the sort who, as the Romans have it, sits like a fly on a chariot wheel and proclaims, 'What a dust I raise'. But Gilles de Rais pursued the dark arts, and sent his many minions in search of those who had knowledge of them. One of those far-flung seekers brought back a man named Prelati who introduced Gilles to the secret pleasures of demonism, though it can hardly be said that he encouraged the carnage that would later overtake Machecoul. For that kind of bloodletting, Gilles needed only his own unrelenting appetite, a fact he himself admitted in his oddly brainless confession. It was to satisfy his 'ardour and sensual delectation' that he tortured and killed, he told his ecclesiastical judges in Nantes, then, in a staggering turn, offered the advice that parents should be 'strict' with their children, that they should 'punish' them. Even in moral instruction, it would seem, Gilles' soul could not escape the sucking mire of his own devouring sadism.

The fetidness of Machecoul, unadorned in its ruin, gives off the sense of this rotted soul, of a putridness at the core. The ground is soft, and at places it seems perpetually oozing, so that I often glanced down to make sure I hadn't stepped into a puddle. The grasses are high, and the branches of the trees hang heavy, and nothing, not even the breeze, feels unencumbered by what happened here. It is a place overgrown, the abattoir as overgrowth, so that it is only from certain angles that the broken towers can be glimpsed through a thick curtain of leaves. Because of that, there is a sense of nature as accomplice to crime, part of the enveloping silence and concealment that allowed Gilles de Rais to prey upon the children of Brittany for so long.

They were brought here in staggering numbers and over a period that must have seemed an eternity to the chateau's cooks and carpenters. To maintain and daily operate Machecoul, there must have been many such people, and for that reason it is impossible to walk its extensive grounds without imagining a scullery maid glancing into the courtyard, her broom stopped dead, her eyes following yet another boy as he is escorted to the tower. Though quite voluble in his confession, Gilles could not say just how many of these boys he had killed. There was one named Guillaume, he recalled, and one named Pierre, but the great majority of his victims remained nameless to him, mere fodder to be ground beneath the wheel of his sadistic lasciviousness.

But at Machecoul, as in all such killing grounds, it is important to remember that though the victims came in droves, they died as individuals, each death unique to the one who suffered it. Bion of Borysthenes once noted that although boys kill frogs in sport, the frogs die in earnest, and so died the boys of Machecoul to the sport of Gilles de Rais.

In fact, there was but one survivor. His name was Étienne Corrillaut, otherwise known as Poitou, a 'page and pimp' as one chronicler put it. Poitou had been brought here to be raped and tortured and killed like all the others, but he was spared because of his great beauty, and so lived to provide assistance to Gilles, and with him take the lives of other boys. On the scaffold, it would be Poitou who remained most loyal to the master who had spared him, encouraging Gilles to be strong of heart as he faced death, then commending his soul to heaven.

At Machecoul, I paused at the very spot where Poitou had been arrested, but could not imagine the thoughts that must have raced through his mind at that moment. By then he had been with Gilles through the most gruesome of his crimes, had been his bedmate and his procurer, this boy who'd been only twelve when he'd first passed through the gates of Machecoul, no doubt like all the others thinking himself the most fortunate of lads.

For all those less fortunate boys, however, a fate other than the moral midnight that engulfed Poitou awaited them in the tower's uppermost chamber. There they would be repeatedly raped and sodomized, hung from a beam and tortured, then cut down and straddled by Gilles who, as their throats were cut, breathed in their dying sighs. The tower where this carnage was carried out is now a shattered wall of stone and mortar that seems to squat upon rather than rise above the untended grasses of Machecoul. It stands alone, surrounded by piles of nondescript rubble. Though Gilles was charged with one hundred and forty murders, it is not known exactly how many boys, along with a few girls, were slaughtered at Machecoul and various other chateaux throughout Bretagne. The highest estimate is eight hundred, and if the true number even remotely approached that figure, then Gilles' appetite for children was fed at a rate of approximately fifty-seven children a year for the fourteen years the silence of Bretagne's nobles, workers, peasants and priests allowed his dominion to continue.

The silence of Machecoul, and which even now seems its chief characteristic, took two quite different forms. First there was the silence of those who wished to remain in the good graces of Gilles de Rais. These were the nobles who enjoyed his banquets, the clerics who received his behests, the tradesmen who sold him goods at the extravagantly high prices about which his heirs would later complain far more vehemently than they would decry his crimes. This was the silence of those who had something to lose, to be sure, but it was a loss they could quite easily have borne, Gilles' generosity a luxury they could have done without. For that reason, theirs was a silence that was self-imposed, a matter of choice. It was the product of their greed or their need to remain within Gilles' favoured circle, and by maintaining it they were complicit in his crimes.

But the other silence of Machecoul was the silence imposed by terror. Gilles was careful always to travel with a heavily armed bodyguard. At Machecoul, knighthood was reduced to thuggery, and Gilles was careful to ride in full display of the tyrannical warlord he was. Watching him prance by, the peasants in the fields and the workers in their shops could think only of their helplessness against such a force. Riding with him were priests, so how could they approach the Church? Riding with him were officers of justice, so how could they approach the courts? Riding with him were the highest of the high, so how, from their lowliness, could the poor of Brittany think of being heard?

The irony for Gilles was that the silence of those he bribed and the silence of those he terrorized equally fed his arrogance, and it was this that sealed his doom. On 15 May 1440, while in the throes of that arrogance, he led his henchmen into the church at Saint-Étienne-de-Mer-Morte while mass was being said. His intent was to regain a castle that had been sold to Jean le Ferron, Gilles' appetite for more and more property unappeased by the fact that he already owned more of it than anyone in Bretagne. Jean le Ferron immediately conceded, but the deed was done. Gilles had, at last, offended a power even greater than himself. In the France of the fifteenth century, a church whose sacred space is nothing less than the house of Jesus Christ on earth is not violated with impunity, especially one overseen by the Bishop of Nantes.

Gilles was at Machecoul when they came for him, thirty men led by a captain at arms. He looked down on the men the Bishop of Nantes had sent to arrest him from the battlements that now lie broken and covered with weeds. He surrendered without a fight, was taken to Nantes, where he confessed to everything, and declared himself ready to die, asking only that his body be buried rather than burned, a request the tribunal later granted.

It was a spectacular fall, and it seemed to me that it was perfectly mirrored in this collapsed chateau, so wholly a ruin, with little to suggest that anyone had ever actually lived here save those few remaining windows from which Gilles must occasionally have surveyed the kingdom whose children he had ravaged.

From the far field, Susan and I stood and watched night begin to fall over Machecoul. The air turned faintly blue, like Gilles' beard, and with darkness descending, we headed back through the grass and over the fetid stream, to where our car waited in a deserted lot.

We had not booked ahead, and so it was now time for us to look for a place to spend the night. But the village streets were deserted, and so while Susan readied to depart, I stood beside our car, hoping that some passer-by would come my way. Finally, far in the distance, I saw a little boy heading towards me on the opposite side of the street. He was riding a bicycle and looked to be eight or nine years old, dark with long hair. As he grew nearer, it struck me that he was quite beautiful, with flawless skin and bright eyes, his body very trim, just the type of boy Gilles de Rais or one of his procurers would have noticed.

I called to him as he drew near. He wheeled his bike around and pedalled up to me. I asked him if he knew of a hotel in the area. He directed me to a highway several kilometres away. There were many hotels on that road, he said. His smile was ready, and his eyes were entirely trusting. He seemed to be in no hurry to be on his way. I was a foreigner, as he knew from my accented French, and for Machecoul, so far off the tourist circuit, somewhat of a curiosity.

And so, more or less to keep the conversation going, I pointed across the road. '*Le château de Barbe-bleue*,' I said. Bluebeard's castle.

He assumed I was asking directions to this castle, and immediately indicated a way through the bramble, a narrow trail I could take in order to approach the chateau. I couldn't help but wonder how often he had taken that shadowy route himself, whether alone or with friends, making a game of it.

We talked on for a minute or so. I thanked him for telling me where I might find a hotel. He then said, '*Au revoir*,' and pedalled away.

I thought how horrible to have been this little boy during the long years Gilles de Rais had inhabited the castle at Machecoul, and whose command, 'Come with me, I won't hurt you,' he would have had no choice but obey.

Five hundred years later and a hemisphere away, a little boy of about the same age, standing in the rain, waiting for his mother, had replied to this persuasive entreaty, 'That's what they all say.' The little boy who was so willing to show me Machecoul had had that same freedom, but it had not been easily won. Vast religious, social and economic structures had been swept away in order to secure it. Thousands of nameless human beings had sat on the Spanish donkey or been locked in the Nuremberg Virgin, had been hanged and guillotined and broken on the rack. Considering all that, I had to give humanity credit for the progress it had made, often against considerable odds and at inconceivable cost.

I glanced up, and through the trees, the chateau's broken tower rose into a pale evening sky. The walls of Machecoul had once protected a monster, but now it seemed to me that its fallen towers could be seen as a monument to the heroism and sacrifice of those countless men and women who had suffered the terrible consequences of their personal commitment to enlightened law and equity, and by their courage and endurance, forged a Western world in which a modern Gilles de Rais could not carry out a fourteen-year reign of terror, slaughter innocents in unknowable numbers, and only be brought to heel at last because he'd offended a bishop.

This, it seemed to me, was the overriding, unexpected and quite hopeful final message of Machecoul, the consoling truth that the debt we owe the past is not always bad debt, and that because so many courageous human beings had paid that debt, the little boys of Brittany were safer than before.

If that isn't progress, I thought, as Susan and I headed out of Machecoul, then I don't know what is.

Snapshot: Granada

The train had stopped before a high wall of mountains and a more powerful engine had replaced the one that had brought us south from Madrid. After that, we'd moved slowly over the mountains, then descended towards Granada, where we had finally arrived in the dead of night. We'd taken a taxi to Hotel California, a booking we'd made before leaving Madrid and which, as it came into view on a deserted street, looked more like one of those crumbling hostels blithely entered by unsuspecting youths who are subsequently never seen again.

'It looks pretty run-down,' I said.

'Who cares,' Susan said with a shrug. 'As long as the room has a bed.'

She had never been one to care about fine accommodations, having long ago understood something that Justine only later stated, that tourists take their world with them, while travellers fully enter the world into which they go. For it is really true, as

Patrick Fermor once said, that life can truly be seen only from the third-class carriage.

'Okay,' I said, and on that word we lumbered up the street to where the hotel's sign blinked its palely flickering welcome.

The rooms were indeed modest. Susan and Justine, who'd just turned twelve years old the month before, quickly disappeared into the one that had two beds, while I headed for the one that had only one. There was a sink and pitcher, as in rooms I'd seen in old movies. The floor creaked and the windows rattled with each kiss of a breeze, but to my weary bones, and no doubt to Susan and Justine in their own room, it was a palace. Like Susan, I would not have asked for more.

Tired as we were from our day-long journey, I'd expected all three of us to sink very quickly into deep slumber. But that was not to be for the simple reason that although the Hotel California was modest, to say the least, its far more daunting issue was the fact that it was situated on a road the sleepless teenagers of Granada used as a racetrack for the very noisy 'motos' that whizzed up and down the road until the cruel crack of dawn. By then, the ravages of a sleepless night were in all our faces.

'Did you sleep at all?' I asked Susan when she and Justine appeared at my door the next morning.

She shook her head. 'No, but I think I passed out occasionally.'

Justine did not find this funny. She stared at me plaintively. 'Can we change hotels, Papa?'

By late morning we'd managed to find somewhat better accommodations, but that had done nothing to relieve whatever bug Justine had caught, so instead of going to the Alhambra that afternoon, Susan and Justine hunkered down in a mercifully air-conditioned room while I went in search of medicine.

The heat of Granada that day was absolutely hellish. It was a heat you didn't so much walk through as sink beneath, a heat that made it hard to breathe, so that you felt, in this parched, land-locked city, an odd sense of drowning.

Enclosed in that suffocating swelter, I hailed a cab, and in the best Spanish I could muster after only a few weeks in Spain, I explained that my daughter was sick and that I needed to be taken to a pharmacy. The cab driver reminded me that it was Sunday and for that reason most of the pharmacies would be closed. We would have to go from one to the other until we found one that was open.

Ah, so I am about to be royally cheated, I thought. This guy certainly knows which pharmacy is open but he will take me to four or five closed ones before he finds it. With that thought, one of the dreads of travel hit me squarely in the head: helplessness. There was nothing I could do. I would pay this driver whatever it cost and chalk it up as one of the usual penalties for being a foreigner, the fact that you can be cheated with impunity, and most likely will be at every turn.

With that recognition, a deep resentfulness boiled up in me, one so strong it instantly turned Granada into a dark place, but one made dark not because of something profound that had happened to someone else here, but by something trivial that was happening to me: a feeling of vulnerability and of being taken advantage of because of that vulnerability; a feeling which called up a ridiculously fierce sense of acrimony at the general larceny of mankind, its ubiquitous and petty corruptions; the fact that Tennessee Williams had been dead wrong, because you could not – and never could – put your trust in the kindness of strangers.

And so, rather harshly, I voiced a doubt about the taxi driver actually not knowing which pharmacies were open on Sunday in Granada.

He shrugged. '*Lo siento, pero no*,' he said. I'm sorry, but I don't.

Not likely, I thought sullenly, then snapped, '*Bueno, vamos.*' All right, let's go.

With that, we were off, cruising down the hill from the hotel and into central Granada, turning this corner, then that one as the driver took me first to one closed pharmacy, then another, and another, with each dead end my resentment growing hotter, as if struggling to match the suffocating heat outside it.

At the fourth closed pharmacy, I shook my head. '*Mierde*,' I said. Shit.

'*Lo siento, señor*,' the driver said with what I assumed to be a wholly counterfeit regret.

Yeah, right, I thought as I glanced at the increasing toll on the meter, I just bet you're sorry.

Then, without saying a word, the driver leaned forward and turned off the meter to the cab.

This took me completely by surprise. '*¿Porque lo haces?*' I asked. Why did you do that?

'*Porque tengo hija tambien,*' he said in a voice angelically kind and sympathetic. Because I have a daughter, too.

It took another twenty minutes before he found a pharmacy that was open, and during all that time he never reset the meter, so that minute by minute, he lost more and more money. As those minutes passed, I cursed myself for having mistrusted him, for falsely accusing him, and finally, for allowing myself to place all mankind unfairly in the dock.

When we finally located an open pharmacy, it was up a pedestrian promenade, so that he could not take me to the door. Even so, we could see the trademark green cross glowing, and knew that it was open. I knew that the driver was aware that I could go there, buy medicine for Justine, then turn left, disappear into the streets of Granada and thus avoid paying his fare. When I told him this, he nodded, and with a gentle smile, said, '*Debo confiar en ti.*' I have to trust you.

When I returned to his cab he said nothing, but simply drove me as quickly as possible to my hotel. He never turned the meter on again. At the hotel, when I paid him, there were tears in my eyes.

Plaza de Mayo, Buenos Aires

Among the many surprises that I've found in dark places is the utterly unexpected way they sometimes present themselves and the equally unexpected lessons they teach. You cannot anticipate in what way you will be touched or what you will learn. You go with your mind and heart open, and the place decides what to put in them. You may suddenly recognize some small truth, or some great one, see yourself in the place of another, or wonder why you don't, dwell upon the place itself or be swept back in time to view and more deeply comprehend, or simply see from a different angle, a far more personal scene. But a dark place may also teach a lesson about itself, as was the case for me at Plaza de Mayo in Buenos Aires, and then later, as we shall see, on the island of Pho Quoc and in the dark labyrinth of Wieliczka.

One beautiful Sunday morning in 2000, now living alone, since Justine was away at college in Boston, Susan and I went walking in Manhattan. We intended to stroll across town to Fifth

Avenue, then turn north towards what is now called Museum Mile. As the name suggests, this is a stretch of Fifth Avenue dotted with museums, many of them very large and very famous, with crowds almost as deep as their endowments. It was early fall, and so the crowds were particularly dense, and given that we'd heard of an interesting exhibit at El Museo del Barrio on 104th Street, we decided to go there.

El Museo del Barrio turned out to be a very modest affair. In fact, it looked very much like a school that had been converted into a museum. It had wide, relatively dark corridors, and its rooms were small and decidedly unadorned. There was little evidence of professional lighting, so that what illumination there was flowed helter-skelter through the windows or from the sort of lights used in public places that make no pretence to lighting art. Clearly this was an underfunded museum that, by all appearances, was barely getting by, a poor cousin indeed to the great halls further south, and from the look of its nearly empty rooms, a sparsely visited one.

The exhibition was called 'The Disappeared', and it featured the work of fifteen artists, all from Latin American countries whose citizens had done precisely that. The photographs and installations were quite varied. In a photograph of an eighth-grade class in Argentina, the faces of the thirty-two of the artist's classmates who had later disappeared are grimly circled in black. A fluorescent ladder displays the names of various Chilean officials accused of carrying out 'disappearances'. One exhibit simply presents X-ray photographs of dental plates exhumed from mass graves. On one wall there is a Chilean flag made entirely from human bones collected by medical students from the exhumed bodies of the 'disappeared'. In this particular exhibition at El Museo del Barrio, I thought, both modern and representational art had joined hands to 'represent' something very dark indeed.

I had heard of the *Desaparecidos*, of course, but until that day, as I walked through the various rooms of the exhibition, I had never actually seen any of their faces. Then, quite suddenly, they were there in pictures modestly framed and lined up against a wall as if, once again, awaiting execution. For the most part, they were strikingly young men and women, most of college age, students who'd been taken in the spring of their lives and never seen again.

In the sixties, I'd been swept up by the same zeal for social reform as these victims of the Dirty War. I'd participated in the marches and protests of that time, even joined the Young Socialist Alliance and hawked their rather silly newspaper on college campuses. For that reason, I could easily identify with these young Argentineans. I also suspected that, like mine, both their activism and their radicalism would have been changed over time, so that had they survived, they would now be working in offices, schools or hospitals, doing social work, volunteering at old-age homes, or handling pro bono legal cases, while at the same time raising families, owning homes, paying taxes, and in general shouldering the customary duties of a fully functioning life. Disraeli had been much maligned for tying political idealism to youthful naivety, but he had not been altogether wrong.

Seeing so many of these young faces was a compelling experience, but it was the power of the next exhibit that surprised me because I am rarely engaged, much less moved, by what is often called 'video art'.

In this case, it was three television screens. They hung a few feet apart, and in the first a hand was drawing a face in black ink on white paper. Once the portrait was complete, it shifted to the next television screen in line, where the face began to dissolve because it had been drawn in some sort of disappearing ink. This disappearance continued until about half the face was gone. Then the portrait shifted to the third screen, from which, seconds later, the face disappeared entirely.

This was a powerfully moving video made all the more so because the ink disappeared in a way that steadily blurred the individual features of each face, and by that means jarringly reproduced the actual process of physical decomposition, a visual effect that gave the sense of these people having been buried, as many of them had been, in garbage dumps and landfills, where they had disintegrated in a slow but thorough process of radical disappearance.

Argentina's mass disappearance might equally have disappeared from human history had it not been for the mothers who'd suddenly appeared one day in Buenos Aires' Plaza de Mayo, and whose passionate search for their lost children had finally captured the attention of the world.

Even so, I didn't go to Argentina specifically to see the Plaza de Mayo. I had never been to South America, and Buenos Aires was said to be a particularly beautiful city, but my real reason for going to Argentina was because I'd always wanted to see Iguazu Falls, where the opening scene of a movie called *The Mission* had been filmed. In this scene, a crucified priest is set adrift on the waters of the Iguazu River. He floats face up in steadily accelerating waters until he finally goes over the falls at the fittingly named point of Devil's Throat. I had always found it a compelling sequence on film, and so, when the question of Argentina came up, I decided to make the trip.

The ten-hour night flight from New York to Buenos Aires is done for the most part in total darkness. And so, during that time, you sit in a dimly lit fuselage while a vast continent passes unseen beneath you. This continent has the highest waterfall, the largest river, the longest mountain range and the driest desert on earth. Its nearly eighteen million square kilometres holds 3.5 per cent of the world's population. More significantly, this population overwhelmingly shares a single language and religion. Even so, Simón Bolívar's dream of unification, the continent's only hedge against the colossus to the north, was never realized, and because of that, South America has had a chaotic history of internecine conflict. I'd recently read about the Chaco War, a grim struggle that would have been operatic had it not been fought over a terrain as relentlessly unforgiving as any on earth and left thousands of hapless peasants dead by bullets, serpents, insects and disease. Such disasters formed much of the history of the continent over which I flew that night, and so it seemed oddly metaphorical to pass over it in an impenetrable darkness that was not unlike Africa's in its anarchic politics, its corruption, and even in the faux-Napoleonic strut of its Mobutu-like military dictators.

But there had also been moments of resistance to all this, and although I was not coming to Argentina specifically to visit the Plaza de Mayo, that earlier exhibit in El Museo del Barrio had succeeded in making it a place that deserved some small act of homage and remembrance, and this, too, it had long seemed to me, was a valuable object of travel, simply to stand silently and recall, which was my modest intent when I set off for the Plaza de Mayo on my second day in Buenos Aires.

The streets of central Buenos Aires are bright and full of energy, with the quick pace of a large city. It has been called the Paris of South America, and in the European style of much of its architecture, it does resemble European cities, though I would hardly compare it to Paris. Nonetheless, that such a city had once experienced a terrible repression did actually make me think of Paris under the Nazi occupation. For the fact is, Buenos Aires, like Paris, is a minefield of grim events, so that to walk its streets and avenues with some understanding of what once happened here is to see it in a very different light. For example, at the Obelisk, that central monument to democracy which towers over Avenida de la República, witnesses once saw a man pulled from a Ford Falcon with a missing licence plate (the vehicle that became emblematic of the Dirty War) roped to the monument itself, then machine gunned, all of this done in broad daylight. As one writer pointed out, this is like Americans witnessing the same scene on Times Square. Although the vast majority of the atrocities of the Dirty War were not carried out in so public a place as the Obelisk, they have nonetheless succeeded in poisoning the geography of the city. 'Camps' were located in schools and hospitals, and even in the basement of Buenos Aires' most prominent department store. Few neighbour-hoods escaped the stain, least of all La Boca, an area of shaded streets and quaint pastel-coloured houses that in the absence of such history could hardly be more charming. Walking those streets with the Dirty War in mind, however, is like strolling the Luxembourg Gardens fully aware that the building whose courtyard they so majestically form had once housed the Parisian headquarters of Herman Goering's Luftwaffe.

Not unexpectedly, the rule of the 'Gentlemen's Coup' had in various ways mimicked that earlier German dictatorship, none more mind-numbingly than its denial of the obvious fact that thousands of Argentineans had disappeared. The more iron-clad the system of control, the more ludicrously extreme this imposed blindness can become, of course. In *The Imperium*, Ryszard Kapuściński writes about how, under Stalin, magazines and newspapers continually reported on stores overflowing with goods despite the fact that the most casual visit to these very stores would confirm that nothing was on their shelves. The various state governments that made up the segregated American South in which I grew up were by no means comparable to Stalinist Russia, and yet their collective 'disappearing' of reality had consistently maintained the fiction of 'separate but equal' school systems for whites and blacks. Never mind that the black football team in my town did not actually have a football, but played intramural games with a stone wrapped in a pair of trousers. Never mind that there was no library at the black high school, nor that one of its math teachers, as was later revealed, had not known that when written numerically, the number one thousand had three zeroes.

In this light, and faced with an Argentine dictatorship that generally denied the 'disappearing' of its citizens, the mothers of Argentina had found it necessary simply to bear witness to the fact that once there had been a young man or woman, and now there wasn't. After all, who but a mother would know for sure that she'd indeed once had a child and demand to know what had happened to it? The government's answer was that these thousands had 'disappeared' into the mountains, into guerrilla movements, into clandestine cells, into exile. The Madres knew better because they knew that here or there or over there, in a city increasingly marked by sites of 'disappearance', a young man or woman had been tossed into an unlicensed Ford Falcon and after that, had never been seen again.

The place the mothers chose to begin this effort to make visible their vanished sons and daughters was the Plaza de Mayo.

I walked there by what I later discovered to be a quite circuitous route, but as Pilar, my Spanish friend, once noted, it is best to get lost in a city. Certainly, I got lost as I wandered about San Martin, with its beautiful trees, then down Avenida Florida, a crowded pedestrian shopping quarter where I watched an outdoor tango performance, and finally somehow onto Avenida de Mayo, which dead ends at Plaza de Mayo.

The Plaza de Mayo has had a violent history. Because Casa Rosada, Argentina's seat of government, overlooks the plaza, it has long been the focal point of Argentina's tumultuous political life. In 1945, it was the massive demonstrations here that first freed from prison, then installed as president, Juan Perón, and it was from the balcony of Casa Rosada that he and Evita greeted their adoring crowds. It was also here, ten years later, that several planes dropped a number of bombs in a failed attempt to remove Perón that left the plaza awash in blood.

There was little activity on the plaza the day I came to pay my respects to its Madres. It is a wide plaza, bordered by government buildings and a large cathedral, all of cream-coloured stone that in the right sun can shine dazzlingly white, and which makes the full-bore pink of Casa Rosada so jarring. For this is the pink of cake icing and prom dresses and a little girl's pyjamas. It is the pink of strawberry milkshakes, a colouring book pink that makes the building look less like a government headquarters than the storybook palace of a fairy princess. As the place from which the Dirty War had been administered, it militantly argues for the unreality it imposed, for how, it seems to ask, could so black a policy come from so whimsically pink a structure? And yet it had, and the mothers knew it.

The Argentine government the mothers of the Plaza de Mayo confronted here on 30 April 1977 was exactly the sort about which any number of people have written, a typical *caudillo* dictatorship, iron-fisted, intractable, self-righteous and cruel. As they began their circle around the plaza (they'd been told they had to 'keep moving' and so they did) these fiercely aggrieved mothers were certain that the men who watched them from behind the high windows of Casa Rosada knew very well what had happened to their children. There were fourteen mothers that day, and to suggest the danger into which they walked that morning, it need only be added that three of them, including the founder of the march, Azucena Villaflor, were later themselves to disappear, their bodies only found and identified years later.

To acknowledge, and in some small way, to honour that courage was what had brought me to the plaza, but I was unprepared for what I found there.

To begin with, thirty years had passed since the Madres' first march, and by then the dictatorship that had carried out the Dirty War had not been in power for decades. In fact, members of three military juntas had already been tried and sentenced to life imprisonment many years before. For that reason, when I arrived at the plaza that afternoon, I'd been unaware that the mothers were still marching, and certainly unaware that they were doing it according to a set schedule: every Thursday afternoon at three p.m.

This struck me as rather odd, though the changed nature of the Plaza de Mayo would have seemed far less surprising had I earlier read a description of the nearby Café de Madres de Plaza de Madres, an eatery-cum-bookstore that offered both a left-wing library and a selection of Italian pastries. Here, evidently, one could buy books about Che Guevara and talk either windily or earnestly about global politics while enjoying table service dining. This did not seem in keeping with the heartrending history of this Plaza, but worse was to come.

The plaza was by no means crowded that day. There were a few people strolling by, and there were others lounging about, doing what people the world over do in such places, reading newspapers, feeding pigeons, eating ice cream. It was only by accident that I lingered there long enough to notice a group of women as they walked casually towards the centre of the plaza. They were unhurried, and seemed quite cheerful. At first glance they might easily have been a tour group just disembarked from an air-conditioned bus.

But as I soon realized, these made up the current version of the Madres of the Plaza de Mayo. There were perhaps fifteen or twenty of them, and although they wore the white headscarves long associated with the original march, only a few looked old enough to have had adult children thirty years before. Walking shoulder to shoulder, the women moved forward in a single flank, circling the dazzlingly white Pirámide de Mayo like the long hand of a clock. There was little fanfare as they began the march, but the tourists immediately realized that the show had begun and in response, they quickly closed in and began to snap pictures of what some thirty years before would have been a searingly authentic gathering of passionate and courageous women.

One of the tourists turned to what he clearly saw as a fellow gringo and nodded towards the long banner behind which the mothers marched.

'Do you read Spanish?' he asked.

'Yes,' I answered.

'What does the sign say?'

'It says "Don't pay the foreign debt".'

The foreign debt? How far the agony of missing children seemed from this. The women still wore their characteristic white scarves pulled tightly down and knotted at the throat, but their voices had lost their charge and now seemed barely audible above the leaden hum of this other, far less desperate demand. *No pagar la deuda externa* the mothers chanted in ideological lock-step, a slogan no doubt selected by some political action committee, and which bore neither the love nor the loss of vanished sons and daughters.

The march proceeded on, careful not to overtake the scattering of tourists who were walking backwards in front of it, snapping pictures as they walked, some kneeling to get a better shot or keep Casa Rosada in the background. The women chanted their slogan and worked to appear outraged, but spiritual fire is hard to mimic, and theirs seemed like a show. In the first marches, they'd been middle-aged, their faces already deeply lined. Rather than banners about foreign debt, they'd carried photographs of the children they sought, and their voices had broken when they'd named the culprits they'd come here to confront: the government, the army, the Church. Those tortured voices had once pealed over this plaza, voices that had to have carried all the way to Casa Rosada and the Metropolitan Cathedral, where Argentina's most powerful men had jealously guarded their power. The first Madres de la Plaza de Mayo had known this, of course, and because they'd known it and raised their voices anyway, their courage in doing so had been scarcely imaginable.

It was to that courage that Plaza de Mayo should eternally have served as monument, but the day I came here, it no longer did. By then, as I learned later, the Madres had been co-opted by an ideology that romanticized Che, and befriended Castro and Hugo Chavez, along with various personality cult dictators in Africa and the Middle East, regimes that routinely 'disappeared' the sons and daughters of other *madres* in those countries. The mothers who marched now had their slogans and their sombre expressions, but the hardness of dogma had entirely driven the tenderness of motherhood from a place that should have been its most passionate memorial.

For a time, I stood with other tourists and watched as the Madres made their ready-for-primetime stroll, a performance that now seemed as staged as an elephant walk around a circus ring. I had not a whit of sympathy for them, but I felt a great deal of sympathy for the Plaza de Mayo. This place had once served as a beacon, and might have been preserved in that light. But now it was like a coin that had had its lustre scraped from it, a tired stage set as false as a cowboy town in some studio back lot.

And yet, there was a lesson to be learned about the fragile

art of remembrance. Left to itself, with nothing but strolling pedestrians, the plaza would have retained its power over anyone who came to it with some knowledge of the inestimable passion and courage that had once found voice here. But as the plaza made clear on that bright Thursday afternoon in Buenos Aires, such places are not beyond desecration. They have a genuineness that can be squandered and an authenticity that is frail.

Once their circle around the Pirámide was completed, the Madres rolled up their banner, pulled off their white scarves, and in little knots of idle conversation, made their way out of the plaza, towards the restaurant that commemorates, though in name only, those women who'd once risked their lives here, perhaps to try some delicacy from its new selection of Italian pastries.

The Forest and the Bridge

Each year, over a million people kill themselves. At a rate of sixteen out of every hundred thousand, this makes suicide the thirteenth leading cause of death on earth. Globally, one person dies by suicide every forty seconds, which means that 1.8 per cent of all deaths on earth are self-inflicted. According to Suicide. org, global suicide rates have increased 60 per cent in the past forty-five years. Far more men kill themselves than women, generally about four times as many, though in the People's Republic of China the female suicide rate is so close to the male that they are statistically indistinguishable. Lithuanians top the list of one hundred countries whose people most often kill themselves, while Haiti, Jordan, Honduras, Saint Kitts and Nevis share the bottom. Among the larger nations, Russia leads the world in suicides, with the Baltic States coming in second. In the United States, according to the Center for Disease Control, more Native Americans kill themselves than any other ethnic group, followed closely by non-Hispanic whites. Fewer Asians and Hispanics kill themselves, and non-Hispanic blacks have the lowest suicide rate of all Americans. Parenthetically, a gay teenager is four times more likely to commit suicide than a straight one.

A World Health Organization study completed in 2006 found pesticides to be the method of choice for poor farmers in the undeveloped world, thus accounting for about one quarter of all suicides on earth. Outside the Third World, hanging was the predominant method, and is most often employed in Estonia, Latvia, Lithuania, Poland and Romania. As you might expect, firearms was the most common method in the United States, but it also topped the list in Argentina, Switzerland and Uruguay. Jumping from buildings, bridges and the like was the means most often used in Hong Kong, Luxembourg and Malta. Drug overdose headed the list in Canada, the Nordic countries and the United Kingdom, though this means was more often employed by women than by men. Recent studies have shown that the British favour Monday, while Americans favour Wednesday. No one knows why.

The social acceptance of suicide has varied widely throughout history. The Athenian polis, of course, permitted it, and even supplied the poison, as it did for Socrates. Most of the world later outlawed it, but recently the majority of European countries have removed legal restrictions against suicide, or attempted suicide, though not always against those who give assistance. Most of Asia and the Indian subcontinent still consider suicide a criminal act, however.

Among Western intellectuals and artists, suicide has often had a certain romantic appeal. Balzac found something great and terrible in the act, and approvingly noted that it had once been in vogue in Paris. In that same city, in 1900, a photograph of the death mask of an unidentified young woman who'd been found floating in the Seine became all the rage among artists. Later dubbed 'L'Inconnue de la Seine', this young woman's image was sold in framed copies that could be hung on the walls of their studios.

Without doubt, suicide has a certain artistic cachet in that it lends a definite sense of the authentic to the artist himself. *You see*, the artist/intellectual seems to insist, *my suffering was real*. In fact, it is rare when such an artist's work is discussed without some dark reference to the fact that he or she committed suicide. A reader may not know that Somerset Maugham stuttered, or that T.S. Eliot sometimes wore pale green face powder, or that Albert Camus died in an automobile accident, as did Nathanael West and his wife, Eileen McKenney, whose sister Ruth famously wrote about her. But if a favoured author killed himself or herself, you know it. You know that Hart Crane jumped off a boat, that Hemingway shot himself, and that John Berryman leaped from a bridge. You know that Anne Sexton walked into her garage, got in her car, turned on the ignition and breathed carbon monoxide until she died. You know that Sylvia Plath put her head in an oven and that Virginia Woolf stuffed stones in the pockets of her coat then walked into the River Ouse. If you are fans of these writers, you know that Primo Levi jumped off a third-floor landing, that Arthur Koestler and Stefan Zweig took pills, that Jerzy Kosinski put a plastic bag over his head, leaving the world with a typically sardonic message, 'I am going to put myself to sleep now for a little bit longer than usual.'

And it's not just writers. If you are a photographer, you know that Diane Arbus took pills. If you are a painter, you know that Mark Rothko slit his wrists and that Van Gogh shot himself. The list, of course, goes on and on.

The notion that suicide is the ultimate proof of authenticity has also had a long shelf life in the East. The Japanese, for example, ritualized it under the name 'seppuku', which means 'stomach-cutting', and so honoured it that the method was forbidden to any but the samurai.

Without doubt, there have been naysayers, people who have found suicide not in the least admirable. For them, it is considered a rash act, done in a moment of despair and often because of a condition that time would likely have ameliorated, such as losing one's job or the death of a loved one. In this regard, Zeno's reason for killing himself was probably the most trivial ever recorded. He had stubbed his toe. He also gets the gold for the most wilful means. He simply held his breath. Joseph Conrad's reason for attempting suicide was considerably more common, the disastrous end of a first romance. According to various sources, he was either seventeen or nineteen when he tried to kill himself. One must consider the loss had he been successful.

Suicide and those who commit it have sometimes even been the butt of jokes. Ezra Pound once said that the only true reason for killing himself would be the prospect of teaching Latin. Jean Genet quipped that Hamlet most certainly would not have killed himself had he not had an audience.

But for all that, to the human being confronting its dreadful summons, suicide is not funny. Rather it is a bleak and shocking act, and probably for that reason, it is usually done in private, most often at home. There have been public suicides, of course. In America, a Pennsylvania politician shot himself at the end of a news conference, and even more spectacularly, a Florida news reporter killed herself while on the air. Some suicides are meant to be flamboyant public statements. The spectacularly showy suicide of Yukio Mishima, one of Japan's most famous writers, was indisputably such a death.

But there are also public areas that attract private suicides, and two of these, the Aokigahara forest at the base of Mount Fuji and the Golden Gate Bridge in San Francisco, have been officially designated as the second and first most 'popular' suicide sites on earth.

The Aokigahara is Japan's most haunted wood. It spreads out from the base of Mount Fuji, an easy day trip from of Tokyo. Since 1950, over five hundred people have come here to die by their own hand. In 2003 alone, one hundred bodies were found by the wood's hikers and volunteer searchers. The suicides are so plentiful that in the nearby town a special room has been set aside to await the dead. It has two beds in it because in Japan the dead do not sleep alone.

Various reasons have been offered as to why Aokigahara has become the favoured spot of Japan's most despairing. In 1963, Seichō Matsumoto's widely popular novel *The Pagoda of Waves* featured a woman who kills herself in the Aokigahara forest, a story later made into an equally popular television drama series. In 1977, the same author published *The Sea of Trees*, in which a pair of lovers come to Aokigahara to kill themselves. This was also a very popular book. But it was Wataru Tsurumi's *Complete Manual of Suicide,* published in 1993, that first described Aokigahara as 'the perfect place to die'.

Long before these books, however, Aokigahara had held an especially dark place within the Japanese psyche, for it was into these dense woods that during hard times the old had been brought to die. They had been the useless eaters of a starving time, and through the centuries their ghosts have been said to haunt the woods.

This ancient sorrow, combined with the more recent suicides, have given Aokigahara a storied creepiness. It is said that compasses do not work in the forest and that there are no birds there. The first assertion has been explained by the fact that large deposits of iron lie beneath the soil. The absence of birds remains unexplained, at least as far as I was able to tell, though I must say that on the day Susan and I visited the forest, we did, in fact, see no birds. But it was a drizzly day, with Mount Fuji covered in dense cloud, and this may have been the reason there were no birds in the forest. In fact, it had rained all during the train ride from Tokyo, so that by the time we reached Aokigahara, everything was drenched.

The forest is large, and though it is completely accessible from the road, there is also an official entrance. At this centre, visitors are encouraged not to enter the forest alone or to stray from the well-marked path. A guide was provided, but he spoke only Japanese, a good indication of how few foreigners travel there. One of the people in our group of four spoke a tiny bit of English, and she was nice enough to translate what she could. From her I gathered that at no point during the tour was there a single reference to the dark fame of Aokigahara. The guide pointed out this plant and that one. He nodded towards the occasional stream or puddle, and sometimes turned over logs and indicated what he found there. He named trees and vines and various other vegetation, but when we reached a sign I later found translated as 'Your life is a priceless gift from your parents. Think about them and about your family. You do not have to suffer alone,' he passed it by without comment, so that I left his service with a sense of having been taken on a very thorough botanical tour, but one that had wholly ignored the hundreds of desperate acts that had been committed within this sea of trees.

But this indifference to Aokigahara's grim function did not succeed in hiding the odd look of the place. The forest was not thick and overgrown, as it is often described, though there may be different regions of the woods that are much denser than the

143

area Susan and I visited. Even so, there is something curiously distorted about it, something that looks unreal, even computer-generated, like a forest set created for *The Lord of the Rings* or some other such fantasy. Susan found the general fetidness of the place unnerving. It was, she said, 'as if the whole forest were a decomposing body'.

And, indeed, a walk through Aokigahara can be quite unsettling. There are places, for example, where the ground abruptly opens like a large black mouth, ragged and toothless, save for dangling brown roots. The ground is covered in dark soil, and everywhere scoured with roots that swell from it and run across it like bundles of exposed nerves. It is easy to trip, easy to fall, and because of that you can lift your gaze from the forest floor only at your peril. But if you do, you see little that is different from the ground because the forest canopy hangs almost as darkly above you, and from that deep shade sends down thick tentacles of leafless vine that give the forest, both below and above ground, a deeply sinister feel. The overall impression is that you have entered a landscape mined with pits and snares and strewn with fierce entanglements, a place fraught with obstacles to progress, which, metaphorically at least, suggests the sort of life, thwarted and ensnared, that many suicides are no doubt fleeing, a world so strewn with entrapments that you cannot move without faltering.

For that reason, I was struck by the strange irony that in Aokigahara, people had found an outer world that perfectly mirrored their inner one: sluggish, webbed, chaotic, closed in and intractable, so that I recalled the 'furiously overheated room' William Styron had wished to flee by means of suicide. Added to this jarring effect, there is a great sense of rot and seepage and decay in these woods, so that it gives the appearance of a forest that is at once lushly alive and weirdly mouldering. I knew the history of these woods, of course, and so I can't claim that my sense of them was unaffected by what I knew. And yet, Aokigahara did feel darkly tinged with hopelessness, a tangled wood that might indeed be thought a perfect place to die by people for whom life had taken on the fatal aspect of an inescapable bramble.

In that sense, it could not have been more different from the Golden Gate Bridge, the place that had long held its title as the number one suicide site on earth. I had walked it a year before coming to Aokigahara, and on the local train back to the Japan Rail station – a brightly painted train, as it happened, with a cartoon Mount Fuji adorned with ribbons and balloons – I was struck by the contrast between the forest and the bridge, the former so thick and entangling, the latter so open and accessible.

The Golden Gate Bridge is as beautiful in its visual simplicity as Aokigahara is in its visual chaos. The bridge is a line. The forest is a web. This difference is important, and far-reaching in its suggestiveness. Aokigahara is perfect for concealment. The Golden Gate Bridge is perfect for display. In the forest, the suicide seems to say: I am to blame for this. On the bridge, the message is: Everything outside me is to blame. The forest admits a failure. The bridge proclaims a martyrdom.

Or at least so it seemed to me on the way back to Tokyo. But our first thoughts are rarely correct ones, and so later, in the cold light of more reflection, I recalled the morning I'd walked the Golden Gate Bridge, and the route by which I'd reached it.

I'd taken a bus early in the morning, and on the way suddenly imagined myself a suicide determined to take my own life when I reached the bridge. Caught in that imagined death grip, I'd suddenly found myself searching for reasons to stay my own hand, choose life, however dismal it might seem at that moment, over death. It was a drizzly day, just as it would be a year later at Aokigahara, and the mist gave the streets an appropriately sad and desolate look. Even so, it seemed to me that there were plenty of quite obvious reasons to think life worth living. To begin with, I noted the variety of restaurants: Chinese, Japanese, Thai, Mexican, Italian. There were plenty of churches, too, places one might go for comfort, guidance, renewal, any of the many services they provide. There was a dance studio to learn a new skill and theatres and bowling alleys for entertainment. There was a statue to firefighters in Washington Square Park, and so I thought of the many men and women who had given their lives in service – firefighters, soldiers, police – and this, I thought, might remind the potential suicide that one should not hastily throw away that which others had so deeply wished to keep. There were pet shops and animal shelters where the utterly companionless could obtain a perfectly serviceable companion.

The night before I'd sat in my hotel room and read one of

the better known of the many books on suicide, a workmanlike analysis with the usual number of penetrating glimpses into the obvious. Suicide occurs because people want to escape pain or illness. People kill themselves because they've been raped or bullied or abandoned by a loved one, because someone near has died or because they cannot find release from an addiction. The enumeration of types of suicide followed, along with an equally weighty listing of the various kinds of unmet needs that can generate it. People killed themselves because they lacked love or because they had failed to achieve what they thought they should have. They killed themselves because they felt shame or humiliation or because they had run into obstacles they were certain they could not overcome.

These were all reasons to die against which I now collected additional reasons to live. There were lovely parks through which to stroll, and small curio shops where one might find that unexpected bargain. There were hobby shops for builders of wooden ships and collectors of coins and stamps. There were places to play video games and places to play chess. There were offices and factories, groceries and bakeries, and somewhere in the city's bustling warren, I – the potential suicide – might yet find enjoyable work. There were museums and art galleries and exhibition halls, many of which were free, and somewhere in all that something might catch my eye or engage my mind. There were libraries and bookstores, and among all those books, I might yet find the one that spoke to me with the age-old power of literature. And everywhere there was music, pouring out of shops and from cars stuck in traffic. It was still quite early, but I knew that in only a few hours yet more music would flow through every park and green space as the city's street performers took up their work, and that when night fell, it would twine out of jazz clubs and dance halls and bars. And if none of this was worth living for, then there was always the caravan of faces. They came in all shapes and sizes and colours, and behind each face was a unique experience of the life I was set on leaving.

So much to lose, it seemed to me, so much to prefer over an eternal darkness.

The bridge was wreathed in cloud when I reached it, and in the bay, the horns of the ships, blinded by the dense morning fog, were calling to each other continually, a sound I found as haunting as the silence of Aokigahara, and which seemed no less chilling and dramatic. It was a bridge from which over twelve hundred people had leaped to their deaths since 1937, some evidently having come great distances to do so, and at that moment, half-hidden in a thick mist, it seemed every bit as forbidding as the depths of Aokigahara.

The deck of the Golden Gate Bridge is seventy-five metres above the water. The fall takes only four seconds, but by that time such a speed has been reached that the velocity at impact makes the surface of water little different from the density of concrete. When a human body abruptly goes from roughly 120 kilometres to zero kilometres per hour, the destructive results are far reaching. The internal organs detach from their moorings and surge forward at fantastic speed, ripping out adjacent tissues and collapsing one into the other to create a misshapen jumble of lacerated flesh. Even the most protected of the body's organs is unstrung on impact, because the sternum collapses, which compresses the heart and causes it to disconnect from the aorta. A similar destruction attends the bones, so that later autopsies become a picking through of broken ribs and vertebrae. To leap from the Golden Gate Bridge is not to descend into the waiting arms of angels. Rather, it is to confront with lethal force the naked facts of physics.

Even so, twenty-six people have survived what for the vast majority proved a fatal leap, thus the tellingly stark statistic that 98 per cent of those known to have leaped from the bridge did not survive the fall.

More than at any other spot, they had chosen lamp post 69 from which to make their leaps, and so that became my destination once I reached the bridge.

It was still chilly and a fog lay thickly all about, so that I could make out only about the first third of the span. Since there are 128 lamp posts on the bridge, I assumed that the sixty-ninth would lie somewhere near the middle.

The actual span of Golden Gate Bridge is only a little over twelve hundred metres, but the approaches are long, and the one on the San Francisco side of the bay had the usual trappings of a popular tourist destination. There was a gift shop, an eatery and a large parking lot. The gift shop was closed, but there were a few people so busy having breakfast outside the eatery that not one of them appeared to notice a small, white-haired man, dressed entirely in black, walking without a coat in this inclement weather, and clearly headed towards the bridge at what, given the fact that I was cold and anxious to get indoors after reaching lamp post 69, must have been a quite determined clip.

Because of the hour, the chill, the fog, I found the bridge pretty much deserted, so that it wasn't until I'd reached what I later calculated to have been approximately lamp post 22 that I encountered a man on a bicycle. He was about my age, and he was coming from the other side of the bridge, riding briskly, glancing towards the water from time to time, but as he closed in upon me, I noticed that unlike the eager breakfast crowd on shore, he noticed me, and for that reason slowed his pace considerably and stared directly at me, his eyes quite penetrating by the time he passed and murmured his soft, oddly tentative and faintly quizzical, 'Good morning.'

'Good morning,' I said, and continued on my way, though now fully aware that my appearance had given this lone bicyclist pause, so that he'd clearly wondered if I might be headed to the middle of the bridge with no expectation of coming back.

As I'd expected, lamp post 69 stood at almost the exact centre of the span, theoretically at its highest point, which made its selection perfectly sensible. From here the fall would be the longest, the sudden impact the greatest, and the chances of rescue the most remote.

That morning it was a lonely place made more so by the fog,

the chill, the drizzle, and, of course, by the mournful horns of those blindly passing ships. Looking out over the water from the exact place from which so many had leaped into it, I was seized by the sheer physical dread that must have preceded that final step. Much has been written about what the suicide must overcome in order to make so fatal a choice. Primarily, it is said, he must move beyond the reach of hope. But in the interesting study of his own suicide attempt, Thomas Joiner points out that at the moment of decision, the suicide must step beyond the reach of something far less abstract than hope. He must step beyond both the fear of pain, which is instinctively very great, and the fear of death, which is instinctively the most basic of them all. The overcoming of these twin fears is the final test of the suicide. From the vantage point of lamp post 69, suspended above that frigid water, I simply could not imagine an isolation so deep, a constriction so complete, a despair so profound or a hopelessness so unrelenting as to compel any living creature to make that fatal dive.

And yet they had.

In Eric Steel's documentary *The Bridge*, you watch them do it. Beginning in January and ending in December of 2004, Steel's film crews photographed twenty-three of the twenty-four suicides that occurred during those twelve months. What you see is hesitation, and a lot of it. There is much pacing before the jump, along with much standing silently, peering down at the water. Not one of those twenty-three suicides simply marches out to a given point and boldly leaps. Here, on this steel precipice, they stopped, at least briefly, and for the last time engaged what Styron called, quoting Milton, 'the darkness visible' of despair. Aristotle had deemed suicide cowardly because it was life taken in order to escape life, rather than for some noble aim. But watching those on the bridge come at last to their fatal choice, you realize that suicide is not a cowardly act at all. You see in them the great pull of resistance, the heavy hand of dread, the fierce grip in which life still holds the living. For that reason, suicide, seen nakedly, is an act of awesome courage, one I frankly, and quite surprisingly at that moment, found myself helplessly admiring.

True, many suicides are rash reactions to some moment of grief or anguish or disappointment, one that might well have passed, and in its passing, opened to a fuller, or at least more endurable life, and these we must do everything we can to prevent. But others are the product of a protracted ordeal, and it is these, if we cannot prevent them, that we must judge more tenderly, as I found myself doing that morning. For it seemed to me that here, on this bridge, a final evaluation had been made, and a final judgement rendered, one that utterly rejected my long, trivial list of why a given human being should find reason to live. For what is food when one no longer cares to taste? What is music when one no longer cares to hear? What is work when one no longer sees its purpose? What is the value of your life if it has grown so torturous that neither the fear of pain nor the fear of death can hinder you from taking it?

Life, like a story, must have a gimmick, it seemed to me,

something that makes it work, and when, after much painful searching one still cannot find it, then it seemed to me not altogether unreasonable to end it.

Such might have been the lesson I drew from the bridge, but for a stunning fact I learned only subsequently, and which radically changed my mind. The bridge had convinced me that some lives were simply too painful to bear, and by that means, it had to some degree inured me to the deaths that had been carried out here. I had stared down at those frigid waters, calculated the terror of the fall, and concluded that if one could make such a leap, then it was surely from a life that could no longer be endured. For such people, it seemed to me, suicide was simply a form of euthanasia. If not the bridge, they would surely have found some other means of escape. But this supposition had already been proved untrue. A study of 515 people whose attempts to leap from the bridge were stopped had shown that a full twenty-six years after the attempt, 94 per cent of those who'd been restrained were either still alive or had died of natural causes. Let me repeat that: 94 per cent. True, a disproportionate number had subsequently fallen victim to violence or alcoholism or drug abuse, but it was at least possible that some had also found happiness and gone on to live productive lives. One thing was certain: the vast majority of those who'd come here to die had later come to terms with life after having attempted quite spectacularly to take it.

This study returned me to my final moment on the bridge that day.

It was still cold and drizzling rain when I stepped away from lamp post 69 and headed back across the bridge to the city. On the way, I saw a man coming towards me, the same who'd approached me earlier, slowed enough to give me a close look, then offered his quiet, quizzical, 'Good morning.' To my surprise, he slowed again, and as he drew closer, an extraordinarily sweet smile lit his face. 'Glad you made it,' he said gently and with great sincerity. There was kindness in his face, relief in his eyes, and in his voice, for that instant, I heard a music as beautiful as any I had ever heard. For a moment, I felt myself the utter opposite of that drowned Parisian girl. Like her, I was '*inconnu*', unknown, but unlike her, someone had set aside the romanticism of suicide and seen, instead, its grim and heartless face, and by that recognition, had been pleased, and perhaps even a little uplifted, by the fact that I had chosen, at least this time, the longer road to death.

'Thank you,' I said, and with those words felt something very soft and warm bloom within me. It seemed infinitely worthwhile to live in a world where one could be so deeply touched by a stranger's regard. He had not known me and so could not have judged whether my life was settled or whether I swirled in a maelstrom of inner pain. Even so, he had wanted me to live, to fight my way through, because there is always a chance that one can find a way.

It struck me later that the care I'd seen in this stranger's eyes and heard in his voice was perhaps life's ultimate gimmick, a reason, in the absence of all others, to live, and I couldn't help but wonder if it was this selfless, anonymous care that had been felt by those who'd been restrained by perfect strangers from leaping from the bridge and for whom this anonymous act – at least for the vast majority – had proven in the end to be enough.

Snapshot: Adanwomase

'The project has not met expectations,' Eric said as Susan, Justine and I prepared to leave Adanwomase. It was the summer of 2011, and as a family we were on the road again, now in the middle of the old Ashanti Kingdom, perhaps fifty kilometres from Kumasi, Ghana's second largest city. This was the Bonwire region, known for its Kente cloth, and Eric, no doubt on instructions, was draped in a brightly coloured robe. This was his costume, and it suggested a hope and pride that was nowhere in his voice.

Two weeks before, Justine, who was now thirty-one and a world traveller in her own right, had met Susan and me in Accra, Ghana's sprawling capital, where she'd been living for the last two weeks, working on a documentary film about the scourge of glaucoma in West Africa, and a particular NGO's efforts to treat it.

We'd embarked from Accra in the early hours in order to avoid its impossibly snarled traffic, and from there made the journey north towards Tamale. This had been hard travelling over the sort of roads that seemed determined to grind human bones to powder, and even now we were only halfway to our destination. For that reason, if for no other, the stop at Adanwomase was a much needed and very welcome one.

We'd met Eric at the town visitors' centre, a one-storey concrete building where various Kente goods were on sale, and where the weaving technique was demonstrated. After that, we'd followed him to a 'factory', which was simply an open shed with several weavers, all of them men, as Susan noticed with particular interest because, in the innumerable villages through which we'd passed on the way to Adanwomase, the men had appeared universally idle while the women were ceaselessly at work.

After the factory, Eric had dutifully escorted us to a cocoa orchard where a revival of that once lucrative crop was being attempted, then to the town's witch doctor who'd conveniently gone in and out of some sort of trance while Eric explained the superstitions that regularly brought townspeople here to slaughter chickens and get news from the future. This had been an attempt to make grotesque superstition seem charming, and Eric, bright and sceptical as he quite obviously was, had clearly not had his heart in it. It was part of the show tourists were said to expect, but I could see that for him it only romanticized a style of magical thinking he found both stupid and dangerous, this local shaman a throwback whom his fellow villagers at Adanwomase had not thrown back far enough. Leaning against one of the cracked walls that surrounded the shaman's house, he'd seemed incalculably lonely. His eyes drifted skyward as the shaman began to mumble and gesticulate, and he did not return his attention to earth until this particular part of our guided tour was over, at which point he immediately reanimated.

'This way,' he said briskly, clearly relieved to be done with the shaman's mumbo-jumbo show.

With that, he guided us out of the small plaza, with its bloody altar and scattering of chicken heads, walking slowly and silently. I could see that he was thinking. Finally, in a soft voice, he said, 'It is hard to succeed here. There is so much corruption. It is hard for someone to stand on his own feet.'

I simply didn't know how to respond to this without making some sort of invidious comparison between the developed world and the one in which he seemed very much imprisoned. Neither did I want to give the impression that I felt sorry for him, for Ghana, for whatever was holding both of them back, though, in fact, I did. And so we walked on without speaking.

Soon we were once again outside the visitors' centre, the end of our tour, and thus a perfect moment for Eric to ponder the fading likelihood of future guests.

'We get very few visitors,' he said.

He glanced out over the dusty streets of a town that, he said, had been 'educated' to attract tourists. There were no pestering hawkers, no gang of young men swooping in on the nearest females, none of the annoying and sometimes unsettling excesses that had earlier turned to nightmare any attempt to see, for example, the Larabanga Mosque, and because of which visitors were now being vigorously warned away from what might otherwise have been a successful local attraction.

Adanwomase had learned the hard lessons of Larabanga and so its inhabitants and tradesmen had been carefully schooled to keep everything low-key. In the shops, proprietors said hello, smiled, and left it at that.

'Maybe two or three visitors in a week,' Eric continued. He seemed to be staring into the desert of his own lost opportunity.

'Why don't more people come?' I asked.

He shrugged as if any further discussion of the 'why' would only increase his despair.

Even so, he seemed to want to talk, and so I pressed him a little. 'What is the problem, do you think?'

He smiled, but sadly. 'Everything is the problem here.'

This was not altogether untrue, as I'd learned by then, because, in fact, the 'problem' was Ghana, and not only its corruption. For there was also the matter of its disorganization, its dreadful roads, the fact that whatever should work (toilets, sinks, electrical outlets) did so erratically or not at all. Save for the occasional exception to the rule, the hotels were flea-infested, the food terrible, the water undrinkable. Ceiling fans weaved and wheezed and banged until they stopped, never to turn again. Ghana was the kingdom of the unrepaired, the half-constructed, the endless repetition of the same goods, this said of what is surely one of the continent's least blighted countries – in fact, a paradise of order and development compared to most. At an earlier stop, we'd watched three full grown men, all employees of this state-funded facility, lounge under a tree while the one woman who worked there cleaned the rooms, washed the linens, cooked and served every meal. It was as if the men of Ghana saw no other point in being men save, unlike women, they could live in perfect idleness.

'Surely the country will find a solution,' I said lamely, unable to think of anything more assuring for fear of being thought arrogant, a Westerner with all the answers, when, in fact, I had none.

Eric smiled that smile of his again, weary, melancholy, fixed in solitude, a smile that gave off the sense of a fertile but unwatered field, a person of great potential locked in a world of little opportunity.

'We are stuck with ourselves,' he said after a moment.

I thought of a line from Conrad, the fact, as he'd said, that colonialism wasn't pretty. Neither, it seemed, was independence. In truth, there was hardly a work on contemporary, post-colonial Africa that did not grudgingly admit that the continent was worse off now than ever. The so-called 'donor nations' had poured trillions of both private and institutional money into its always outstretched hands, but there was little to show for it. In fact, only a few weeks before our stop at Adanwomase, the British had suspended any further bequests to Uganda because that country's officials could not account for a full seventeen million pounds in aid that had simply vanished. If Paul Theroux's description of a 2003 journey from Cairo to Capetown could be credited, Africa was pretty much a three-C's study in unrelieved nightmare: crime, corruption and chaos. I'd recently read Tim Butcher's account of his journey in the Congo, a harrowing, life-threatening trip that his aunt had made without the slightest difficulty, and barely any inconvenience, in 1955. Africa had not simply declined during the post-colonial period, such works suggested, it had plummeted into the abyss.

All of this bad news was in Eric's disenchanted eyes.

'Well, I'll certainly tell everyone back home how much I enjoyed our stop at Adanwomase,' I said.

This silly effort at encouragement seemed to have the opposite effect. Rather than brighten slightly, Eric simply offered another disheartened shrug to Africa the intransigent, Africa the disordered, Africa the incompetent, Africa the corrupt, the tribal, the ignorant, a hopeless shrug to the benighted and blood-soaked Africa whose realities past, present, and in the foreseeable future, turn the extravagant nonsense of *The Lion King* into little more than a cruel joke.

To this shrug, I could add nothing. I was just another outlander, soon headed out of a place that Eric could not leave, so that he seemed suddenly like a sane man trapped within the insurmountable walls of a madhouse, doomed to live forever among its inmates and according to its lunatic customs and traditions.

From there, my mind might have gone to anywhere on earth, this dark place a springboard to another even darker. Instead, it returned me to Madrid, a city I had left nearly twenty years before. It was a hot summer day, and Susan, Justine and I were just getting back to our apartment on Francisco Silvela. There was a bus stop directly in front of our building, and our next door neighbour, Pilar, was standing there, waiting for the famed Circular. She was in her mid-fifties, a very refined woman from a noble Spanish family that had no doubt flourished under Franco, but which had later fallen on bad times. As a result, Pilar, with her extensive knowledge of art and her perfect English, now worked as a guide at the Prado. She had been the best of neighbours, particularly helpful early on when we'd spoken so very little Spanish.

We knew little of her private life, save that she had never been married and had only a sister who lived far distant from Madrid. She never had guests in her immaculately clean apartment, and I never saw her in any of the local bars or restaurants nor in any way take part in the highly animated nightlife that is so much a part of Madrid.

Even so, she seemed quite content, always friendly, ready for a chat either in Spanish or in English. For that reason, it seemed strange that day when she didn't smile and wave to us as we approached. Something was clearly wrong.

'Are you okay?' Susan asked when we reached her.

For a moment she seemed unable to answer, then, with a vehemence that was all but shocking she said, 'I would leave here!' Her eyes flashed. 'I have wasted my life here.' She seemed on the verge of explosion. 'If I could have my life again, I would get out!' She was silent for a moment, then her arm shot up, and her voice lifted in a frantic declaration. 'I would go to AMERICA!'

On the heels of that memory, now facing an equally dispirited Eric, I said, 'You know, a lot of people feel trapped.'

Eric nodded. 'Trapped,' he said softly. 'Yes.'

For a moment we stood in silence. Then, quite suddenly, one of those ubiquitous white Range Rovers pulled up, and out popped a gaggle of tourists, these from Australia. Eric's eyes flashed with surprise and appreciation and he quickly stepped forward, welcomed them with a big smile, then escorted them inside the visitors' centre.

'Where are you from?' asked the man who'd brought the Australians here and who, as he told me, was the owner of the local hotel in which they were staying.

'The US,' I answered.

'Well, you should be happy about what you've done here,' the man said, who, as it turned out, was also Australian. 'This whole Adanwomase project is paid for with US tax money.' He smiled brightly. 'So, thank you.'

'You're welcome,' I said, instantly accepting his generous compliment at face value.

But some weeks later I was not so sure. Now back from Africa, and again on the crowded streets of New York, I ran into one of my old students, a black girl I'd taught in high school and who was now a woman of around thirty.

'I'm glad I ran into you, Mr Cook,' she said warmly. 'I always wanted to thank you for something you said in class one day.'

'What was that?'

'You said, "If you think of yourself as a victim, you will always

163

be one,"' she answered. 'I remember going home and thinking about that and deciding right then and there that I WAS NOT going to be a victim. I think that changed my life.'

It was one of those gratifying moments that sometimes comes into the lives of teachers, and I thanked her for it, then we parted.

But as I continued on my way, I thought again of Adanwomase and wondered if my tax money, or anyone else's, had actually been well spent here.

In recent years, there has been a large and steadily accumulating literature on the paradoxical nature of aid. A list of such works would fill a large bibliography, and most focus on aid as encouraging tribal or ethnic antagonism, prolonging civil war, serving the aims of a new imperialism, enriching corrupt governments or arming warlords. But it seemed to me that there might be an element of aid that ran deeper and was more damaging than any of these, and which, once firmly established, might never be eradicated.

Could it be that in the end, all those innumerable grants and hugely funded projects were merely part of a complex of public and private charity that extended the continent's infancy, nurtured a sense of inferiority and helplessness and failure, taught Africans with every dollar or euro they accepted that they were children, incapable of working out their own destinies, that if the 'donor nations' did not lift them, they would forever crash and burn? There is an old African proverb: *He who gives, rules.* Might this hard truth of largesse's dominion not equally apply to the enslavement of the spirit and the colonization of the will?

On that thought, I recalled the quick step with which Eric had moved to welcome those typically cheerful Australians. Was there something of the dance of subservience in that movement, or was he simply a responsible employee greeting the latest customer in a way no different than one might observe in a waiter or a sales clerk in a Western department store? I could not be sure, and yet, I couldn't help but fear that although the manacles that had once bound African bodies had been broken long ago, the ones that now threatened to bind their hearts and minds were still being forged.

Okinawa/Hiroshima

The journey to Hiroshima should be made by way of Okinawa, a small island only thirty kilometres long, but upon whose thickly shrouded hills and shadowy ravines was fought the last battle of the largest war humanity has ever waged, and which was, in terms of its later impact upon the human future, perhaps the most decisive of all time. It is a two-hour flight from Tokyo over a sea that had once bristled with arms. The approach is over Naha, Okinawa's capital city, and it is possible to gaze out the window and see the narrow contours of the island as American pilots would have seen it on the morning of 1 April 1945, when 545,000 American troops attacked Okinawa by land, sea and air, in the largest such military assault in human history.

On that day, American pilots would have flown over an expanse of heavily wooded hills and vine-choked valleys. They would have seen few, if any, Japanese troops, and from their apparent absence might have surmised that plans for the island-by-island defence of Japan had been superseded by the more desperate method of kamikaze attack, itself the largest organized suicide effort in the history of man.

Susan and I had come to Japan at a time of school trips, and so the airports both in Tokyo and at Naha were crowded with hundreds of neatly uniformed students, not one of whom was anything but Japanese. There were no black students, no Caucasians, no Indians, no Hispanics, no Polynesians, no South-East Asians, no Chinese among the throng of impressively well-behaved young people we so often encountered as we moved throughout the country.

This homogeneity remains a holdover from the nation's long adherence to a form of ethnic purity that is based not on a tragic history of ethnic conflict followed by ever changing oppressors, as is the case, for example, in the Balkans, but purely on Japan's policy of keeping the country ethnically Japanese. Thus, in 2005, when Tarō Asō, then Japan's Communication Minister, declared Japan to be 'one culture, one civilization, one race', no Japanese in either public or private life so much as blinked an eye. After all, Japan's policy of banning all immigration has pretty much remained unchanged since it was first promulgated in 1899.

In this sense, Japan has enforced a profoundly exclusionary policy that cannot but remind the travelling American that it was this same sense of their own uniqueness, infused at that time with military bravado, dreams of empire and the shared national fantasy of imperial divinity, that fired the nation's bellicose ambitions, thus contributing not only to the gut-wrenching horrors Japanese soldiers inflicted upon the people of Nanking, but which, by its blind arrogance and sense of invulnerability, also paved the way for Japan's own destruction.

Within that ethnically conscious scheme of things, the Okinawans of 1945 were a people who were but nominally Japanese, their status compromised by Chinese and Mongolian influences. For that reason, the Japanese of the mainland regarded them as inferiors and during the battle treated them as such, conscripting them for forced labour and at extreme moments even using them as human shields. Caught between American invaders and Japanese defenders, one third of the island's indigenous population would be dead by the end of the campaign.

Okinawa is a generally undistinguished island of fewer than five hundred square miles. Naha's population is around 300,000, and there is no other city on the island. Neither is Okinawa high on the tourist agenda for the Far East. For all those reasons, no visitor to the island could expect to find much English spoken here. Even so, Susan did not want to see Okinawa by way of a guided tour or trail with lock-step rigidity after a guide. I was less adventurous on this particular occasion, but her argument that this trip was focused on the darker elements of the island's history, 'not a visit to Okinawaland', had proved telling and thus had finally won the day. For that reason, she had planned to tour the island by car, and had already arranged to rent one. Unfortunately, when we arrived at the rental company, we quickly realized that absolutely no one spoke English. Even so,

Susan continued to stand her ground until I finally said, 'Look, if we do it your way here, we will spend all our time being lost in a country where no one can give us directions we can understand.' To this argument, Susan at last acquiesced though with the obvious disappointment of one who believed that the true riches of travel could only be gained by freedom of movement and the risk of folly, which, in fact, is true.

Neither seemed possible on Okinawa, however, particularly given the very short time we'd planned to be here, and so I went about making less adventurous arrangements.

Such arrangements turned out to be easier than expected. The wonderfully accommodating employees of the rental agency clearly recognized our problem, cancelled our reservation without prejudice, and even had one of their drivers take us to our hotel. More than that, no one could have asked.

At our hotel the next morning, it was suggested that we hire a guide to show us the island.

His name was Hiroko, a short, stocky man with a bright, welcoming smile. In a jolly, hugely accommodating way, he asked us where we wanted to go, then listened as I ticked off the dark places I had come to see: the Japanese Naval Headquarters, Shuri Castle, the Himeyuri memorial and museum, the southernmost cliffs, where the final tragedy had unfolded.

'Hmm, okay,' Hiroko said with a certain lack of enthusiasm, then added a few decidedly lighter suggestions of his own: the striking beach rock of Manzamo, the American air base, a 'recreated' Ryukyu village.

Susan cast me a doubtful glance, then said, *sotto voce*, 'Where we can see lots of plastic stuff.'

This was typical of Susan. She did not like replications, miniaturizations or any attempt to render history somehow less immediate than it had been for those who had actually experienced it. At Waterloo, for example, she had been singularly unimpressed by the Lion Monument. It was not the grandiose that spoke to her. Rather, she sought what she once called 'the feel of the real,' and in pursuit of that, she would sometimes bend forward and touch the grass of some sacred field or take up a handful of soil. For her, there was more to be found in the touch of the wind or the play of the light than in sweeping murals or cycloramas.

'Habu at Ryukyu village,' Hiroko told us.

'Habu?' I asked.

'Snake here on Okinawa.' Hiroko smiled broadly, and perhaps a tad too proudly. 'Very bad.' He snapped his fingers and chuckled. 'Kill you like *that*.'

For the next few hours Hiroko happily whisked us all about the island. We went to Manzamo, in the far north, then turned back south, where we were shown the scenic beaches and the Ryukyu village Hiroko had suggested, and where, sure enough, there was a glass enclosure featuring the dreaded *habu*, Asia's longest pit viper, a slender little snake, but famously sluggish, so that most people are bitten by it because they've inadvertently roused it from its usual torpor. There was also, as Susan had earlier predicted, a lot of plastic stuff.

For the rest of the day, we moved north to south, the same direction the invading American troops had taken, so that it was possible for us to see the tortuous hills and valleys over which they had fought and from whose hidden redoubts the Japanese had rained down a relentlessly hellish fire.

Faced with the American advance across the Pacific, Japan's lethally determined military leaders had hatched a simple plan: to show the invaders that the Japanese would fight absolutely to the death and by that means demonstrate just how much American blood would have to be spilled per square inch of captured Japanese soil, a price they hoped the Americans would ultimately be unwilling to pay and thus relent on their demand for 'unconditional surrender'. For the Japanese, any dream of actual victory had long ago slipped into nightmare. Now the hope was simply to end the war on terms that would prevent invasion and subsequent subjugation, Japan to be ruled, as always, by its ancient imperial system.

Okinawa found itself situated, both geographically and ethnically, at the cross-hairs of this plan.

The result was a brutal campaign that lasted nearly three months, much of it fought in monsoon rains that turned the island into a muddy swamp. The fighting was often at close quarters, with a consequent hardening on both sides, each now determined utterly to eradicate the other. It was a brutalization that E.B. Sledge, a soft-spoken Alabama boy, had eloquently recorded in his classic account of the battle, a journey, as he said, that had turned his heart to stone.

At the end of the campaign, the Japanese had proved their point. They would fight to the death, as an astonishing 107,539 Japanese soldiers out of an army of approximately 110,000 actually did.

Towards the end of the day, we reached that part of Okinawa, its southern quarter, where the last desperate days of the battle had been waged.

'You go in here,' Hiroko said when we reached the Japanese Underground Naval Headquarters. 'I wait for you.'

The Underground Headquarters proved to be a series of tunnels, the first of which was hung with the paper 'peace cranes' that have become the number one tourist buy at such places throughout Japan. But just beyond this bright, multicoloured display (with their long tentacles, the peace cranes look more like peace octopi) the underground environment abruptly turns as stark and unadorned as the spare life that was lived here. The walls are uniformly brown, and every aspect of the tunnels, from the electrical wires to the nakedly hanging lights, testifies to the grim nature of a desperate stand. The tunnel complex is 430 metres long. Inside it lived men, mostly very young men, who had no expectation of living very long, men who must have carried the usual baggage of their pasts but with no anticipation of a future.

No guide takes you through the tunnels. You simply walk from room to room listening to sporadic recorded narrations and reading the small plaques that identify the military functions that were carried out inside them. Most people move through them quite quickly, but at one, they inevitably linger. It is a small room, and it was no doubt chosen for that reason. In so confined an underground space, the explosive impact would be extreme and the devastation absolute. A plaque informs the visitor in less than perfect English of what happened here: *Wall Riddled With A Hand-Grenade When Committed Suicide.*

The wall is indeed riddled and large chunks of it are blown away, though the major impact of the grenades had been absorbed by the heads and torsos of the Japanese officers who'd gathered tightly around the point of detonation and thus had taken the full force of the blast as their final act of defiance. Added to the terror of the tunnels was the fact that this was one of many such suicide rooms inside them, for space is required for 175 men to kill themselves, which is what happened within this gloomy warren thirty metres below ground.

Horrible though it was, the mass death that occurred in the Japanese Underground Naval Headquarters bore the mark of ritual and for some might even offer the grim reward of a starkly formal beauty. Madness though this mass suicide surely was, there had been method in it. Outside the tunnels, however, a much more frenzied self-inflicted carnage descended upon Okinawa as the Americans pressed closer to the sea. At Chibi-chiri Gama, a one-hundred-foot deep limestone cave, Okinawan civilians slaughtered their own children, then killed themselves, an act repeated in the murder-suicide sites that now dot the southern reaches of the island, and which make this tightly enclosed landscape, quite bright and beautiful in so many ways, surely one of the darkest places on earth.

The southern tip of the island was the last place we visited that day, and as we made our way there, Hiroko suggested what I later came to think of as his antidote for what we were about to see.

'You should go to Okinawa World,' he said.

'What is Okinawa World?' I asked.

As I listened to Hiroko's description, it became clear that Okinawa World was a theme park devoted to Okinawan culture. It had caves, and a recreated village that Hiroki said was 'even better' than the one we'd seen earlier. It also had a snake museum with a far greater number of *habu*.

'I think we'll skip that one,' Susan said before I could agree to it, then glanced towards where we could now see the southernmost tip of Okinawa, and surely its most tragic place. 'Those are the cliffs,' she said gravely. 'And the caves.'

I knew the ones she meant.

In the final sweep of the island, flame throwers and hand grenades had been used to destroy caves in which Japanese soldiers were thought to be hiding. Among the most horrific results of this policy was the deaths incurred by the Himeyuri Corps, which consisted of some 222 girls, formerly students at the Okinawa Daiichi Women's High School and the Okinawa Shihan Women's School, and who, on 23 March 1945, were conscripted by the Japanese to serve as nurses. Three months later, as the Americans began their final assault, the corps was disbanded, but not before the girls were told that American troops would rape, torture, and murder any who were later captured. As a result, scores of these terrified young women, cast adrift in a field of battle, were either shot, blown apart or committed suicide. To escape such a fate, some sought shelter in what has since come to be known as the Cave of the Virgins. According to Ruri Miyara, one of the three student-nurses who survived the Cave, an American soldier had 'pleaded' in Japanese for any people who might be hiding inside the cave to come out immediately as it was going to be blown up. The Japanese soldiers inside the cave refused to answer this plea or allow the nurses to answer it. Nor were the nurses allowed to leave. The cave was subsequently blown up and some fifty of these nurses were killed.

The memorial to these girls is lovely and dignified. In the sombre photographs on display there, they are dressed in their school uniforms, their dark hair neatly combed. Himeyuri means 'star lily' in Japanese, and these girls surely were the enchantingly lovely flowers of this island. In the photographs, they give off their youth like a steady light, and it is a youth filled with expectations of service and achievement. These were serious girls, and in their calm and noble faces, one senses how full of purpose they must have been, how wide they must have imagined their own horizons, and with what terror, anguish and dismay they must have watched those horizons close.

A few minutes later, we walked along the outer rim of the Peace Memorial, then up a small hill. From there the 'suicide cliffs', a jagged expanse of coastline at the southern tip of the island, could be seen in the distance. Those who'd been driven to them in the last days of the battle must surely have thought themselves at the end of the world. By then, the Japanese army was no more, and they could look northward only into the advancing ranks of a second army, this one American, and which they believed bent upon inflicting cruelties even greater than those they had endured at the hands of the Japanese. Staring at those cliffs, I found I had only one question: *To what extremity must you be driven, and in expectation of what agony, that casting your child over a cliff and into the sea can be conceived as an act of parental love?* 'Terrible,' I said to Hiroko when we rejoined him in the parking lot of the Peace Museum.

He nodded briskly. 'You see everything you come to see now?' he asked, like a man with a checklist.

'Yes,' I answered.

'Okay,' he said, started to turn, then looked back at Susan. 'You not forget Okinawa.'

'No,' Susan answered him solemnly, clearly moved by all we'd seen together. 'No, I won't forget Okinawa.'

I knew that I would not forget it either.

And in fact, I was still thinking of it, thinking of the shrapnel-sprayed suicide rooms inside the Japanese Naval Head-quarters, the murdered children inside Chibichiri Gama, the terrible fates of the Himeyuri girls, along with the cliffs at the end of the island where countless other suicides had been carried out, still thinking of all this as we made our way towards Hiroshima a few days later.

The train from Tokyo to Hiroshima passes through the city whose dreadful place it took. Kyoto had been chosen to suffer the first atomic attack, but Henry Stimson, the American Secretary of War, had visited the city as a young man, thought it beautiful, and for that reason, scratched it off the target list.

Until the morning of 6 August 1945, Hiroshima had been lucky. While most of Japan's comparably sized cities had been destroyed, it had remained untouched. For that reason, many of the city's residents had come to believe that it would remain so, and thus had felt little alarm when the air raid sirens sounded and a single B-29 was sighted, moving not at all hurriedly, over the city. The time was 8.15 a.m.

Seconds later and 580 metres overhead, 560 grams of uranium-235 were converted into energy.

Curiously enough, as one chronicler of the bombing has noted, for those directly beneath the point of detonation nothing actually happened because the human nervous system is simply too slow to record the velocity of a nuclear explosion. Thus, in terms of the actual experience of those situated directly beneath the blast, Hiroshima was never bombed. The women waiting at the entrance of the Sumitomo Bank remained unperturbed, as their shadows on its steps attest. A man working in a nearby garden felt nothing of his own end. Nor did those who were crossing the T-bridge or riding in the buses that had stopped at the Prefectural Industrial Promotion Hall see the light that flashed brighter than the sun nor feel the heat that was hotter than its core. Perhaps for the first time in human history, to those instantly vaporized, death gave no hint of its own experience.

To those who were not instantly vaporized, however, the horrors of Hiroshima – the waves of boiling heat and blinding light and sheer concussive force that raced in ever-widening plumes across the city – remain almost unimaginable.

The Peace Museum, at the city's centre, makes a valiant effort to give those horrors expression despite the fact that it is a very modern building, one so architecturally undistinguished it might easily be mistaken for simply another of Hiroshima's many office complexes. A precisely manicured park, which is more an expanse of grass and flowers, fronts the building. This area is dotted with peace memorials of one sort or another. There is the Peace Clock Tower, which chimes every day at precisely 8.15 a.m., and a Peace Bell whose surface displays a 'map' of the world without national borders. As it was a gift of the Greek Embassy, the bell is inscribed with Socrates' famous dictum, 'Know Thyself', written in Greek, Japanese and, unaccountably, in Sanskrit. Visitors are encouraged to ring this bell, but while I was there, no one did. The Peace Park also contains the Flame of Peace, first lit in 1964 and which proposes to burn until the last nuclear weapon has been destroyed, and the Pond of Peace, which surrounds a memorial cenotaph holding the names of each of the human beings killed at Hiroshima, and which lies beneath a concrete arch that is said to provide shelter for their souls.

I have to confess that I found a childlike naivety in much of this. The one-world bell stuck me as very Kumbaya, and if a list of the ancient epigrams most ignored by human beings were ever compiled, surely 'Know Thyself' would top it. I also came away thinking that the worldwide gas reserves needed to power the Peace Flame would more likely run out before the last nuclear weapon was destroyed by anything other than another nuclear weapon.

Susan was similarly unmoved, and for that reason we didn't linger very long at any of these memorials, but instead headed for the Peace Museum in hope of finding a spot in the Peace Park which, rather than envisioning some futuristic fantasy of peace, recorded the first use of the most destructive weapon in the history of war.

The usual crowds of Japanese students were gathered outside it, all very orderly, their teachers in full command. Clearly, the Peace Museum was a celebrity site, a place educators felt it important for their students to visit. Some students were carrying single sheets of yellow paper, and at one point a few of them, spotting Westerners, tentatively approached us.

The girl who first spoke to us looked to be but a little younger than the youngest girls of the Himeyuri Corps, so that it was easy to imagine her not here, at Hiroshima on a bright summer day, but on Okinawa sixty years before, drenched by rain and caked with mud, listening to voices outside the cave she cowered in, fixed in terror, unable to move, waiting, as it turned out, for the flame.

Very carefully, slowly forming the words, she asked, 'Where . . . are . . . you . . . from?'

'New York City,' I answered.

She gasped, turned to her fellow students, and excitedly said something that made them gasp, too,

'New . . . York . . . City?' she asked again, as if unsure as to whether I were telling the truth.

'Yes.'

She looked at the sheet of paper she was carrying. 'Why . . . are . . . you . . . at . . . Hir-o-shi-ma?'

'I visit dark places,' I told her.

'Why are you at Hiroshima?' Susan asked softly, and with it, offered a reassuring smile.

The girl smiled back very brightly. 'We . . . are . . . here . . . to . . . practise . . . English.'

The other students nodded vigorously and smiled.

'And . . . to . . . work . . . for . . . brotherhood.'

'Well,' Susan said, again with a smile. 'I suppose Hiroshima is a good place for that.'

The girl glanced down at her paper, and as she did so, I saw that it was a series of questions, all in English. She turned to me.

'What . . . do . . . you . . . think . . . of . . . world . . . peace?'

'I'm for it,' I said. 'I suppose most everyone is.'

The girl nodded, though I was by no means certain she understood my uninspired answer to her question. Then she looked at her paper, asked a few more questions, but gave only the faintest hint as to whether she understood the answers. With her homework finished, she then wished us a good day, and with the other students trailing behind her, all very animated now, strolled away.

Inside the museum, there were yet more students. In fact, I

saw few visitors who weren't students. Certainly there were relatively few adult Japanese visitors at the Peace Museum that day, nor were there very many at the somewhat similar museum at Nagasaki when we visited it a few days later. This did not surprise me, for it seemed reasonable to suppose that for older Japanese, the atomic bombings were perhaps not events of which they wished to be reminded, nor of which they could be reminded save within the grim context of their catastrophic defeat. The French don't exactly flock to Agincourt, after all, and were not the two warring parties reunited after the war, I doubt that many Southerners would add Appomattox Courthouse to their 'must see' lists.

In any event, had the Peace Museum for some reason been closed to students that day, its rooms could have been walked with less possibility of brushing shoulders with Japanese tourists than at, say, the Eiffel Tower or the Empire State Building.

As a commemoration of Hiroshima, the Peace Museum is fittingly arranged to narrate the events that led first to the war, then to the bombing. A large photograph of a clock with hands stopped at 8.15 a.m., the exact moment of the detonation, was being used by students as a photographic backdrop. Small group by small group they arranged themselves in front of the clock, posed for a picture, then smiled into a flash of light perhaps a million times less intense than that which other children had faced in this same spot sixty years before.

Beyond the clock the other rooms revealed themselves in a light whose sombreness seemed fitting, given the poignancy of the articles on display: the tattered remains of school uniforms, the single wooden shoe of a child whose body was never found, a crushed tricycle, the bones of a human hand encased in melted glass, part of a wall streaked with the black, radioactive rain that had fallen over the city as the river and harbour waters that had been drawn into the mushroom cloud descended once again; all exhibits that attested to the physical horror of the bombing, the terrible wounds human flesh had suffered on that August morning.

Paul Tibbets, the commander of the *Enola Gay*, which he named for his mother, and which dropped the bomb on Hiroshima, later said that he 'didn't think about what was going on down on the ground'.

It was this: a mushroom cloud that reached 13,700 metres high, a point of detonation temperature of one million degrees Celsius, and a flash of light as bright as the surface of the sun.

In the seconds following detonation, the ground temperature descended to a mere three thousand degrees, roughly twice the heat required to melt iron. The surface waters of Hiroshima instantly boiled. Wood burst into flame. Glass melted. Flesh peeled away from bone like molten wax. Then came the blast waves, hurtling across the city at 440 kilometres a second and instantly flattening everything in their paths. In their wake, tens of thousands of Japanese lay dead or quickly dying, while others moved in dazed disbelief towards whatever water they could find, particularly the Ota River, which runs through Hiroshima, and in which thousands more, charred by flame or eviscerated by flying debris, would later die. Those who lived a little longer saw fires converge to create gigantic firestorms whose smoke was so black and dense it blocked out the sun and shrouded the city in darkness. Then an equally black rain began to fall as the water that had evaporated in the blast condensed overhead and fell back to earth.

In the wake of this cataclysm, only one building, the Prefectural Industrial Promotion Hall, remained standing in central Hiroshima, and although many residents later wanted it torn down because of the painful memories it evoked, it has remained untouched, a reminder of the city's destruction, and has since become the most recognizable symbol of the international peace movement.

In terms of dark places, other than this building, which is now called the 'Peace Dome', human memory has lifted only the 'Arbeit Macht Frei' gate at Auschwitz to similarly iconic status. But unlike the Auschwitz gate, the Peace Dome represents not only a seminal event in human history, but the dawning of a fearful age, the first in which the annihilation of every life on earth could actually be carried out by human agency alone.

No man-made structure could possibly suggest such an awesome change in planetary affairs. In fact, only the film and photographs of that biblically billowing mushroom cloud come close. The Peace Dome, on the other hand, is curiously uninvolving. It is relatively small, and the fallen stonework and gutted interior give it the appearance of a structure currently under demolition rather than one long ago destroyed. It is surrounded by an iron fence and, as expected, there are numerous historic markers, all in Japanese and English, which relate the events of that catastrophic August morning. The words that carry this history are similarly inadequate, a parade of facts, the unprecedented single-bomb destruction of an entire city related in the passionless prose one generally encounters in official military histories. But then, would poems have been any better, or paragraphs of overreaching prose? After all, when asked to commemorate august occasions or awesome events, writers usually prove themselves quite unable to meet the challenge. Beyond that, however, the fact is that certain events require the eloquence of silence, and the Peace Dome does rest silently and with great dignity at the heart of what is now a bustling, modern city. The sight of it demands a pause, a thoughtfulness, a drawn breath, and that is rightly so for any place at which a large number of human beings ceased to breathe at all.

As I tend to do, I'd paused to read the historical narration that was displayed at the dome. When I'd finished, I turned to find that Susan had drifted away and taken a seat on one of the nearby benches. She was sitting silently, staring off into the middle distance. When I came up to her, she looked at me and shook her head. 'There's no way to get your mind around something like this,' she said, then shrugged. 'So what can you say?'

'Saying nothing is fine,' I told her, 'and it's certainly better than ringing that silly bell.'

A few minutes later, a woman approached us. She was one of the many volunteer guides who take up positions in and around

Left: My father, 'somewhere in Africa'

Below: My mother at twenty, the determined maker of a happy home

Above: With Susan in Spain, our first 'year of living dangerously'

Above: Justine on Juliet's balcony, Verona

Left: Our daughter, Justine, at twelve, the year we left for Spain

Above: Republicans shooting at the Alcazar during the Spanish Civil War (Bridgeman)

Left: Alcazar, Toledo (Bridgeman)

Above: The barracks at Auschwitz, taken by Justine

Above: Ingeniously shaped spoons that could be held by fingerless hands

Above: Kalaupapa, Father Damien's grave

Above: The Ossuary
at Verdun

Right: Inside the
Ossuary, with floor
to ceiling plaques
bearing the names
of French soldiers

Below: Sleeping
area within Fort
Douaumont, Verdun

Left: Kamakura: hundreds of Jizos, standing in ranks like little frozen soldiers

Below: The ruins of Gilles de Rais' chateau at Machecoul

Above: Child murder as tourism: the prettified chateau of Gilles de Rais at Tiffauges

Above: Plaza de Mayo, moments before the scheduled arrival of the Madres

Above: The creepy depths of Aokigahara

Above: The Golden Gate Bridge on the foggy morning I walked across it

Above: Adanwomase

Right: The suicide room on Okinawa

Below: Suicide cliffs on Okinawa

Left: Peace Dome, Hiroshima

Above: Monument to the courage of the elementary teachers of Hiroshima on the day of the attack

Below: New Echota, Georgia, the Cherokee capital, where the Trail of Tears began

Above: The clock stopped at the moment of the blast, Nagasaki

GEORGIA 1776

TRAIL OF TEARS

The New Echota Treaty of 1835 relinquished Cherokee Indian claims to lands east of the Mississippi River. The majority of the Cherokee people considered the treaty fraudulent and refused to leave their homelands in Georgia, Alabama, North Carolina, and Tennessee. 7,000 Federal and State troops were ordered into the Cherokee Nation to forcibly evict the Indians. On May 26, 1838, the roundup began. Over 15,000 Cherokees were forced from their homes at gunpoint and imprisoned in stockades until removal to the west could take place. 2,700 left by boat in June 1838, but, due to many deaths and sickness, removal was suspended until cooler weather. Most of the remaining 13,000 Cherokees left by wagon, horseback, or on foot during October and November, 1838, on an 800 mile route through Tennessee, Kentucky, Illinois, Missouri, and Arkansas. They arrived in what is now eastern Oklahoma during January, February, and March, 1839. Disease, exposure, and starvation may have claimed as many as 4,000 Cherokee lives during the course of capture, imprisonment, and removal. The ordeal has become known as the Trail of Tears.

Above: Elmina Castle, Ghana, through which passed the 'black gold' of slavery

Right: The door of no return, Elmina

Below: The beaches of Melos, upon which the residents of the island were slaughtered during the Peloponnesian War

Above: Uluru, at the centre of the Red Desert, Alice Springs

Above: The Killing Fields, Choeung Ek

Above: A torture bed at Tuol Sleng

Left: The Children's Tree at Choeung Ek

Below: Tuol Sleng, the Khmer Rouge's central interrogation and torture centre, Phnom Penh, Cambodia

Above: A wall of victims, Tuol Sleng

Below: Bou Meng, one of the centre's few survivors, selling his book in the courtyard of Tuol Sleng

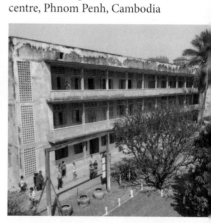

Above: Justine on the road as an adult, now a world traveller on her own

the Peace Park and she was very friendly. Like other such people we encountered in Hiroshima, she was intent upon pressing the city's varied pleasures upon us, rather than its tragedy.

'You should not leave Hiroshima without trying *okonomiyaki*,' she said, her eyes fixed on Susan. 'It is the dish of Hiroshima. Very good. Please, try it.'

We agreed to do just that, lingered at the dome a while longer, then moved on through the surrounding park, now in search of a monument I'd read about but not seen. No one seemed to know where it was, and so it took us quite a long time to find it. Time well spent, as I knew instantly, once I saw it, so simple, so eloquent, the one piece of memorial sculpture in Hiroshima that is wrenchingly heartfelt.

It is the statue of a woman holding an obviously dead child. The memorial was erected in honour of the elementary school teachers of Hiroshima, and in its stark simplicity it manages to convey the grim bedazzlement of both the event itself, how confusion must have reigned in the immediate aftermath of unprecedented horror, and the astonishing capacity of human beings to deal with whatever befalls them. In the statue, the woman's body seems to have melted into her tattered dress, while the child she carries, with its head lolling backward and arms flung wide, appears to drip rather than fall from her grasp. Nothing I saw at Hiroshima, nothing in or around the dome, nor in the nearby museum, sombre as that museum was, and despite the dome's iconic status, held a similar power. Only here, in that dazed and bedraggled teacher, bravely carrying her unspeakable burden, could one feel the sheer anguish of what happened here on that August morning.

I was aware, of course, of the long-voiced argument that the bombing of Hiroshima, then of Nagasaki three days later, had, in fact, saved both American and Japanese lives. In defence of that claim, it was often pointed out that more Japanese had died in the Okinawan campaign than in the bombings of Hiroshima and Nagasaki combined. On the American side, it had also been noted that prior to the bombings, military commanders in the Pacific theatre had already ordered the manufacture of 500,000 Purple Hearts in anticipation of a long and very bloody Japanese defence. It was Okinawa that had demonstrated the fierce nature of that defence, of course, so that the fate of that island and this city were uniquely connected. That determination to fight to the death had not been altered by the terrible losses incurred by the Japanese on Okinawa. And so, in service to that defence, and at the moment the bomb detonated, army trenches were being dug in Hiroshima by a youthful contingent of Japanese soldiers, engineering students were trying to figure out a way to use wood to make triggers, woodworkers were carving bullets out of mahogany, factory workers were manufacturing two-shot wooden pistols to be distributed to mothers and children, and doctors at a hospital near the hypocentre had already been ordered to teach boys as young as fourteen to strap on bombs and dive under cars and trucks and tanks. Such had been the still unyielding determination of Hiroshima on the day of its destruction.

It was the destruction of this will to defend Japan to the point of complete annihilation that became the central aim of American power after Okinawa, and it had been in service to that aim that the most destructive force yet devised by man had been unleashed. Even this had not been enough to move Japan's military leaders to countenance the unconditional surrender that anything but fantasy demanded. But for a few days fantasy still reigned, now more or less fuelled exclusively by delusion. America had only one atomic bomb, the hardliners argued, and therefore the war should continue. And so on 9 August 1945, the second bomb, the one Japan's generals had convinced themselves did not exist, fell on the quarter of a million people who lived in Nagasaki.

A black stone monolith now stands at what is called the 'hypocentre' at Nagasaki, the exact spot where the bomb detonated 500 metres overhead, instantly vaporizing the three hundred or so families who lived directly beneath the explosion. It is estimated that another seventy thousand died more or less immediately, to which were added yet another seventy-five thousand wounded. Concentric circles radiate from the cenotaph and quite effectively suggest the percussive and thermal waves that swept out from the hypocentre, reducing the city to the same fiery rubble in which Hiroshima still smouldered. In the nearby museum, stopped clocks record the exact time of the detonation: 11.02 a.m. There are also stark reminders of what those who died must have felt, however briefly, before they died: melted coins, a mound of glass bottles fused by heat.

But most moving of all, I thought, was the installation of grey 'clouds' that hung from the ceiling of one room of the museum and which represented the ones that had parted just in time for the bomb to be dropped. These same clouds had protected Kokura that day, and forced the American bomber to proceed to Nagasaki, the mission's secondary target. It was over this spot the clouds had parted at 11.02 a.m. and it seemed to me that nothing, neither here nor in Hiroshima, better suggested the fickleness of war.

The various memorials that commemorate the city's subsequent destruction are plentiful (forty-eight) and varied. There is the Fountain of Peace whose lifted waters take the form of a dove's wings. There are statues of children peacefully sitting on a park bench, of a child praying, of a young girl releasing a dove. Quite a few were donated by what were then some of the world's most benighted dictatorships. The Soviet Union provided the sculpture of a woman holding an infant child. Communist China's *The Maiden of Peace* is a young woman with a dove perched on her arm. *The Sun Crane of Peace* places the faces of dead children inside a sun surrounded by the wings of one of Japan's ubiquitous peace cranes. It was sent by Fidel Castro, who, in October 1963, urged Nikita Khrushchev to attack the United States with nuclear weapons even if it meant the total annihilation of his own people, a good many of whom, of course, would have been children. The loud jangle of such mind-numbing hypocrisy tended to drown out what should have been the tragic music of Nagasaki.

This unpleasant sense of Nagasaki's commemoration of its own bombing might have lingered somewhat longer had Susan and I not strolled back into the museum, where we soon found ourselves standing before a remarkable photograph. It was of a young Japanese boy. He is alone, save for the infant strapped to his back, its head tilted far back and with its arms hanging slack, clearly dead. He is barefooted, and his slender legs are coated with dirt and ash. He stands at attention before one of the city's crematory pits.

This photograph was taken by an American photojournalist, Joe O'Donnell, in Nagasaki in 1945. He later described the scene to a journalist.

'I saw a boy about ten years old walking by. He was carrying a baby on his back. In those days in Japan, we often saw children playing with their little brothers or sisters on their backs, but this boy was clearly different. I could see that he had come to this place for a serious reason. He was wearing no shoes. His face was hard. The little head was tipped back as if the baby were fast asleep.

'The boy stood there for five or ten minutes. The men in white masks walked over to him and quietly began to take off the rope that was holding the baby. That is when I saw that the baby was already dead. The men held the body by the hands and feet and placed it on the fire.

'The boy stood there straight without moving, watching the flames. He was biting his lower lip so hard that it shone with blood. The flame burned low like the sun going down. The boy turned around and walked silently away.'

In this photograph, it seemed to me, one saw the dignity, sto-
icism, and will to go on in the face of unimaginable loss that has
so characterized and ennobled the Japanese people since the war.

Susan and I stared at this photograph for a long time. We both
knew that it would remain foremost among the many memories
we would take back with us from Japan.

On the train leaving Nagasaki, I looked out over the city. From
a distance, it is like most other Japanese cities of comparable size,
its buildings a clutter of glass, steel, and ferroconcrete. As usual
at such departures, I thought of the experiences one encounters
in travel, and whose irony and poignancy are generally greater
in dark places. I remembered the girls practising their English
in Peace Park, and the woman who'd recommended Hiroshima's
favoured dish, which we'd later tried and very much enjoyed.
Then, for some reason, I thought again of Okinawa, whose
desperate defence, so utterly brutal, had sealed the fate of both
Hiroshima and Nagasaki, and this thought returned me to the
Himeyuri girls, how their young lives had been trapped between
two mutually desperate forces, and in the terror of that death
grip, those same lives had come to be so radically devalued.
One might argue forever as to whether it had subsequently been
necessary to drop atomic bombs on Japan, but the tragedy of its
having been done seemed simple enough to understand within
the terrible calculus of the time.

Such, I thought, is war, and once again recalled the terrible
fate of the young nurses of Okinawa, then the fact that before
returning us to our hotel after visiting their memorial, Hiroko

had suggested a respite and had taken us to a stunningly beautiful highland park. In deep shade, Susan and I had walked through a landscape whose lush vegetation was occasionally broken by dramatic towers of stone. It was a world hung in vine, cool and green and infinitely serene, and we'd left soothed by its calm.

'Beautiful place, yes?' Hiroko asked when we returned to his car.

'Very,' I said.

He smiled. 'We go back to hotel now?'

'Yes. Thank you.'

We'd been halfway down the mountain when I'd noticed a yellow butterfly sweep abruptly down, directly towards the windshield of the car. Hiroko saw it, too, and swerved to avoid it. For why should a butterfly now needlessly be killed on an island upon which, fifty years before, and without a blink of concern, a hundred 'star lilies' had been burned alive?

Such, I thought now, as I recalled this moment once again, Nagasaki retreating into the distance, is peace.

New Echota

In the car on the way to New Echota, my mother played Christmas music. It is the only music she has ever played, and she plays it all year round.

'What is the place we're going to?' she asked.

'New Echota,' I answered. 'The capital of the Cherokee Nation.'

'I didn't know Indians had a capital,' my mother said.

'The Cherokee once did,' I said.

In an eloquent passage, William Bartram had described them in 1791:

> *The Cherokee people are tall, erect and moderately robust; their limbs well shaped, so as generally to form a perfect human figure; their features regular, and countenance open, dignified, and placid, yet the forehead and brow are so formed as to strike you instantly with heroism and bravery; the eye, though rather*

small, yet active and full of fire, the iris always black, and the
nose commonly inclining to the aquiline. Their countenance
and actions exhibit an air of magnanimity, superiority, and
independence. Their complexion is a reddish brown or copper
colour; their hair, long, lank, coarse, and black as a raven . . .
The women of the Cherokees are tall, slender, erect and of a
delicate frame; their features formed with perfect symmetry;
the countenance cheerful and friendly; and they move with a
becoming grace and dignity. (Bartram's Travels)

Two hundred years later, the Cherokee are still remembered in northern Georgia, but in trivial ways. On the drive to their reconstructed capital, I noticed that there was a road named for them, and a car lot. There is a Cherokee County in Georgia, as well, but no Cherokee live there.

Among all the tribes of the New World, the Cherokee had been the most determined to live in peace with the people who ultimately banished them. In that effort, they had fought long and hard, always in the courts, never on the battlefield, and in the course of that protracted struggle, they had generated leaders of enormous skill and courage: John Ross and John Ridge, Major Ridge and Elias Boudinot. These men had worked ceaselessly to convince the governments of Georgia and the United States that because the Cherokee had never posed a threat to the people around them, they deserved to govern themselves and to remain in their ancestral home. Their struggle was to preserve the Cherokee Nation, but along the road that led to the place of their last, and quite peaceful, stand, I could see only how little other than their name remained.

The route to New Echota runs north from Atlanta, first along a teeming expressway and then by way of a local road bordered by strip malls. The velocity of the way of life that expelled and replaced the Cherokee was the most telling feature of this landscape. It was in the fast food restaurants and the one-stop shopping emporia, in the one-hour glasses and the five-minute car wash. There was nothing that any longer attended to the changing seasons or the phases of the moon. All that had once been carved of nearby wood or sewn with nearby cotton had disappeared, and with it, the simple, and often idiosyncratic, charms of localism.

There are no doubt gentle things that gentle people everywhere believe, as Stark Young, that most eloquent defender of outmoded life, once said. But the way to New Echota gave little evidence that so kind and generous a sentiment had ever been applied to the Cherokee. In that sense, the tragedy of their removal seemed to have been only the opening curtain in the longer tragedy of the small-farm Southern agrarianism Stark Young had championed, a fact that made their mutual doom all the more ironic in that it had been Thomas Jefferson, that great defender of a farming people, who'd decreed that the Cherokee had to go.

Even so, the route to their departure had been long and halting, and there had to have been moments when their hope was genuine, intervals of judicial or legislative delay during which they had surely dreamed their old dream of remaining on their ancestral lands, among the oak and pine, tilling the rich soil that had immemorially been theirs.

Dispossession is a melancholy enterprise, and by the time the Cherokee lost their final effort to remain in Georgia, there'd already been plenty of destruction of native populations, particularly on the eastern seaboard, much of it done by microbes imported from Europe and strewn into an air breathed by an indigenous people who'd had no immunity to them, and by which nearly a third had perished without the firing of a single shot. There'd been battles, too, and soon there would be outright massacres, particularly among the transient villages of the nomadic western tribes who, though they had often and quite viciously fought each other, had been mutually opposed to the white man's penchant for deeds and fences.

The Cherokee, however, had had no such reservations regarding the sanctity of private property. They'd been an agrarian people, rooted in a kingdom that encompassed lands so extensive nine separate states would later be carved out of it, a fertile and prodigiously watered land that was among the richest on earth. By 1820, this vast Cherokee nation had shrunk to little more than 10 per cent of its original sweep. By 1838, almost all the Cherokee had been dispossessed of their lands despite the fact that, as a film on the New Echota website frankly states, the Cherokee had been the most 'progressive' of all the native tribes. They had fully adopted Christianity, Western dress, the tools of modern farming, the English language, and even European dinnerware. They lived in log cabins, not tents. They farmed corn and cotton and raised pigs, chickens and cattle, and in that way they were indistinguishable from their white agrarian neighbours. Others owned taverns, grist mills, and blacksmith shops. They operated ferries and what amounted to local motels. To complete their utter assimilation to local practices, some of them became wealthy planters and owned slaves.

None of this was enough for white Georgians to become less insistent on the federal government's implementation of the Cherokee removal it had promised them in the Georgia Compact of 1802. With growing impatience, Georgia moved towards this removal, first by passing fiercely discriminatory laws against the Cherokee, such as barring them from testifying against whites in court proceedings, then by ever more vociferously proclaiming that its citizens had waited long enough for the state to be made Cherokee-free, a choir that became a chorus once gold was discovered on Cherokee land, and which precious ore, it should be added, the Cherokee themselves were quickly banned from mining.

By then the Cherokee Nation had established its own government, characteristically modelled on the American one, complete with executive, legislative, and judicial branches, and presided over by a two-house legislature.

Its capital was New Echota, a settlement lost for almost a hundred years after resettlement, but which the state of Georgia had recently decided to recreate as a historical site and tourist attraction.

Only a few cars were parked in the lot out front on the day my mother and I came here, and this being full summer, the height of the tourist season, their number rather pointedly suggested that New Echota had not succeeded in luring visitors on their otherwise determined way to the greater attractions further south, whether Atlanta as an urban centre, or the family friendly extravaganzas in neighbouring Florida. Even my cousin, a museum curator and Civil War re-enactor, had been less than thrilled that I'd chosen to visit New Echota rather than Andersonville, the Confederate prison camp whose commandant had been the only soldier prosecuted for war crimes after the Civil War. 'There's really nothing in New Echota,' he'd warned.

But it seemed to me that New Echota was worth seeing. Some places are dark because something began there, the Atomic Age at Hiroshima, for example, and some are dark because something ended there, and at New Echota a dream of coexistence had ended, not just for the Cherokee, but for all of America's native peoples. For if the Cherokee could not be accepted into the body politic of America, then surely no tribe could.

We arrived at around ten in the morning. Throughout the trip, my mother had talked about family matters, and I'd gotten the usual update on marriages and births, accidents and hospitalizations. She had said nothing more about New Echota once I'd added that it was here that the Trail of Tears had begun. I was by no means sure she'd known what the Trail of Tears was, but she hadn't asked, and so I'd added nothing more.

'I'll just stay here,' she said as we walked into the air-conditioned 'welcome centre'.

'You don't want to see the grounds?' I asked.

She shook her head. 'No, I'll stay here, but you don't have to rush.'

I noticed a small museum in an adjoining room. 'You want to look at the museum?'

My mother eyed a padded bench a few feet away. 'You go ahead. I'll sit right there.'

And so for the next few minutes I perused the welcome centre's modest exhibition of Cherokee artefacts, then with still some time to kill before the guided tour began, walked out the back of the centre.

And there it was, New Echota, the deathly still capital city of a nation that no longer existed.

Even from a distance, perhaps especially from a distance, it was clear that the buildings that had housed the hopes of the Cherokee for self-government had been uniformly modest. They were made of wood, mostly unpainted, and sat upon stone foundations. As currently maintained, they had a manufactured, unreal look, as if New Echota had rested beneath an invisible dome, its buildings eternally unaffected by wind or rain or snow. More than anything, the replications looked like a movie set long after the last scene had been shot, the structures mere façades that could be disassembled in minutes. In contradiction to the deeply established people who'd built and by every peaceful means fought to keep it, New Echota appeared impermanent and collapsible.

There was irreverence in this, it seemed to me, a failure to convey what a rooted people the Cherokee had actually been, and because of that, a failure to approach the tragedy of dispossession that had occurred here, and which had contributed to my final sense that of all the monuments to the forcefully uprooted I'd visited, New Echota was the saddest.

A guide arrived and I obediently trailed after him. He was dressed in a beige knit shirt and green flannel pants, and these tones perfectly mirrored the drab nature of his presentation, its concentration on historical dates and population statistics, what buildings were 'restored' (one) as opposed to which were 'recreated' (ten), and, of course, the never ignored and always mind-numbing enumeration of local flora and fauna. Never had the traveller's bane of TMI (Too Much Information) been more soporifically exhibited.

I was not alone during the tour that day, and so the guide's presentation was often punctuated by the scuffle of bored children convinced that the fences and porches of New Echota were playground equipment and who entertained themselves climbing onto and leaping from them while their parents occasionally hissed for them to 'Quit it!'

But even these noisy distractions failed to diminish my initial impression upon actually entering New Echota, which was its eerie stillness. I felt it in the emptiness of the roads and buildings, the motionless wagons and never used farm tools, in the hayless barn and carefully tended fences that fenced nothing in. In fact, save for the children and the guide's tedious recitation of desiccated facts, the 'town' was so quiet it was hard to imagine that anyone had ever actually lived here, let alone a thriving people to whom it had been of such precious value that they had struggled mightily to hold it as their capital for all time.

The standing monument to that effort was in the little buildings that had either been restored or recreated. There were smokehouses and corncribs that might have been part of any early nineteenth-century farming community. But the Cherokee had added a council house and a supreme courthouse, along with a print shop whose very first book had been the Bible. These buildings stood in peculiar isolation, reached by narrow earthen paths and surrounded by a spectacularly green grass whose specific genus I had every faith the guide would at some point reveal.

Fearing that revelation, along with others of similarly critical importance, I soon slipped away from the scuffling children and scolding parents, and headed off on my own.

By then, my cousin's warning seemed justified. In some sense, there really was nothing at New Echota. The acreage was small and for the most part wooded. Roads had been laid out, along with a few trails that wound out into the forest and along which it was easy to conjure some ghostly Cherokee, stereotypically feathered and armed with bow and arrow, making his way homeward at the end of a hunt. But such a phantasm would have been a Hollywood version of these people, of course, for the Cherokee had been one of the so-called 'civilized tribes', a farmer more likely to have grasped the handles of a plough or the reins of a mule than the Great Plains weaponry of the Sioux. Because of that, New Echota had been in all ways a typical rural town, not a gathering of wigwams, and during the years it had flourished as the Cherokee capital, it had been both a trading centre and a seat of government.

One can only now imagine what New Echota must have been like in the 1830s, but imagination is what the place required, the ability to envision, quite literally, what once had been but was no more, and without which imagining it would have been impossible to feel anything for it, particularly that sense of something lost that the place most emphatically demanded, the vision of a once bustling town with its ceaseless movement of people, horses, wagons, everything that had given it life.

So what, I asked myself, would I have seen in New Echota on any given day in, say, 1833? First, I would have seen scores of Cherokee. They would have spread their blankets beneath the shade, and like villagers throughout the world, talked politics and the weather, told jokes and gossiped about family and friends. In that adjoining field, which was only empty grassland now, children and adults would have played their native game of stickball, blown darts from handmade blowguns, challenged each other to a round of 'chunkey', a game vaguely like croquet, or 'Cherokee marbles', which the first Christian missionaries to the Cherokee had banned because it encouraged gambling, but which – and tellingly – had recently been reinstituted in Oklahoma schools as a way of combating the methamphetamine plague.

Here or there around a bustling New Echota, others would

have danced or chanted to the gravelly beat of gourds filled with pebbles. Everywhere within these abandoned acres, there would have been motion, noise, life, where now there was only a pervasive, eerie silence.

But for me it wasn't just its stillness that so profoundly characterized New Echota. Rather, it was the fact that this was a stillness of a particular kind, one imposed not by some unknown mystery of abandonment as at Roanoke, nor of massacre as at Oradour-sur-Glane, nor of natural calamity as at Pompeii, nor even by the spectre of early death as I would later feel it among the snow-white crosses and Stars of David at Romagne.

The silence of New Echota was beyond what any memorial could evoke, deeper and more dreadful because it had been imposed slowly, methodically, and implacably not upon a native people in full resistance to 'civilization', but upon one that had done everything possible to prove to those who threatened it that they were already, and for centuries had been, 'civilized'.

A few yards away, so modest it barely made an impression in the surrounding fields and forests, the print shop seemed to symbolize the ultimate failure of that effort. Sequoyah had completed his Cherokee syllabary in 1821, and within only six years the first Cherokee newspaper, the *Phoenix*, had rolled off the presses at this very place. The actual press had long ago vanished, but as I entered the shop, I saw that the custodians of New Echota had made an effort to restore the look of the printing shop by adding a replica of that first and only press, along with a polished editor's desk, complete with inkless inkwell and motionless quill pen. There were even a few sample copies of the *Phoenix* under the desk, all of them more neatly stacked than anything in a busy printing shop ever would have been.

A printing shop is a noisy place, and the actual one that had once toiled on behalf of the Cherokee must have clinked and clanked considerably, which only made the silence of the one that had replaced it add its dollop of ghostliness to the surrounding landscape, the empty council house and supreme court, so that I felt only the abandonment of the place, as if the Cherokee Nation had departed New Echota like a great, withdrawing wave.

The sense of that wave brought an entirely different vision to mind: New Echota on the hot June day in 1838 when the removal began. During the preceding weeks, seven thousand federal troops under the command of General Winfield Scott had rounded up and herded as many as fifteen thousand Cherokees into stockades earlier built to hold them. The Cherokee of Georgia had been rounded up on 26 May, with later round-ups in North Carolina and Tennessee. The last were the Cherokee of Alabama, who were detained in my own hometown of Fort Payne, a disturbing fact never once mentioned during all of the years I was growing up there.

In New Echota, the Cherokee leadership penned a final plea:

Were the country to which we are urged much better than it is represented to be, and were it free from the objections we have made to it, still it is not the land of our birth, nor of our affections. It contains neither the scenes of our childhood nor

*the graves of our fathers . . . What must be the circumstances
of a removal when a whole community embracing persons of
all classes, and every description, from the infant to the man
of extreme old age, the sick, the blind, the lame, the improvi-
dent, the reckless, the desperate, as well as the prudent, the
considerate, the industrious, are compelled to remove by odious
and intolerable vexations and persecutions brought upon them
in the forms of law?*

To no avail.

Though its historical accuracy has been questioned, Private
John G. Burnett's eyewitness account of the round-up and
removal that followed is the one most often quoted with regard
to what happened next:

*Men working in the fields were arrested and driven to the
stockades. Women were dragged from their homes by soldiers
whose language they could not understand. Children were often
separated from their parents and driven into the stockades with
the sky for a blanket and the earth for a pillow. And often the
old and infirm were prodded with bayonets to hasten them
to the stockades.*

The westward trek for each of these Cherokee assemblies was
begun on a specific date and hour, and typical of such moments,
people had seen omens in the sky or commented on the ironic
brightness of the day as opposed to the darkness of its events.

But surely what the soldiers assigned to carry out the removal had seen and heard in New Echota that hot summer day was a chaos of dust and the rustle of hundreds of Cherokee as they gathered up their possessions and began their long trek towards Oklahoma. By the time the bedraggled survivors of this horrible forced march reached their destination, thousands had died of disease and exposure. Those who had not died had been so weakened by hunger and weariness that at the end of their Trail of Tears, they'd looked to those who observed their arrival like a tribe of ghosts, gone from their place of origin, and never to return.

But that was not the end of the New Echota story. That final episode came a few months after the last of the Cherokee had finally staggered into the wastes of Oklahoma. At dawn on 22 June, scores of assassins set out from various locations within this arid new kingdom. Their mission was to carry out the so-called 'Blood Law' by which anyone who ceded Cherokee land was to be put to death. More than twenty-five men were assigned to murder John Ridge, while smaller parties were assigned such less notable figures as his son Major Ridge and Elias Boudinot. These men and others had signed the Treaty of New Echota on 29 December 1835, an agreement that had purportedly traded all Cherokee land east of the Mississippi River for land in present-day Oklahoma. But the document had never been approved by the Cherokee legislature, nor authorized by John Ross, the tribe's principal chief. These complexities didn't matter to the assassins who set off to enforce the Blood Law, however, and so within a few days the murders were carried out with rifles and knives, sometimes in view of the victims' terrorized families. By the time this final act of ancient Cherokee tradition had been completed, the leadership of the most prominent of the Five Civilized Tribes lay buried in the inhospitable land to which they had led their people only weeks before. None of equal eminence or influence would ever rise again.

'There's nothing in New Echota,' my cousin had warned me.

Now it seemed to me that he'd been right in a way more sorrowful and absolute than he'd intended. There really was nothing left of New Echota.

I turned and headed back towards the visitors' centre. Inside, another group was viewing a short film on the Cherokee, their customs, their religion, their social structure, all of it gone, with nothing that remained of them, as I noticed suddenly, but the Cherokee words for 'men' and 'women' on the bathroom doors.

It was a gesture no doubt meant to honour the Cherokee, but it struck me as both hollow and curiously apt. For the Cherokee had been so completely flushed down the drain of history that even their capital had been cleansed of every trace of them.

My mother was still sitting on the padded bench when I returned to the welcome centre.

'Ready to go?' she asked.

'I think so,' I told her. 'There's really nothing here.'

On the drive back to my mother's house, I fell into the silence that often follows any visit of a dark place; not depression, but the sombre acknowledgement of a suffering you avoided by the simple fact of being born at a different place, or in a different time, or to a people whose race or religion or ethnicity did not doom you or your fellows to destruction.

During my visit, my mother had chosen to remain seated in the welcoming center. It seemed strange to me that she had done so wondered why, rather than view the small museum or walk the grounds of New Echota, she had preferred to sit quietly, patiently, and merely wait for me.

I related all this to Susan when I returned to New York City, where we were living then. Her job as a medical editor had prevented her from joining me on this particular trip, so she'd been anxious to know how the visit to New Echota had gone.

'And so it wasn't particularly eventful,' I admitted at the end of this narration.

She didn't seem at all concerned. 'Give it time,' she said. 'Things hit you later.'

This was true, and by then I'd certainly learned not to force the issue. Dark places, once you've let them in, might well curl up and lie dormant for a long time. You go to them, and if, after that, they recede with no further commentary or effect than your initial impression, then so be it.

But New Echota did rise again a few weeks later, and in doing so, returned me to my mother in the unexpected way the Alcázar had returned me to my father over twenty years before.

It happened as the result of a conversation with Susan during which she remarked, 'People who've had happy childhoods are more free than people like me. They don't use up any space in their brains thinking about how shitty things were when they were growing up. They take happiness for granted, and from there, they move on.' She gave me the penetrating look for which she was noted. 'Like you did.'

In the wake of that remark, and of all unlikely things, I thought of New Echota, of how determinedly the Cherokee had struggled to stay on their homeland and how sad and unfair it was that despite all that effort they'd lost the one thing they'd most wanted to keep. Then, inexplicably, this thought brought my mother to mind. I recalled how she'd come with me the day I'd visited New Echota, a thought that directed me to one yet more poignant, the fact that throughout my childhood in Alabama she had always been with me. I recalled the hard work she had done, holding down a full-time job while at the same time carrying out all the usual household labours of cooking three meals a day, washing all our clothes, dusting, vacuuming. Since my father did almost nothing about the house, there had hardly been a time when she had not been busy at some largely unappreciated task. But the real work of her life had been in keeping a home that was perpetually fixed in the mood of a warm, family Christmas. By succeeding in that strenuous effort, she had single-handedly bequeathed me the illusion of a happy home, and just as Susan had earlier pointed out, that illusion had allowed me to grow up mercifully free of the terrible stress and anxiety that goes hand in hand with an unhappy or disordered or loveless family life. As a result, I had been allowed to let my mind wander, to chart my own course. The sadly ironic thing for my mother was that this freedom had led to what must have seemed to her an ultimate abandonment, my leaving my home, my town, my region, my people, heading off to New York City the minute I graduated from college, leaving without a return ticket or any intention ever of returning save for brief visits. Like the Cherokee, my mother had done everything she could to protect her traditions and her way of life so that they might be passed on to her only child. And like the Cherokee, she had failed. In the wake of that failure, all her sacrifice had come to nothing, because she had reared a son so entirely unburdened by a troubled childhood that he'd had not the slightest hesitation in carrying out his own dispossession, walking a trail of gladness to New York City, rather than one of tears, and from there making a life as far from hers as she could possibly have imagined, a celebrant, as it were, of removal.

'Youth is a country with closed borders,' I'd later written in one of my books. 'All that is valuable must be smuggled in.' Despite its stillness, the scrubbed façade of its display, and the boring nature of its presentation, the abandoned capital of the Cherokee had risen to prove once again that dark places are great smugglers. They sneak thoughts and impressions past the border guards of time, as New Echota did in the case of my mother, and as the Alcázar had done years before with my father, and as Verona would do with regard to Susan, and for which, on that night in New York City, I could offer only a simple, heartfelt, 'Thank you.'

Snapshot: Kumasi

We'd driven to Kumasi over roads glutted with traffic, often stalled behind trucks belching a toxic black smoke that enveloped our dust-coated Land Rover. We'd moved at a snail's pace along a tortuous route that crawled up inclines or suddenly lurched left or right in order to avoid chasm-sized ruts. Justine had taken a hilarious picture of Susan and me, both so dog-tired that we were dead asleep despite the fact that our bodies were being tossed around like two marbles in a whirligig.

And so it was with great relief when at last we made it through Kumasi, the former Ashanti capital, and towards evening found ourselves at the place Susan had booked us for the night, a compound for mentally handicapped children that rented rooms as a way of supporting itself. She had become very adept at finding such places by then, but I think that in this case she may have been driven by an odd nostalgia for the place where we'd first met, a school for people not unlike the ones who immediately surrounded us, save that the ones in New York City had returned to their homes at the end of the day. I never asked her if this nostalgia had, in fact, played a role in her having selected this place, but I do know that when it came time for me to write about our experience here, I was overcome by a memory of our first encounter, and this, too, is a gift of dark places, the fact that in remembering them, you remember those you were with in a way that is often richer and more touched by tenderness than memories made in places less charged with emotion or deepened by gravity.

That first encounter had happened a week or so after I'd taken a job as a typist at a school for what were then called 'retarded' adults, a word no longer in common usage, of course. Susan worked as a speech pathologist, and although we barely knew each other, I'd noticed that anytime she introduced herself, she was careful to spell her last name: t-E-r-n-er. Sometimes she would explain, 'It's not the English "Turner", it's Austrian.'

My job was to type the reports of the agency's staff, one of whom, of course, was Susan. While typing one of her reports, I came upon this line: 'Stephen's bathroom habits are à la Portnoy.' I was only a typist, but I felt I needed to address this sentence before typing it into an official report.

'What's the problem?' Susan asked when I summoned the courage to go to her office. I handed her the report she'd given me to type. 'I'm not sure "à la Portnoy" would be understood,' I said.

'Why not?' Susan asked. A comic glitter lit her eyes. 'They're all Jews here.' She looked at me pointedly. 'So am I, by the way.'

I couldn't help but wonder if she'd added this last comment because she'd heard my southern accent and with a Yankee's foreboding, suspected that I might be an anti-Semite, closet or otherwise.

She glanced at the paper I'd just handed her. 'You're probably right about the "à la Portnoy".'

She snatched a pen from her desk, made a few quick marks on her paper and handed it back to me. I looked at what she'd done, an arrow here, a cross-out there. It was a perfectly seamless edit. *This*, I told myself, *is one bright woman*.

Now, over thirty years later, we were still together, so it was those same comic yet pointedly serious eyes that now settled upon me in a way that told me she'd noticed my uncertainty about her latest choice of accommodation. 'You can have a nice room, Tom,' she reminded me firmly, 'but the chances are, you won't have an experience.'

True enough, for in point of fact, the compound had already provided one of those moments when images seen in films or read in books come fully to life. A clanging iron gate had opened to let us in, and when it closed behind us, it had seemed to seal us in a world completely divorced from what sprawled around it. This was a place of refuge that held within it a way of life entirely different from the one outside its gates. In that way, it had the feel of a precarious existence, one briefly granted rather than permanently secured.

Even so, there was no actual sense of the compound being threatened. In fact, once inside the gate, the world that opened up to us was a very peaceful one. People casually strolled about, and in the distance, I saw a great many children frolicking in a large fountain.

After dropping off our things, we walked back outside, found a few chairs and sat down to watch the residents of the compound either at play or strolling about the grounds. Even from a distance, it was clear that some of these 'children' were in their late teens, while others were perhaps no more than four or five years old.

'Where do they come from?' I asked when a middle-aged man who turned out to be the director of the place took a seat next to me.

'They were all abandoned,' he answered. 'Found on the streets, that sort of thing.'

He was Dutch, and like everyone I've ever met from Holland, his English was perfect.

'And where will they go?' I asked.

He looked at me, clearly puzzled by the question. 'Go?' he said. 'They won't go anywhere.'

'They will always stay here?' I asked.

He nodded. 'There's no place else for them to go.'

'But that means that eventually this place will become a home for the aged,' I said.

Again, he nodded.

'Then what about the others?' I asked. 'The children years

from now. Where will they go if there is no room for them here?'

He settled his gaze on the children at the fountain. Several had come out of the water and were towelling themselves off. 'Well, that's the sort of thought people can't dwell upon too long.'

Before that moment, it had never occurred to me that the fact that my ability not to dwell on certain thoughts for 'too long' was what made dark travel possible. I could go to dark places, read about them, even write about them later, but if I truly dwelled upon them 'too long', if I truly let these tragic shores settle into me in such a way that I could think of nothing else, then I would become dysfunctional not only in my work, but in every aspect of life. Denied that capacity, even people like the director who'd sat beside me as the sun went down over Kumasi that afternoon would sink into a black malaise. Compassion for the world had to have a limit in order to be effective, a fire escape in the mind and heart by which you could exit those thoughts that would otherwise char your soul.

And yet how very odd and contradictory that we should be rescued from complete ineffectiveness by being able to eat while others are hungry, enjoy shelter while others have no homes, warm ourselves while others freeze, provide for our own comfort despite the many miseries of which we are aware.

The morning I was writing this particular snapshot, I went to the 'Bring Back Our Girls' website and found this:

Today is the 39th day since 273 Nigerian school girls were kidnapped. We ask that all of you, from whatever city/country you live, to continue to march and hold rallies. Continue to call your government leaders and tell your friends. We will not be silenced.

It is very good indeed that this 'we' will not be silenced.

But it is also necessary that this 'we', once having written or called or participated in a rally for these lost girls, should be able to go on with their lives, pursue whatever form of personal happiness and fulfilment they deem most appropriate for themselves.

I have no doubt that I, along with all the others who make up this 'we', will do precisely that – distance ourselves from these girls, compartmentalize their fates – because we are designed to do exactly that, a fact that is not so very comforting, though it is surely embedded in the human DNA, a biological fact that, by the way, 'we' perhaps should not think about too long.

Monte Sano Mountain/
Copenhagen Harbour/
Landet Churchyard/
Père Lachaise/Verona

As a boy, I'd lived for a year or so in Huntsville, Alabama, within view of a mountain called Monte Sano. One legend that gave the mountain its name told of a beautiful Indian maiden named Monte who'd once loved a young warrior. Unfortunately, this warrior had died, and so her father had later chosen another of Monte's many suitors and demanded that she marry him. Faced with marrying a man she did not love, or even know, for that matter, Monte had eventually found herself pondering her father's demand while standing on a cliff at the top of a mountain. There, the wind brought her the voice of her dead lover: 'Monte,' he said to her, 'say "No".' Beguiled by her lover's voice, the beautiful young Monte had leaped from the mountain to join her beloved in death.

The legends we hear in youth can work quite insidiously, as this one did in my life. It was only a story, but it came to represent romantic tragedy to me, so that long after I'd learned that Monte Sano had never existed, my idea of romantic love continued to be mingled with notions of passionate torment occasioned by various dramatic obstacles. Lovers were thwarted by parents, by society, by religion, and from time to time, these obstacles had proven so overwhelming that these passionate beings had chosen death. Marked by the notion that specific outside forces most imperilled romantic love, I'd found myself attracted to places that spoke of the lethal nature of Cupid's arrow because it was such places that seemed most to represent love's doomed course.

And so one frigid evening, I braved the bitter cold of Copenhagen Harbour to see the famous statue of the Little Mermaid, that sad heroine of romance who'd given up eternity for the love of a human prince. It had been too dark to get a glimpse of her, as it turned out, but a friend took a photo of me shivering at the edge of the water, the Little Mermaid somewhere out there in the arctic darkness, but wholly invisible to me. 'You are the only American ever to be photographed in this place alone,' my friend joked. 'They all come in groups, take a picture, then head straight back to their buses and rush off to Hamlet's castle.'

Later, I took a train to Odense, where the Little Mermaid's creator, Hans Christian Andersen, had been born. Though he'd lived in a continually boiling stew of unrequited love, Andersen's considerable torments had never resulted in anything truly tragic. The same could not be said of the two doomed lovers who lay in a country churchyard not far from Odense, however, and whose tragedy was world renowned.

Landet churchyard is small and immaculately tended, with the tidiness common to everything in Denmark. As such, it hardly befits the final resting place of the celebrated lovers who lie buried here. In my fanciful imagination, something wilder seemed required, something far more physically sensual, a grove hung in vines, perhaps, steamy and faintly overripe. Landet Churchyard, however, is neatly pruned, its paths among the short grey stones as straight and narrow as the life the Danish Church had been determined to impose a century ago, when these two lovers' bodies were interred. In fact, the site is so entirely well-ordered, all the stones more or less indistinguishable, that what I noticed most were two graves whose headstones appeared to be parts of an aeroplane propeller.

'Two RAF pilots are buried here,' my friend Borg explained. 'They crashed near here in 1944.'

Briefly, we paid our respects to these brave pilots, then Borg said, 'The doomed lovers you're looking for are over there.' He pointed towards two squat grey stones. 'Since the movie, more people come to see them,' he added.

Elvira Madigan and her lover, Sixten Sparre, are buried side by side, the only surprise being that Elvira's stone bears her real name, Hedvig Jensen, rather than the more musical name she'd chosen to promote herself as the tightrope walker and trick rider she had been.

'Sad story,' Borg said.

Very sad indeed, so that as I stood, staring down at the graves, I thought of just how lethal romantic love can be.

Elvira Madigan had been a beautiful, twenty-one-year-old circus performer when she met the dashing cavalry officer, Sixten Sparre, a thirty-five-year-old married man with two children. They'd run off together, Sparre even going so far as to desert the army, a very grave matter, in order to be with the lovely Elvira. But lovers, no matter how overarching their passion, must also have bread, and by the time these two fiercely reckless creatures reached the little Danish island of Tasinge, their flight had so utterly depleted their resources that they'd found it necessary to forage the island's woodlands for food. At some point during this bleak struggle to sustain themselves on the meagre gleanings of the forest, Sparre had made a fateful choice, reached for his service revolver and shot Elvira, then himself, an event that immortalized them both, but particularly Elvira, whose name later became the title of a movie and a song. It had even been the name chosen by a Swedish musical group for its symphonic black metal band.

It was a moving place, Landet churchyard. The solemnity of the lovers' graves was an effective symbol for their romantic tragedy despite the intrusion of reality into the myth of their romance – the fact, for example, that Elvira might have been less in love with Sixten than seeking a way out of the circus, and that Sixten had been a gambler and wastrel throughout most of his misspent life. Like most tales of overweening romance, that of Elvira Madigan and her love-crazed paramour had played fast and loose with the facts, always erring in the direction of unblemished passion so that anyone who heard or read it would be convinced that the lovers would surely have lived happily ever after had not the rigid rules of the social order stood in their way.

Death had abruptly brought down the curtain on Elvira and Sixten's tale of romance, but some passions have had a longer shelf-life, and so after visiting Landet churchyard, I decided to pay my respects to what is, perhaps, the most famous of them all.

To my surprise, I felt the same solemnity at the graves of Héloïse and Abélard at Père Lachaise cemetery, in Paris, that I had felt in that Danish churchyard. So much so that it seemed only fitting that these doomed lovers now lay quite near to Edith Piaf, unquestionably the world's greatest songstress of romantic tragedy.

The timeless love story of Héloïse and Abélard had always struck me as even more harrowing than that of Elvira Madigan and Sixten Sparre. Elvira and Sixten had died early, after all, but Héloïse and Abélard had lived for years in the aftermath of romantic catastrophe.

Theirs had been a story that in some sense mirrored that of Romeo and Juliet, at least to the degree that a family objection was the root of the problem. Héloïse's uncle, Canon Fulbert, hired Abélard to tutor his brilliant niece, then became convinced that Abélard had seduced her. Abélard had, in fact, done exactly that, a conquest he seems to have had little wish to conceal.

Fulbert's revenge on Abélard is perhaps the most famous in all the literature of love, a castration Abélard detailed in his aptly titled book, *The Story of My Misfortune*. As an act of avuncular vengeance it proved titillating in the extreme, so that the story of Héloïse and Abélard came to be recounted in plays, songs, operas and films. In almost every case, Héloïse's love emerges as very nearly perfect. She adores Abélard through eternity, and appears simply not to see the vain, self-absorbed, and endlessly self-pitying man he actually was. All her life she writes to him. In his long illness, she nurses him. At his death, she brings his remains to the convent over which she presides.

The problem with Héloïse's devotion, however, was that it seemed to speak less of enduring love than of the enduring power of romantic imprinting. But this only added to the tragedy, at least on Héloïse's part. She had been a mere girl when she'd fallen under Abélard's spell, after all, and she'd gone into a convent almost immediately after his castration. For that reason, she had burned in the fire of first love all her life.

The ferocity of that love is nowhere in evidence upon the tomb in which Héloïse rests side by side with Abélard, their remains having been moved a few times before finally coming to rest in Père Lachaise cemetery in Paris. In fact, there has been some dispute regarding whether these celebrated remains are actually to be found in the tomb at all, though the evidence seems to favour Père Lachaise's claim that the two lovers do, indeed, share this single crypt.

As a tomb it is large by most standards, but not so large that it could not be easily missed among the crowded walkways of the cemetery. In fact, on the day I came here, only one tomb was really easy to find, Jim Morrison's, the leader of the Doors, his resting place indicated by a number of chalk-scrawled directions left by his fans, people evidently unaware that Balzac also rests here, along with Colette, Oscar Wilde, Gertrude Stein and any number of other such luminaries.

The truly striking thing about the tomb, however, is its thorough lack of passion. A stone cupola with a peaked roof rises above the recumbent figures of Héloïse and Abélard, both lying very straight and with their hands folded in prayer. As such they look like actors on a set, backs to the board, motionless, awaiting more make-up. It is a militantly cautious representation in death of two people who, in life, were anything but cautious. Their story, perhaps more than any other, suggests the recklessness of passion. As a matter of fact, after writing one of his passionate missives to Héloïse, Abélard literally climbed over the garden wall in order personally to deliver it, at which point he discovered that she was already pregnant with his child (a boy she later named Astrolabe after the scientific instrument). Abélard then begged Héloïse to flee with him to Brittany, which she did. She would not marry him, however, citing as her reason the fact that it would hinder the career of her beloved. This is Héloïse at her characteristically self-sacrificial, a star-struck teenager still in awe of her smooth-talking teacher – ten years her senior – who seduced her, a bleary state of being with regard to Abélard that she never subsequently abandoned.

It was the blinkered nature of Héloïse's passion, along with

Abélard's nearly inconceivable vanity, that made my visit to their resting place far from edifying. True, their passion, like that of Elvira and Sixten, had been very great indeed. And yet, for all the suffering and death that had accompanied it, I found something rather pathetic in these two famous tales of romantic tragedy. I knew that such tragedy existed, of course, but it seemed to me that the lovers who occupied the graves I'd visited in Landet churchyard and Père Lachaise cemetery had been prisoners of a somewhat lugubrious romantic melodrama they'd had neither the insight nor the resourcefulness to escape.

But at least Elvira Madigan and Sixten Sparre had been real people, as had been Héloïse and Abélard, and so, beside their sad fates, fictional representations of romantic tragedy would surely pale, it seemed to me, even the most famous of them all.

And so, on that summer day in Verona when Susan, Justine and I visited it, I had little anticipation that there was much to be learned from visiting the 'tragic shore' of 'Juliet's Balcony'. In fact, I had fully expected to leave the town remembering only the cell phones, which, while new in the United States at that time, were so numerous and so continually in use by the testosterone-charged young men of Verona that I had found it difficult to focus on anything but their steady stream of chatter.

We had taken a table at a small outdoor café not far from the town's famed arena. An opera was soon to be staged, and the area around the arena was filled with pieces of what was clearly to be a very large and elaborate set. It was the middle of the day, and on the plaza surrounding the café, workmen were lounging about, usually with their legs stretched at full length in the relaxed way of southern Europeans at that time, when the lunch hour had a tendency to extend deep into the afternoon. It was a scene that would have given concern to an Englishman and appalled a German, but we were used to it, having lived in Madrid where, although shops were said to open at nine in the morning, the city's rush hour was at ten.

We had spent the morning strolling Verona's winding streets. Even in summer, they were remarkably uncrowded, probably because the city is about halfway between Milan to the west and Venice to the east, tourist magnets with which modest little Verona simply cannot compete. Even so, Verona has had its share of visitors, the most famous of which was probably Charles Dickens, who found it 'pleasant'. He had feared to come here, he said, lest the city throw him 'out of conceit' with Shakespeare, but had, after a short tour of the old marketplace, gone straight to what was then called the House of the Capulets, and which he'd found to be a 'miserable little inn', with a muddy courtyard, patrolled by a gaggle of quarrelsome geese and guarded by a nasty dog. Thus put off, he'd left Juliet's house immediately, and if his own account is any guide, without a thought in his head.

Dickens' lacklustre response to this most famous of Verona's small treasures might easily have been mine, particularly given the fact that cell phones were still ringing in my head as we made our way there. Certainly, I wouldn't have expected to find the house said to have been Juliet's a site destined from then onward to represent romantic tragedy to me far more deeply than Landet churchyard or the tombs of Héloïse and Abélard in Père Lachaise cemetery, and in so doing, become one of the saddest places I have ever seen.

It was a tourist attraction, of course, though at that time I saw no sign that 'Juliet's Balcony' could be rented for a wedding ceremony as it can now, nor was the façade of the house covered with the multicoloured love Post-it notes I saw in a recent photograph of the place. The courtyard was small, and there was a bronze statue of Juliet, looking demure and maiden-like, but with her right breast and, somewhat disturbingly, her crotch, rubbed to a sheen by the touch of thousands of hands, a ritual touted to bring good luck.

Juliet's balcony hung above us, a modest affair, and quite small, so that only a few people could crowd onto it at a time. A steady stream of tourists were doing just that.

Justine was standing beside me, peering up at the balcony.

'Why don't you go up there,' I said. 'It isn't really Juliet's balcony, of course, but it's a renowned place anyway.'

She shook her head. 'It's crowded.'

'Oh, come on,' I urged her. 'I'll take a picture of you from down here. You'll be glad you did it.'

A few minutes later, I saw her appear on the balcony. She leaned over, waved, then returned immediately to where Susan and I waited for her in the courtyard. With that, our visit to the House of the Capulets was over, and we made our way back towards the streets of Verona.

And so this little journey might have ended, had we not

subsequently passed beneath an archway that led from the courtyard to the street. I hadn't taken much notice of it as we'd headed towards the house, but now, it suddenly captured my attention.

It was a low archway, without great distinction, but its interior walls had become the canvas for hundreds of romantic messages written in various languages. I could read the ones in English, French and Spanish, and since love's vocabulary, when not written by Shakespeare, is anything but complicated, I could pretty much understand whatever had been written in German and Italian. I didn't notice any Japanese or Chinese symbols or any messages written in the Arabic or Cyrillic alphabets, but I have no doubt that had there been such messages, they would have expressed the same feelings as those in the more familiar European languages.

I stopped to read a few. They were exactly the sort of declarations people carve into trees or spray-paint on rocks, and I suddenly remembered how the Live Oak, a magnificent tree outside Charleston, had been covered with the same romantic graffiti. Here, as there, the expressions themselves were staggeringly inane, hearts with names inscribed inside them, for example.

And yet, something deep and resonant somehow rose from all that inanity, something not carried by the words, which were commonplace, but embedded in the sentiment, which was universal.

I glanced back towards Juliet's balcony, where Justine had

stood only minutes before, and in that brief glance, it struck me that in this little tunnel I had stumbled upon one of the saddest places I would ever see. For it seemed to me that had Juliet only her parents' objection with which to contend, their hostility to Romeo the only obstacle to their enduring love, then she would have been far, far luckier than most, her love for Romeo not really star-crossed at all. And if all the people who'd written on this little archway's walls had died as Elvira Madigan had, or lived their lives in a state of romantic delusion, as had been the fate of Héloïse, then they would have avoided all the terrible obstacles that genuinely and formidably lie in the path of enduring love. They would have their victory, but it would be the victory of a fighter who fights only the first round.

By the time I paused in the archway that day in Verona, I had seen my share of weddings, some quite elaborate, black-tie affairs, the bride and groom resplendent, dancing in a sea of smiles. Susan and I, on the other hand, had been married in a county courthouse by a judge with other business on his mind. During the ceremony, Susan had suddenly burst out laughing and had laughed uncontrollably for some few seconds while the judge looked on with a baffled expression before asking if he should go on. Susan, still laughing, had told him that he should, so the ceremony, such as it was, had been completed more or less in the five minutes allotted to it, and after which, we had been asked to contribute to the 'coffee fund' as payment for his services. As we'd headed out the door, I remembered that during Susan's laughing interruption, the judge had glanced at me with a half-troubled, half-quizzical expression, as if to say, 'Are you sure about this?'

Are you sure about this?

That was the question that occurred to me that afternoon as I stood in the little archway, staring at all those passionate avowals of eternal constancy and devotion.

No one can be sure, of course, a truth that made the confident declarations that covered the walls of Juliet's archway all the more poignant. Here people had given little evidence of understanding that enduring love will inevitably have much to endure, that it may dim, change, that Juliet and Romeo, had they lived, might finally have come to find each other rather tiresome, or at the least to acknowledge how deep and numerous had been the pits that lay ahead. Indeed they might have lived to smile ruefully at the old English bromide that marriage is a long boring dinner with the pudding served first.

Are you sure about this?

No one can be, and yet we have no more passionate hope than the one these lovers had paused to express before continuing into the courtyard to touch Juliet's breast or stand on her balcony. Nor do we harbour any hope less likely of fulfilment, so that as one romance fails, we seek another and another, marry and divorce again and again, forever in pursuit of a lasting romantic passion that by its very nature cannot last.

A few minutes later, we passed through the far side of the archway and out into the bright streets of Verona. Justine dashed ahead, ready for the next adventure, leaving Susan and me to walk alone.

'That place meant something to you,' Susan said. 'I could tell.'

She meant the archway with its multilingual messages.

'I was just thinking about all those lovers,' I said. 'I wonder how many of them are still together.'

'Not many,' Susan said. 'And some of ones that still are may wish they weren't.'

'Yes,' I agreed. 'That's probably true.'

I stopped and looked at her. 'Are you glad we're still together?'

She smiled and took my hand. 'Yes, I am.'

I never looked back towards Juliet's archway, but over the years it has quite often returned to me, a scattering of names united in a moment of supremely romantic hope, and each time I've thought of it, I've considered my own version of enduring love, how despite our many inadequacies as human beings, Susan and I had managed to hold on to something as fragile as it was ineffably dear. Together we had seen good times and bad, sickness and health, endured the rigours of less than spiritually satisfying work, struggled through the bramble of parenthood, painfully questioned the lost opportunities that bedevil every life, learned that love is often strangled by the very ties that bind.

And yet, through all of the stresses that had threatened to tear us apart, we had remained together not because we had to do so, but because in the end, no matter what life tossed us, we had continued to believe that we could better absorb its blows together. This was a rigour of love neither Elvira Madigan and

Sixten Sparre nor Héloïse and Abélard, nor Romeo and Juliet, so early dead, had ever had to face. Time is, after all, the test of love, and although no one at any particular moment can be sure that his or her own love will stand that test, I felt that my love for Susan and hers for me at least had a chance of doing so. On the wings of that possibility, I looked forward to a time when we might return to Juliet's archway, perhaps in old age, on our last voyage together, and I would take a pen and draw a heart and inscribe our names inside it, careful, of course, to put that 'E' in Terner.

Elmina

Eight hours out of London you descend into another world, one where the usually dazzling lights of a metropolitan airport are blurred by a haze of pollution. Once on the ground, a dense heat surrounds you because you are not ushered into a gleaming, air-conditioned terminal, but into a sweltering room where at a snail's pace you proceed through customs. Posters welcome you to Ghana, but what you notice is sagging electrical wires that seem to have been abandoned in the midst of installation. You don't know it yet, but these dangling wires will become emblematic of the country: not dangerous, just desultory.

Nearly twenty-five million people live in Ghana and every one of them seems prone to smile at the first eye contact. These are warm smiles, welcoming smiles. This is not the Africa of solid, travel-story nightmare, where your luggage is pawed over by 'customs officials' who have no uniforms or identification, and who charge a 'tax' on every item they find. It is a country with plenty of militarized roadside inspections, yes, but none of them is conducted by club-wielding thugs, and the barrier that halts your progress is an official one, duly marked, not a rusty chain lying across the road and only lifted as a Western car approaches. At such stops in Ghana, you are asked for your passport, not your money or your watch. Whether stopped by soldiers, or by the police, all are friendly. In fact, everyone is friendly. Several days after entering the country, and while Justine and Susan and I were on an isolated jungle walk, I noticed a man approaching us in the distance. He was rhythmically swinging a machete, but as he closed in upon us, I felt not a whit of fear.

You are not frightened *by* Ghana. You are frightened *for* it.

I had come to see Elmina Castle, once called Al Mina, which means simply 'the mine' in Portuguese. It is arguably the most notorious location south of the Sahara. It was the first building to be erected by Europeans in the southern latitudes of Africa, a coastal fortress constructed by the Portuguese in order to protect their trading interests along what would later be called the Gold Coast. Its construction was no small project. It took ten caravels and two transport ships to haul everything, from the foundation stones to the roof tiles, all of it pre-fitted, so that Elmina is, in some sense, a modular construction. At the time, 1481, Portugal's main concern was in securing its trade in gold. But as the tide of trade shifted from precious minerals to frighteningly expendable people, so did Elmina's purpose, and with that shift the clanking streams of manacled 'black gold', slaves, began to flow in and out of its stone gates.

We were advised not to go from Accra to Elmina by public transport, our preferred means of travel. As a family, we'd long ago learned that such is really the only way actually to experience the daily life of a people, the places they go, the hardships they endure, the markets where they shop, the houses in which they live, in short, to borrow Tim O'Brien's efficient and oddly moving phrase, 'the things they carry'.

But as the smiling owner of the inn in which we were staying made clear, the problem was not that we might get ourselves into trouble on the way to Elmina, but that we might not get there at all, or at least, only after a very arduous and bone-crunching journey. This struck me as quite odd, since the 'journey' was only about seventy-two kilometres. When I said this, her smile only widened. 'You do not know Ghana,' she said. 'You will not be robbed. You will not be kidnapped. But the road is bad, and things break down.'

This was true, as I discovered some days later, when a second journey of approximately four hundred kilometres took two days, requiring a full stop for the evening, and whose final eighty kilometres were, as a fellow Dutch traveller put it, 'pure hell'.

I am far from a fearless traveller, and so I take the warnings of locals seriously. For that reason, we decided to tag along with two women from the same inn who'd hired a car and driver to take them to Elmina early the next morning. They were West Indian, and thus admirably in search of knowing more about what their captive ancestors had suffered there.

We set out at dawn's early light and were soon engulfed by a sprawl of traffic that immediately reduced all forward movement to a crawl. At some point later, perhaps an hour – for by then I'd somewhat lost track of time as we know it – the bumpiness of badly potted pavement gave way to a road that was not paved at all, so that to the din of hundreds of roadside hawkers was added a continual boil of red dust, clouds of it that rose explosively from each tread of a foot or revolution of a wheel. It was a dust so ubiquitous it coated your skin and lay upon your eyes, a dust so fine you could not keep from breathing it in, or sometimes eating it.

The towns through which we passed on our way to Elmina that morning revealed that outside Accra small businesses become minuscule businesses, a lively, noisy, dusty commercial roadside life, much of it conducted from open-air stands whose names revealed the deep religious fervour of Ghana's people. Out the window I saw the 'Blood of Christ Hair Salon', 'Salvation Mechanics', and 'Jesus is Mine Appliances'. These enterprises were stationary, while a wholly separate and completely mobile economic life was vigorously pursued by people carrying their trading goods on their heads or shoulders, huge piles of brown cakes, bags of fruit, nuts, chips, towers of water contained not in bottles, but in small plastic bags that have no openings at all. 'You bite off one corner and squeeze out the water,' Justine, who'd preceded Susan and me by a couple of weeks, and thus was now an old Africa hand, explained. Unfortunately, biting off a corner of this water-filled bag was far from easy due to the incessant bump and jangle of the road, along with the sudden violent swerves that were repeatedly necessary to avoid both human and nonhuman obstacles: swarms of hawkers, deep ruts, other cars, chickens.

I'd travelled in Eastern Europe just after communism's ignoble collapse, so I knew that distance and time were not often relatable, but nothing could have prepared me for the slough of Ghana, a quagmire created by the press of humanity, the obliviousness of animals, the sheer concentration of traffic and the abominable condition of the roads.

At one point I saw something that, given the situation, I briefly took for a mirage. It was an elevated highway, quite modern in its design, a miracle of engineering compared to anything around it, but which, as I suddenly noticed, abruptly ended, literally in suspension, an impressively well-built skyway that simply, inexplicably stopped. There was no equipment, nor any workers either on or around it, so that it appeared less like a modern roadway than an ancient ruin.

'That will really help the traffic situation when it's finished,' I said to the driver.

He laughed. 'It will never be finished,' he said.

And he did mean 'never' literally.

For much is never finished in Ghana. On all sides as we made our way towards Elmina, I saw buildings whose construction had stopped at various levels of completion and which gave no sign of ever being finished.

The structures that surrounded these unfinished buildings bore the singular mark of Accra's suburban sprawl, collapsibility, a sense that much of the city could be quickly broken down and carted away. This feeling of impermanence, of things not built to last, pervaded the string of towns that stretched for miles and miles beyond the capital, and which gave the impression of a short-lived bustle, a world not quite nailed down in which energy was released in spurts that could not be sustained. Nothing in Ghana seemed focused on the long haul.

The entire journey to Elmina was crowded with this jumble, along with its accompanying human tide of vendors whose wares were remarkably undifferentiated, the toys and baked goods all the same, along with the pervasive products of cassava roots, Ghana's chief means of nourishment and which is everywhere pulverized, usually by hand, then refashioned into a paste known as *fufu*, a staple whose texture is a sticky goo, and which has no taste at all.

Elmina Castle first appeared as a block of white perched on a promontory that overlooked the Atlantic, a structure strikingly different from the teeming coastal town that pressed in upon its walls. It was the product of invasion, conquest and massive exploitation, and the nearer I came to it that morning, the more it looked the part, large, forbidding, built to last forever, a huge structure that could not have been more alien to the unfathomable tangle of wood and corrugated tin that huddled around it.

There was a modest parking area adjacent to the castle, and like the entrances and exits of all such attractions in Ghana, it was staked out by young men, all of whom rushed hurriedly towards Justine and the other women. 'Just say you're Canadian,'

Justine told the West Indians. 'They'll lose interest in you if you tell them that.'

This advice worked, and employing it clearly amused the two women.

It was the last time they would find amusement here.

Elmina loomed ahead, and the radiant light that surrounded it proved insufficient to lift its darkness.

It has been estimated that one third of the population of Ghana was enslaved before the Portuguese arrived. Africans had been immemorially enslaved by rival tribes and for ten centuries by Muslims from the north, an estimated fourteen million transported to ports along the Indian Ocean or across the Sahara. The Atlantic Slave Trade provided considerable fuel to this already flourishing traffic, thus adding vast numbers to the human cargo.

Though neither designed nor built with slavery in mind, Elmina nonetheless became a central point of embarkation, its door of no return incontestably one of the busiest in Africa. As such, it also functioned as a holding depot where slaves captured by Africa's many warring tribes were traded to the Portuguese, who held them in dungeons before finally herding them into the small boats that would convey them to the much larger slave ships at anchor in the harbour.

A few minutes after entering Elmina, we were taken to one of these dungeons, and almost instantly, the actual experience of the place, of what its walls could speak, fell over me. The dungeon was relatively small, and its hapless prisoners had been driven into it in a mass so thick that lying down, or even sitting, had been impossible. For days, hundreds of men (for this was the 'men's cell') had stood in the near complete darkness of its interior, lighted as it had been by nothing beyond a small square of open window set high in the wall, its light highly diffused, so that almost none of it reached the dungeon floor. The tightly packed mass of humanity imprisoned in this room had been fed and watered through that same window because the door, once closed, had opened again only when the waiting ship was ready to receive them.

When that door closed upon us, the darkness became a blackness so thick it was only with a powerful flashlight that we could see the shallow troughs that had been cut into the floor of the room, and which had been used to flush out body waste and vomit, along with the leaking fluids of the dead.

The room was cool that day, as almost all stone rooms are, but heated by hundreds of bodies for many days, it must have become a furnace of sweltering flesh. The drains suggested the smells that must have assailed the nostrils of those who stood shoulder to shoulder in this impenetrable darkness, a nauseating combination of sweat, defecation, vomit, the mouldering bodies of those already dead. Alone, this foulness, this daily accumulating filth, would have been enough to turn this now nearly empty room into a hellish pit, 'the very air a shriek of death,' as W.E.B. Du Bois rightly called these cells, an 'agony of hurt'.

One of the West Indian women couldn't take it. I saw her rush outside, closely followed by her friend. When I came out of the dungeon a few minutes later, both were wrapped in each other's arms, and both of them were crying. Susan, who is Jewish, had done the same at Auschwitz. From her experience I'd learned that although certain cruelties in themselves are dreadful enough, it is experienced more deeply when the sufferers are among your own, their suffering inflicted simply because they were Africans or Armenians, Hindus, Muslims, or Jews. To know that at a different moment, you would have been herded into a gas chamber or onto a slave ship or into a ravine to be shot down like an animal adds a measure of frightful vulnerability to the already incalculable vulnerabilities of life and history. There is something in the human sense of things that insists that one should suffer for having done something, not for having been born something, and when this simple moral equation is distorted, life itself become a hideous funhouse mirror in which nothing can ever be seen quite the same again.

Against the fierce storm of that horrendous truth as it was being exhibited by these two West Indian women that day, I found that I could offer only a paltry, 'You okay?'

They both nodded, and once again as a group, we proceeded on, first through the castle's sunbaked courtyard, then into the women's dungeon and after that, the shadowy holding cell used to isolate recalcitrant prisoners, a room designated by the skull and crossbones over its door, and where, in complete darkness, the prisoners taken here were starved to death.

By then I'd noticed that a dense, oddly patchwork darkness pervades Elmina, and that it does so in stark contrast to the blindingly white light in which the castle bathes, a brilliant, sub-Saharan sun that glitters on the water that surrounds Elmina and sinks so deeply into the white walls of the castle that they take on the whiteness of a wedding cake. Only the upper quarters of Elmina are spared this darkness. This part of the castle is made up of the spacious, airy rooms used by its European masters, and which make the lightless, ebony chambers upon which they rest seem darker still. In these rooms the ceremonies of domestic life had proceeded without interruption, with windows open, and gentle sea breezes lifting the lace curtains, with food steaming on the long wooden tables, and candles glowing everywhere. And yet . . . below. Standing in one of these rooms, enjoying that light and those breezes, it seemed scarcely imaginable that one could live here, on the rim of hell, and simply carry on, eat your dinner, sip your port, enjoy a good cigar, then go off to a sweet, untroubled sleep. How utterly subhuman must those in agony below have seemed to those at leisure above? There are places where man's abject failure to share even the slightest element of another's pain simply numbs the mind, and Elmina is one of them.

It was in these upper rooms that the history of the slave trade was told in various drawing and narrations. I strolled about, reading, looking at the drawings, quite content to do so for a long time, until I heard one of the women who'd come with us suddenly cry out.

'Get away from me,' she shouted.

I walked around the corner of the exhibit I'd been looking at and found her facing a tall young man, well dressed, wearing glasses, his arms at this sides.

'Can't you let me *feel* this place?' she screamed angrily.

He stepped back, but did not retreat.

'I'm not going anywhere with you!' the young woman cried. 'And I'm not taking you back with me to England! So just get away from me!'

The man did not move. He did not look threatening, only determined to continue to press his case, whatever that might be.

'Get away from me!' the woman cried again.

By then, Ishmael, her driver, had arrived. 'Leave her alone,' he told the young man, his tone very stern. When the young man did not respond, he added a look that would have sent a shiver down the spine of Attila the Hun. 'Did you hear me, asshole?'

At that point, the young man turned and walked away, though not without glancing back at the young woman in a way that conveyed his complete shock at her reaction.

'He won't bother you any more,' Ishmael assured the young woman. 'These guys are desperate to get out of here, that's all. Somewhere they get the idea that they're irresistible. That they're studs or something. But really, they're just idiots.' He smiled. 'But they wouldn't hurt you.'

'Thank you,' the young woman said, then returned to the exhibits. She looked much more relaxed now, reading carefully, staring at the various renderings of the life, death and suffering that marked Elmina as surely one of the saddest places on earth.

Even so, she often glanced about to assure herself that Ishmael was nearby. He always was.

At last we came to Elmina's celebrated Door of No Return.

It is shockingly narrow, the slaves pressed through it, one by one, their numbers ticking off until, collectively with similar fortresses dotted along Ghana's coast, it reached somewhere between eleven and twenty million, depending upon the estimate one chooses from the Atlantic slave trade's many, and sometimes argumentative, histories. No estimate was given as to how many slaves passed through Elmina's particular door, but since the Slave Trade continued for many decades, even the lowest estimates would be sufficient to indicate the vastness of the enterprise.

Vast, yes, but as this narrow door made clear, the enormity of the number – whether eleven or twenty million – was made up over decades as one person was added at a time, a single person squeezed through this narrow passage and hauled into a boat and rowed out to a ship, and taken aboard, and led down into the bowels of the ship and manacled hand and foot, one person waiting in a darkness only little relieved from the dungeon he or she had survived, and which would not lift until that same ship laid anchor once again in a land so foreign it must have seemed like what it was – a country on the other side of the world.

Before leaving Elmina, I walked up the stairs and stood on the ramparts once again. The coastal town was small, its streets chaotic. Below, lines of fishing boats rested in the sand, mostly unattended. A few children were playing in the surf. One of them hurriedly exited the water, rushed to the castle's wall, pulled down his swimming trunks, quickly defecated, then rushed back into the water. To treat Elmina with such contempt, offer it so vile an insult, rather paradoxically struck me as oddly fitting in an African boy. Still, it was a sight that made me turn away, so that I looked out over the harbour, rather than back towards the town.

Had I been standing on this same rampart on 6 September 1781, I would have seen the *Zong* resting at anchor, small boats moving back and forth with their cargoes of black gold. Two months later, on 29 November, the captain would order one third of the ship's slaves to be thrown overboard in order to reduce the vessel's liability for 'lost cargo'. One hundred and thirty-three Africans were subsequently tossed into the sea, though the final ten, according to an eyewitness account, disdainfully broke free of their executioners, mounted the gunwale and jumped into the heaving waters.

A lawsuit ensued, one that brought a great deal of very bad publicity to the Atlantic trade. The Quakers began gathering signatures on a petition for its abolition, a voice that, once raised, could not subsequently be silenced. As a result, the trade was abolished in 1807. No Africans would pass through Elmina's Door of No Return after that, nor any ships await them in the harbour any more. Outside its high walls and beyond its deep moat, only cabs and buses waited now.

As we made our way to them, the same group of young men by whom we'd earlier been accosted closed in upon us. Usually in such places, those who descend upon you have something

244

to sell, but these young men were offering only themselves, a curious lack of wares we would encounter often over the coming days, young men approaching women, smiling brightly as they attempted to start a conversation. 'What's your name?' Big smile. 'Where are you from?' Even bigger smile.

'What do these guys want?' one of the West Indian women asked after we'd all managed to get back in the van.

'To get out of Ghana,' Justine answered, the same response Ishmael had given earlier.

The irony was obvious. Here, at Elmina, untold numbers of young African men had been forced to leave their ancestral home. Now men of that same age were urgently trying to leave it.

The fierce hopes of these young men stayed on my mind during the next few days. Neither did it take much investigation to understand why their hope of leaving Ghana was such a driving one, why, as Ishmael had said earlier in the day, 'they are desperate'. For the fact is, life in Ghana is hard, though by no means as hard as it is in some of the far more blighted countries that make up the continental patchwork of sub-Saharan Africa. In comparison, Ghana is stable by almost any measure. Here there are no rebel armies wiping out whole villages, no tribal ethnic cleansings, no hallucinatory warlords with their *khat*-chewing boy armies, no mass kidnapping of school girls. In Ghana the nightmare recedes, but in many ways the country remains, at least by Western standards, a pretty bad dream.

During the next week or so, as we moved north towards

Kumasi, Ghana's sprawling second largest city, then over impossibly brutal roads to Tamale, we found precious little evidence of anything but a marginal existence. Outside the cities and towns life seemed to return almost immediately to a pre-industrial age, though one that offered scenes that could only be described as surreally anachronistic, for example a woman with a great heap of clothes balanced on her head, taking that great bundle to a nearby stream while talking on a cell phone.

The curious thing, of course, is that Ghana, like a great deal of Africa, is rich in resources. Ghana's poverty is not a poverty that should be natural to it. The soil could grow most anything, but for the most part, it is used only for *fufu*, the staple diet of most Ghanaians. 'We eat it because we have to,' Ishmael told Justine, 'not because of taste.'

So why only cassava? Certainly it is not a crop imposed by colonialism. In fact, Western advisors and aid workers have made many attempts to replace cassava – which, in addition to having no discernible flavour, has very little nutritive value – with corn. To be fair, some corn is grown in Ghana, but what you see throughout the country is cassava, and only cassava, its thick roots carried in great bundles on the heads of (always) women.

And if the evidence of the eyes holds any merit, it is women who provide the lion's share of all physical labour in Ghana. While men lounge about, sitting in that idle way that has often been described by travellers in Africa, women are busy as bees. Everywhere, they are in motion. And when not in motion, they are found tending the hundreds of makeshift stands that line the roads of Ghana, groups of men often some distance away, slumped beneath the nearest shade, either playing cards or doing absolutely nothing.

Could this explain the failure of corn to replace cassava as a flourishing crop in Ghana? I asked myself. Corn hangs from stalks and is planted in rows. It requires cultivation and harvesting. Cassava lies buried in the ground and grows without any need for human attention. It can do so for two years without the slightest application of labour. Cassava, as such, is the perfect crop for a world in which men have no wish to work. It can be dug out of the ground by a woman, beaten into a paste by a woman, heated and served by a woman. For these reasons, it is surely the ideal crop for providing the pleasures of male idleness. Ghana seemed to give an ironic new meaning to James Connolly's famous remark that women were the slaves of the slaves.

Given that thought, I couldn't help but wonder if any society can finally progress if its women remain in shackles. True, female oppression is probably not the only cause of stagnant societies, but the evidence of life seems to be that any people that keeps half its human genius from asserting itself will forfeit half its achievement. Where might even the most advanced of modern societies now be if, from the beginning, its women had been free to enquire and to discover? How many of the thousand natural shocks that flesh is heir to might have been softened by their liberation? We shall never know nor reap the benefit of what they might have learned, the many maladies they might have cured, the many heartbreaks they might have mended. For that reason, the loss already incurred, invisible though it may seem, will forever be incalculable.

Once back in Accra, and with one final day in the country, we decided to walk to a small 'exhibition hall' said to display the work of local artists. The route took us through a warren of unpaved alleys and along an open sewer whose noxious smells no doubt wafted into every nearby window.

The exhibition hall, by contrast, was light and airy, a good deal of its space given over to the odd wooden coffins for which Accra is noted. Some were in the shape of buses, others took the form of rocket ships and soda bottles. In such conveyances, evidently, were the souls of Ghana transported to heaven.

Just off the main hall, there was a room devoted to wooden carvings, mostly ceremonial masks, and as we'd earlier noticed in our travels about the country, so unvaryingly repetitious in both design and execution they seemed more likely the product of a Chinese factory than of some distant villager with a carving knife.

Still, there was time to kill, and so I wandered slowly among this crowd of wooden carvings. Nothing caught my eye until I spotted a shape that was a tad distinctive. Well, perhaps not really distinctive, but at least not a mask. The figure was a robed African woman, squatting on her haunches, very thin, holding a staff while simply staring out into the middle distance as if helplessly awaiting an answer to this continent's benightedness, its tribal wars and farcical dictators, this rich land continually swept by famine, this world of child armies and female servitude, where slavery, worst irony of all, is said still to exist.

Now my mind shifted, and I recalled an earlier incident that until that moment I'd entirely forgotten. We'd been in our car, headed out of Elmina, now on our way to Kumasi and points north. Ahead, I saw a line of soldiers, rifles at the ready. As we approached, one of them motioned our car to the side of the road.

He came forward with a soldierly stride and peered into the car.

'Where are you going?' he asked.

'Kumasi,' I answered. 'Then further north to Tamale.'

He peered about the interior of the car, his eyes fixing briefly on Susan before settling on Justine.

'Maybe you marry me,' he said to her with a big smile.

Justine smiled back, though in a way that she hoped might discourage any further talk of marriage.

Unfortunately, it didn't.

The solider cocked his head to the right slightly, his gaze still levelled on Justine.

'You are very beautiful,' he said, his tone now less playful. 'You don't want to marry me?'

'I don't want to marry anybody,' Justine told him firmly.

Now the soldier looked at me. 'Where you from, Papa?'

'New York.'

He smiled very broadly. 'Ah.' There was a pause. 'Maybe you take me to New York, eh?'

'I don't think that's possible,' I said.

He laughed. 'I know, Papa. I know.' He shrugged. 'Too bad,

eh?' With that, he smiled the smile I'd later see on Eric, the young man who'd escorted us around Adanwomase. They were very different young men, one deferential, the other brash, but both were bright and ambitious, and I sensed that each of them was seeking some way either to change Ghana in fundamental ways or leave it entirely.

After a moment, the young soldier glanced up the road ahead. 'It is too hot in Ghana,' he said, as if this were enough to sum up its many ills. When he returned his attention to me, he was smiling. 'Goodbye,' he said, then motioned us forward.

Later, considering all this, I recalled an incident once considered vaguely comic, but which now took on a certain melancholy gravity. Upon leaving Zaire, after his famous 'Rumble in the Jungle' with George Foreman, Muhammad Ali was asked what he thought of Africa. His response had taken everyone off guard because it had been shockingly frank: 'Thank God my granddaddy got on that boat,' he said.

Now, upon leaving Elmina, I couldn't help but wonder if perhaps the sons and daughters of those forced through its Door of No Return might consider themselves the similarly fortunate progeny of the millions who'd endured the horrors of the Middle Passage, the decades of enslavement, the long struggle towards social equality. Given the pre-colonial, colonial and post-colonial history of poverty, slaughter and famine that has made up so much of Africa's sad history, might the West Indian woman who'd been so moved at Elmina have felt much the same as Muhammad Ali, that those millions of anguished ghosts are due not just a soft 'I am sorry for your suffering,' but also a heartfelt, 'Thank you for enduring it.'

There is a tragic irony to this, of course. For who would wish to journey to a better life on the back of one taken from his or her own people, transported to a foreign place under unspeakable conditions, then reduced to absolute servitude? And yet, history teaches nothing so thoroughly as this cruel irony, the fact that although each generation stands on the triumphs and discoveries of the generation that preceded it, the latest generation also stands, as it were, on the shoulders of past suffering, reaps the benefit of its forbearers' endurance and survival, drinks a life-giving water seeded by their sweat and blood. Here is perhaps nothing more insistently gnawing to the moral conscience than the unpayable debt each of us owes to those who felt the lash, bore the battle, gave, willingly or not, the last full measure of themselves. Faced with their sacrifice, even as we enjoy its fruits, what can we offer, save a simple, heartfelt, 'Thank you'.

Snapshot: Phu Quoc

Over the years I have visited the dark places where Confederates did terrible things to Union soldiers, where Australians did terrible things to the aborigines, where Germans did terrible things to Jews, where the British did terrible things to the Irish, where the Japanese did terrible things to the British, where Cambodians did terrible things to each other. But on this occasion, I was headed to a place where the South Vietnamese, an American ally in a long, brutal war, had done terrible things to the North Vietnamese who were their prisoners. In the past, I had seen what others had done, but at Phu Quoc I would see what 'we' had done.

The island of Phu Quoc is now part of a united Vietnam, reachable by ferry crossing from the city of Ha Tien, which lies just across the border from Cambodia at the southernmost tip of Vietnam. It now advertises its beaches, and there is a large pearl farm in which tourists can see how pearls are made, then stroll into a brilliantly lit showroom and purchase as many as they can afford.

The prison at Phu Quoc was built by the French in 1949–50 as part of their ill-fated attempt to hold on to their Indo-Chinese empire at the end of World War II. It is often referred to as the Coconut Prison, a curiously pleasing name for what was certainly a very unpleasant place. Travellers who have gone to Phu Quoc have often described it as either unknown or avoided by tourists, but on the day I came here, it was actually quite crowded, mostly with Vietnamese in tour groups, though there were a few Westerners as well.

At first, the prison appears to have been preserved in the way of others I had seen, cleaned up, of course, but at the same time allowed to remain starkly itself. There is a visitors' centre, and the small museum it houses displays photographs of the prison in the days when it was operational, and in that way, it presents a justly harrowing view of the place at the time it was under South Vietnamese control.

The prison itself is hemmed in with barbed wire so dense one cannot imagine a mouse getting through it, much less a man, regardless of how emaciated he might be.

Guard towers rise at various places over the barbed wire, and it is here the trouble begins. For the towers are not empty. Guards survey the prison from these wooden perches. At first, one sees them only as distant, motionless figures, but very soon you find yourself surrounded by similarly life-size models, all of them meant to portray both the prisoners of Phu Quoc and the guards who so mercilessly tortured them.

And merciless is the word. In the various barracks of Phu Quoc, guards drive nails through the hands and into the organs of usually half-naked prisoners, break their legs and arms with truncheons, submit them to electroshock, hammer out their teeth, crack their toes, whip them with cord, and even boil and fry them in human-sized woks.

The problem with these displays is that they fail to convey what was actually suffered here. The models are so crude that they almost immediately became objects of humour for the generally youthful visitors at the prison that day, almost all of whom were Vietnamese and thus should have been appalled by the horrors perpetrated upon their fellow countrymen by their fellow countrymen. I saw a young man put an unlit cigarette in the screaming mouth of one of the victims, while others on the tour simply took the opportunity to pose amiably with a guard or shake hands with a prisoner. Outside the barracks, notably at the celebrated tiger cages, it got worse. These airless, metal containers were packed with models of starving prisoners, and at these displays, tourists actually stepped inside the cages, nestled up to one or more of the emaciated figures, and took a selfie.

Such irreverent, mocking acts would have been unthinkable in a prison that succeeded in conveying its own darkness. Simply to have walked the grounds, observed the barbed wire, the watchtowers, the implements of torture, the tiger cages would have been enough. But other such places have made similar, if less egregious mistakes, in their efforts to portray levels of cruelty and suffering that must be imagined because they simply cannot be conveyed. Phu Quoc's error, the one that made my visit there memorably sad, was also its parting lesson. For it was as I left Phu Quoc largely unmoved by what I'd seen here that I gained some admittedly rudimentary sense of what must be taken into account in the turning of such a place into a public museum or memorial. It is not just that its history should be accurate and shorn of ideology. For no less important is the need to keep the foibles of human nature in mind, the fact that given the opportunity to miss the point, to trivialize events, to act silly, a certain part of mankind will inevitably do so. For that reason, in places of solemn com-memoration, the lights must be kept low, (as they are at the Holocaust Museum in Washington), the symbolism stark (as it is at Oradour-sur-Glane), and the graphics largely dependent upon the mind's capacity to engage the sombre (as they are at Kilmainham Gaol in Dublin). If they are not, then that which is frivolous and forgetful in human beings will triumph over anything that might otherwise be profound and memorable, and you will leave it with the added sadness that here a dark place missed its opportunity to shed light.

Melos/Kampot/Krong Kep/Saigon

On Melos I began to discover that over time, as travel widens and experience accumulates, a network begins to form. One dark place reaches out to touch another and another and another, and with each interlocking fibre, the tapestry becomes more vivid and the fabric of your understanding stronger. You begin to feel connections rather than simply learn about them. As was once said about atrocity, you may read about a thousand, hear about a hundred, but you need see only one. In that sense, tragic shores are as close as the present can come to allowing you to 'see' what the past inflicted, and when they begin to reflect and reinforce and inform each other, what you finally begin to apprehend is a dark fraternity whose mission is to enlighten every aspect of your life. Melos allowed me to glimpse the early work of empires, but it was only later, through these other connections, all of them far less ancient, that I came to understand my own minuscule place in the history of foreign intervention, and just how uninformed and misguided it had been.

Thucydides makes short of work of Melos. He uses scarcely more than three pages to detail its moral argument and barely a paragraph to recount its fate. But my first professor of philosophy had made a great deal of what happened there, and so when I came to do this book, it returned to me as one of the darkest places on earth. For it was here, on this tiny Cycladic island in the Aegean Sea, according to my professor, that something ugly (the concept of might makes right) had been established, and something beautiful (the concept that right makes might) had been destroyed.

In the sixteenth year of the Peloponnesian War, Thucydides tells us, the Athenians embarked for Melos with 'thirty ships of their own, six Chian, and two Lesbian vessels, sixteen hundred heavy infantry, three hundred archers, and twenty mounted archers from Athens, and about fifteen hundred heavy infantry from the allies and the islanders'. This was an overwhelming force in that the island's population is estimated to have been perhaps no more than three thousand at that time. The Melians understood that victory in the military sense would not be theirs. For that reason, they had rested their only hope in moral argument.

Thucydides goes on to tell us that 'before doing any harm' to the Melians, Athens sent a small delegation to speak with island representatives. The exchange that took place between these Athenian envoys and the representatives of Melos is what the French call a *dialogue de sourds*, a conversation among the deaf.

The Melians make a moral argument that they have a right to remain free. The Athenians declare that moral argument itself is irrelevant because only power matters.

The Athenians are quick to note that they are not the first to consider strength of arms the determining factor in the affairs of men. 'You know as well as we do that right, as the world goes, is only in question between equals in power,' one of the Athenian envoys baldly informs the Melian representatives. This statement is but the opening gun in a dialogue during which Athenian cynicism will know no bounds.

Even so, to the tin ear of the Athenians, the Melians offer a soaring song of moral right. They have offended no one, they insist to the increasingly impatient Athenians. They are willing to be neutral in Athens' war with Sparta. They wish only their independence. They are 'friends' to Athens, and have no intention of ever being anything else.

None of this matters to the Athenians. References to the past do not matter. References to the future do not matter. Only the present matters, and as for the present, well, it is what it is. For that reason, the Athenians make it clear that they are not here to waste their valuable time listening to the soft strains of a Melian lyre. They are not even here to negotiate the island's fate. They are here to issue an ultimatum: surrender or face destruction. 'The strong do what they can,' an Athenian envoy declares with the same, barely restrained irritability and naked arrogance that runs throughout the dialogue, 'and the weak suffer what they must.'

And suffer the Melians did. After refusing to give up their independence, they held out against the Athenians for many dreadful months before starvation, internal divisions and, at last, betrayal forced them to surrender.

As might be expected, Melian intransigence did not go over well with the Athenians. And so, to punish this impudent Melian resistance, they subsequently slaughtered all the adult males they could track down. The women and children were spared annihilation, but only to be sold into slavery. The Melians, as a free people, ceased to exist.

The execution or enslavement of Melos's entire population is generally considered the most heinous of Athens' acts during the Peloponnesian War. It is also considered a crime of empire, instigated and carried out by imperialists who firmly believed, as the Athenians shamelessly stated in the Melian Dialogue, 'that by a necessary law of nature they rule whenever they can'.

It had been a very long time since the Greeks had ruled anything on the day Susan and I flew from Athens to Melos. We had come here at a time when their capital city was still reeling from economic crisis, a riotous time of trouble that had considerably thinned the tourist crowds that might otherwise have filled the streets of the Plaka even during the off-season. Though not deserted, these streets no longer pulsed with their usual commercial energy, and the heights of the Acropolis could be walked without fear of bumping into anyone. 'There was a time,' the concierge at our hotel told us wistfully, 'when Greek people were happy.'

But they weren't happy any more. Athens was deeply depressed in a way that reminded me of New Orleans when I went there shortly after Katrina, and of New York City, where I lived, after September 11. On the way to the airport on the day we flew from Athens to Melos we saw scores of empty shops and showrooms, evidence enough of a battle for economic survival that thousands of Athenians had waged and lost. The great capital of a once far-flung empire was no more. It remained to be seen if the inhabitants of the island it had once, and quite brutally, conquered were faring any better.

The first islander we met was the owner of the inn where we'd booked our room.

He spoke some English, and after we'd registered he said, 'Why do you come to Melos now?'

I took this to mean that it was off-season, a time when there was little to do on Melos.

'I came because of what the Athenians did here,' I answered. 'During the Peloponnesian War.'

'Oh, yes.' He looked perplexed. 'Why do you care about that?'

I gave the only answer I had. 'I don't know. I just do.'

He took this as sufficient answer. 'Well, I hope you like Melos. If yes, tell other people. We need tourists here.'

And with that he gave us our key. We took our things to the room, settled in for a few minutes, then, as was our habit, set off to explore.

Melos is not one of the iconic Greek islands about which travel books rhapsodize. The breathtaking beauty of, say, Santorini is not to be seen on Melos, though it has very lovely places. Its claim to fame, of course, is that it was here the Venus de Milo was found, a site, as Susan and I later discovered, that is designated by nothing more impressive than a sign that looks little different from any other you might encounter along a rural Greek roadway. In fact, the most immediate perception of Melos is of how small it is, and how bare. There is some vegetation, though it could hardly be called lush. For the most part, the island is rocky and hilly, and much of the landscape is little more than scrub brush and stone. For that reason, you cannot help but be aware of just how few hiding places there are, and how desperately they must have been sought out during the Athenian outrage.

The island's harbour town is called Adamantas, and on the morning after our arrival, Susan and I made our way up the hill that overlooks it and which turns into a landscape of rounded hills, some bare, some topped by small towns.

As we walked these hills, the sea almost always in view, we were again made aware of why we'd come here, and that had we been Melians in the sixteenth year of the Peloponnesian War, I would have been in search of refuge from death and Susan in search of refuge from lifelong enslavement for herself and Justine. The attempt to put oneself in the place of someone else at a different point in human history is an enterprise fraught with disingenuousness, of course, and yet, in Melos, it was hard not to do just that. It was so small and rugged, so tightly encircled by water, a land area so easily swept by the lethal Athenian dragnet, that it was impossible not to see the land itself as cruelly antagonistic to the Melians' desperate hopes. As a citizen of this island, you had acted bravely and suffered horribly in an effort to keep your homeland free of Athenian domination. And now, it would seem, the island had turned against you, refused to harbour you, exposed you to the sword of your enemy, offered you only a stony bosom in whose few recesses you could find no place to hide.

Walking these same rocky hills, these terrified Melians would ultimately have found their backs to the sea. In the fishing village of Klima, which was only a short walk from the harbour, the adult males would probably have been cut down at the water's edge. Imagining such a slaughter, I recalled Homer's description of how 'warmed in the brain, the smoking weapon lies,' the red eyes of the slaughterers 'like furnace doors ajar'.

There is no chronicle of the actual day-to-day carrying out of Athens' revenge against Melos. Even so, the hideous labour required to track down and brutally put to death roughly a thousand men by sword or spear or arrow, then round up and enslave everybody else had to have taken some time, particularly given the fact that the women and children of Melos, presumably every single one of them, thus a number that approached two thousand, were later hauled onto ships and transported to some other part of the Athenian empire. Melos, according to the Athenian plan, was to be Melian-free, the Melian question, like the Jewish one in Germany, the Armenian one in Turkey, the Tutsi one in Rwanda, and the Muslim, Hindu or Sikh one depending upon which part of India you occupied as that country lurched towards independence, was to be settled, once and for all.

The conquest of the earth, as Conrad once wrote, is not a pretty business, and on Melos, since the island encompasses a mere sixty-one square miles, that unpretty business would have been very visible indeed. Neither night nor fog can conceal so widespread and time-consuming a crime. Add the screams of the slaughtered echoing through the hills, the woeful cries of the women and children as they were captured, the milling of this terrified aggregation as it waited for the slave ships to bear them away, and finally the loud commands of the Athenian officers and foot soldiers as this huddled mass was herded onto the boats, and one can, at last, get a sense of what occurred on Melos during that 'sixteenth year of the Peloponnesian War'. For that reason, Susan and I felt that although we saw not a single reference to this slaughter while on the island itself, we had traversed its length and breadth so many times that by the time we left it, we'd gained some idea of the tragedy that had occurred here, and just how bloody and protracted that tragedy had been.

But while the violent suppression of Melos might serve to represent the moral benightedness required at the birth of empire, it was Kampot that later came to represent empire's squalid end.

Melos and Kampot are separated by thousands of miles, one a Greek island, the other an inland Cambodian town. But dark places speak to each other, as I began to learn the day I went to

Kampot, and found myself thinking of Melos, and the arrogance of the Athenians that had so enraged Euripides, and whose words I later looked up:

> *How are ye blind,*
> *Ye treaders down of cities, ye that cast*
> *Temples to desolation, and lay waste*
> *Tombs, the untrodden sanctuaries where lie*
> *The ancient dead; yourselves so soon to die!*

I'd come to Kampot by way of Sihanoukville, the town on the Gulf of Thailand in which I'd spent the last few days, stranded by Chinese New Year, during which the local Vietnamese consulate had been closed for a full eight days. Once it opened, I'd gotten my visa in just a few hours, then headed immediately for Ha Tien, where I intended to take a ferry across the Giang Thanh River, then move on to Saigon.

I had not planned to stop for any length of time en route, but neither had I expected to encounter Kampot, nor walk its streets for several hours, during which, at some point, I thought of Thucydides, the Melian Dialogue, of Euripides' outrage, and last, of how Kampot itself had unexpectedly returned me to poor, defeated Melos.

Despite its name, Kampot is not a Cambodian town, or at least it was never meant to be Cambodian. Its wide central boulevard is purely a French design, as are the galleried buildings that border and spread out around it. For decades, it was a

French administrative hub, a seat of government that intended to tower over this part of Cambodia in the impregnable way of the Bokor Hill Station that still rests in the heights that rise above it, and which is now in the same state of ruin as the town itself.

Tourists sometimes make the journey up Bokor Mountain in order to see this abandoned station, but it is really Kampot that for me best symbolizes the French empire's languorous slide into oblivion, and in doing so returned me to Euripides' stark reminder that empires are doomed to die. In that sense, it seemed to me, the circle of human experience connected Melos and Kampot with the kindredness that always, and often poignantly, joins beginnings and endings – in this case the arrogant beginning and the squalid end of empire.

As the terminus of that line, Kampot now slumps beside the Prek Kampong Bay River, within view of the Elephant Mountains. At one point a vaguely modern bridge spans this river. But a second bridge, known with ironic poignancy as the French Bridge, spans it too, though only for pedestrians or motorbikes as it is not wide enough to accommodate a car. As if to ladle an extra helping of symbolism upon a town already weighted with it, the French bridge is an utter hotchpotch of design. It was built by the French, then in part destroyed and rebuilt by the Khmer Rouge in an entirely different style. Later, the Vietnamese destroyed then rebuilt yet another span of the bridge in a third style, so that the French Bridge now looks as improvised and chaotic and ill managed as were the final years of French rule in Cambodia.

But it is the town itself that so vividly brings to mind the death of empire. In block after block, it squats in melancholy disrepair, the ghost of its own abandonment. The once graceful galleries slope and wobble, the pastel paint peels, the wide boulevards remain largely without traffic. Long ago, the life support of empire breathed its last breath here, and in its wake, there remains nothing but this enervated town, as pale and unmoving as a corpse. Walking its streets is like strolling through the mortuary of empire, everything slow and sluggish, everything drained, the city still vaguely clothed in a tattered French finery, but listless, purposeless, an imperial phantom, as solitary in its way as the fallen pillars of Ozymandias.

'After Kampot, you should see Krong Kep,' a friend suggested as we lingered by the river, staring at the old French Bridge. 'The French built their villas there. Now they look sort of . . . surreal.'

And indeed, they did.

The French called Krong Kep by another name, Kep-sur-Mer, Kep 'on the sea'. It was built in 1908 as a seaside resort for high French officials who wanted to enjoy the breezes that waft inland from the Gulf of Thailand. For a time, I drove through the hills that overlook the town, and upon whose heights the French had built their great houses. From that lofty eyrie, seated on these spacious balconies, they had surveyed a country they considered theirs and which, with an Athenian reliance upon might, they had expected to be theirs forever.

Their villas are now abandoned, the great rooms empty, the high walls shrouded in jungle vine. From a distance they appear bound in thick green rope. It was as if the land over which their owners had once ruled was itself determined to reclaim dominion. There were quite a few of these long-deserted villas, but after a time, they all began to look alike, faded, faltering, like frail old men, barely standing. In these mouldering rooms there had once been fine china and crystal, on their walls had once hung paintings of Paris in the rain. Here dinners had been served by candlelight, and for entertainment, there'd been renderings of Molière. The high life of empire had once been lived on these heights, but now there was only evidence of its demise.

'. . . yourselves so soon to die' had been Euripides' warning to empire, and so it had been with Athens in the Adriatic, and so it had been with France in Cambodia, and, indeed, with all its far-flung empire in South-East Asia.

From Krong Kep, I journeyed to the Cambodian border, crossed the Giang Thanh River by ferry at Ha Tien, and then proceeded along the Mekong Delta towards Saigon. With Chinese New Year having just ended, the villages along the route were still hung in holiday decorations, the most prominent of which was the Vietnamese flag, a single yellow star on a field of red. It was so ubiquitous it was hardly ever out of sight during the long, seven-hour drive from Ha Tien to Saigon.

'What's with all the flags?' I asked. 'There must be hundreds of them.'

'They have to hang them out,' the driver informed me matter-of-factly.

267

'Have to?'

He smiled. 'You know . . . if someone didn't . . . it would be noticed.'

'I see.'

Night had fallen by the time we reached Saigon, crossing into it over a gorgeous bridge. The nightlife of this fiercely energetic city teemed all around us, a city whose lights made Phnom Penh, even at its best and brightest, seem dull and shadowy. Thousands of sparklingly polished motorbikes whizzed about in all directions. Here was a city on the move, young, vibrant, a people whose past suffering did not hang over them like a shroud. Even so, I knew that a great effort had been made to keep the memory of the war alive, most notably in the War Crimes Museum, which friends had told me was very dark indeed.

I went there the next day and found it less dark than I'd expected. It is housed in a large stone building whose spacious interior is designed primarily to display photographs, along with accompanying narrations of such atrocities as the My Lai Massacre and the Thanh Phong raid. Most of the photographs are in dramatic black and white, and the written accounts are stark.

Various sombre displays accompany these presentations, a few household goods from My Lai and a sewer pipe from Thanh Phong. It is from this sewer pipe that American forces under the command of former senator Bob Kerrey allegedly pulled three children, then immediately murdered them, one by disembowelment. The details of what happened in Thanh Phong on the night of 25 February 1969, the accusation of a horrifying atrocity that involved the wanton shooting of scores of unarmed villagers during the course of a late-night raid conducted by US Navy Seals, may be lost in the fog of war, though even by American accounts something dark and bloody incontestably did.

There is a terrible poignancy in the simple presentation of these things. Lined across a dark floor, or paled by a soft light, the bowls and serving implements of My Lai and the storm drain from Thanh Phong speak with melancholy eloquence of rural villagers momentarily at the mercy of soldiers fully equipped with all the modern implements of war. Faced with such a reminder, and particularly as an American, you do not so much consider what side you were on in this conflict as confront the fact that here a farming people went to war against the mightiest industrial power on earth, and consider how, during the course of that struggle, and despite an inequality of force so immense it can hardly be imagined, David managed not to kill, but certainly to survive Goliath's fierce assault.

Once outside the museum, I toured the large stash of captured weapons that were on display, everything from bombs to jeeps to the Huey and Chinook helicopters whose firepower seemed impossibly ferocious when you considered the vulnerability of their targets: rural Vietnam's exposed hamlets and rice paddies.

I left the museum early in the afternoon, strolled along Saigon's perfectly friendly streets, then ambled my way back towards my hotel, thinking once again of all the hundreds of flags I'd seen on the way here from Ha Tien, and particularly of what they suggested with regard to the larger issue of freedom in

Vietnam, and by which is meant the freedom to speak, read, go, and more or less do whatever you like, all of which are rightly to be cherished and defended.

In 1965, as a high school senior in my small Alabama town, I had written an editorial for the local paper in which I'd fully advocated American involvement in Vietnam for the very purpose (and a very noble one indeed, as I saw it) of securing the right of the Vietnamese people to have and to hold these very freedoms. If we did not fight for them in South-East Asia, I sonorously declared, then we would eventually have to fight for them on our own shores. I'd only been piping back the rhetoric of the day, of course, but even so I'd been convinced that the Americans really were fighting both for ourselves and for the Vietnamese, and that the area of contention was truly the issue of freedom, our wish to extend it, Ho Chi Minh's wish to deny it, as all such communists did.

You know . . . it would be noticed.

Now, nearly fifty years later, it was obvious that the particular sort of 'freedom' we Americans had been told the Vietnamese should have had not yet been won by the Vietnamese themselves. The result was that it would be 'noticed' if you didn't hang a flag outside your house. Genius was not required to figure out just how and by whom this notice would be taken, nor imagine the consequences to those who, once their malfeasance had been noted, did not ultimately correct themselves. Clearly, by Western standards, the Vietnamese were not free.

In Graham Greene's *The Quiet American*, the worldly English journalist Thomas Fowler scoffs at the notion that the Vietnamese have any idea of freedom. They are, he says, too occupied by securing their next meal to concern themselves with such American notions of individual liberty. I had no idea if this had been true in the Saigon of the 1950s, or if it were true now. But to be bereft of that freedom, or even the urge to have it, nonetheless seemed sad. Shortly after 9/11, when President George Bush was asked his reaction to the fact that many people hated America, he had answered that he was 'amazed' that such feelings could exist. This was surely naivety at its most basic, and in the mind of one so powerful, at its most dangerous. And yet, for all that, freedom as a goal still made its eloquent call to me, and for that reason, and again remembering those flags, the absence of which would be 'noticed', I couldn't help but wonder what Vietnam might now be like had the Americans achieved what they'd claimed to be their aim here, the freedom of its people.

At some point I turned onto a less crowded street. It was lined with small shops selling various artefacts. Nothing caught my eye until I noticed several pots that were not unlike the ones from My Lai that I'd seen on display in the museum. Those pots had been empty, of course. The ones before me now were filled with scores, perhaps even hundreds, of Zippo lighters. All of them were metal, and most bore some kind of American military insignia on the front.

'Souvenir?' the woman in the shop said. 'You want souvenir?'

'What exactly are these lighters a souvenir of?' I asked.

I couldn't tell if she understood. 'You look,' she said with a nod towards the overflowing pots. 'We got many, many.'

Many, many, indeed, I thought, so very many, the discarded or captured or stolen goods of so many young men, themselves but the sword point of an enormous effort, according to the rhetoric of the day, to bring 'freedom' to Vietnam.

I picked up one of the lighters. It had a screaming eagle on the front. I turned it over and read what had been inscribed on the back.

Happy day.
Without a care.
Just blowing gooks
Into the air.

I picked up a second:

Red mist in the sky
Watching gooks
Blow up and fly

Others had similarly bloodthirsty and racially charged inscriptions. Gooks were 'lit up', and 'turned to spray'. Soldiers were enjoined to 'Kill 'em all. Let God sort 'em out.' It was disheartening to read such bloodlusty cries. They were expressions of violence, of racism, all the worst aspects of a foreign army fighting an indigenous people.

It was in order to be free of this foreign intrusion that the Vietnamese had struggled so relentlessly, of course, not only against the

Americans, but the French before them, and the Chinese before the French. How could being 'free' in the Western context have any value without first being 'free' of foreign invaders, I thought now, and who would not be willing to confront impossible odds in order to secure this most basic of all freedoms, and how could any foreign power, regardless of how overwhelming its weaponry, ever ultimately defeat a people resolved to 'free' itself from the foreign domination that denied them so fundamental a liberty?

One dark place now reached out to touch another, and I thought again of Cambodia, a country that undoubtedly has its problems. The literacy rate is low and the poverty is deep. In terms of health care and education, its people languish in a swamp of official indifference. It is ruled by Hun Sen, an old-school dictator drawn from the ranks of the Khmer Rouge, and who is kept in power by a military elite whose huge black Hummers cruise the streets of Phnom Penh, brandishing licence plates that allow their owners to ignore the traffic rules of a traffic-choked city. And as everyone knows, the country's institutions, from top to bottom, are utterly corrupt.

And yet, for all these difficulties, Cambodia is at least Cambodian, its evils and corruptions ones that Cambodians alone have the right, perhaps at some point the duty, to overcome.

Suddenly, I thought again of Kampot, of how, after leaving it, I'd driven to a town no longer called by its French name of Kep-sur-Mer, but which is now known by its original Cambodian name of Krong Kep. Chinese New Year had just ended, but many of the families who'd journeyed down from Phnom Penh and other inland cities were still enjoying the wide crescent-shaped beach that runs along the Gulf. They rested beneath the shade of brightly coloured canopies, eating their traditional *pho* and sipping their much favoured drink, iced coffee with condensed milk. This food and drink were truly Cambodian, along with this beach, the thick jungle hills, the old French-built city a few kilometres away, the old French Bridge that stretches its mongrel arm across the Prek Kampong Bay River. All of this was now Cambodia, as were the distant Elephant Mountains, and beyond them, the wide plain that sweeps towards Sihanoukville to the west and Phnom Penh to the north and further still to Siem Reap where still stands in stony grandeur their ancient capital of Angkor Wat. It was a gorgeous expanse of land that, before the French, had immemorially belonged, and now belonged again, to Cambodia and to Cambodians, and the simple fact that they had reclaimed it seemed the final lesson of the dark places I had seen in Melos and Kampot and Saigon or wherever the pillars of foreign intervention lie fallen on the earth, or are destined yet to fall.

And why destined?

For the simple reason – implicit in all human history, and taught by numberless dark places on the earth – that the animating passion, the first and foremost desire for freedom of any occupied people from Melos to Baghdad, will have nothing to do with freedom of speech or religion or of the press or of any other freedom save the one that allows them to be free of . . . *you.*

Snapshot: Alice Springs

I grew up in a fully segregated American South. In fact, mine was the last segregated class at my high school. The year following my graduation, Frederick Douglas, the black high school, was simply closed and all its students transferred to the white high school. I was an eyewitness to demonstrations in neighbouring Gadsden, and, of course, there was a great deal of television coverage of the far more violent confrontations in Birmingham. But my most searing memory of segregation was a story told by a friend. He was walking down one of the side streets of our town on a sidewalk covered by a tin roof. It was raining very heavily, and as he made his way along he saw an elderly black woman coming towards him. My friend was a large, strapping high school student of seventeen, but as he approached this frail old woman, she stepped from beneath the cover, off the sidewalk and into the pelting rain, where she stood, patiently waiting until he passed. 'So this is what it is,' he later told me, 'our cherished Southern way of life.'

So I'd seen my share of segregation, and certainly of separation, but no youthful experience of the American South could have prepared me for Alice Springs.

The woman for whom Alice Springs was named never came here. She was the wife of an Overland Telegraph official and there is no evidence that she ever so much as contemplated the trek into central Australia that would have been required to visit the remote desert town that bears her name. Nor is Alice Todd alone in having found the journey to Alice Springs far too long and difficult to undertake. Though more visited in recent years, the town still has a sense of being cut off not only from the rest of the world, but even from the coastal hubs between which it lies more or less equidistant, Adelaide to the south and Darwin to the north.

It was somewhat by chance that Susan, Justine and I came here in February of 2008. Justine, now in her late twenties, had been travelling in Tasmania, and had met Susan and me in Adelaide, where I'd been invited to speak at the city's literary festival. I'd also been scheduled to attend a convention of independent booksellers in Australia's famed outback, and so after the Adelaide festival, we flew to the capital of that remote region, Alice Springs.

On our first evening there, we congregated in one of our rooms and watched a television programme about Australian wildlife. At one point, the exuberant narrator was proud to declare that Australia was home to the most dangerous spider in the world. Fortunately, he said, this spider's habitat was very limited. With that declaration, a colour graphic zeroed in on Alice Springs. Justine, as sardonic as her mother said, 'Well, I guess they didn't have a photograph of our actual hotel room.'

The next morning we walked through scorching heat from our hotel on the outskirts of town into the far from bustling business district of Alice Springs. In Adelaide and Sydney, we'd seen hardly any aborigines, but in Alice Springs there were quite a few, most of them sitting on the grass outside the welfare centre, men, women and children gathered together under whatever shade could be found. They sat in the weighty idleness Ryszard Kapuściński has described with regard to Third World peoples, a motionless waiting that is nearly trance-like, and which suggests that some need for activity is, itself, a vital spark within human beings, the dearth of which creates problems of its own.

In the nearby galleries it was possible to see at least one sort of activity that remained alive among the first inhabitants of Australia: art. It hung from every available wall, paintings that were for the most part varied repetitions of curling and parallel lines. Justine strolled about, looking at each painting, then turned to me. 'If these weren't done by aborigines, would anyone take notice?'

I had to admit that the same question had occurred to me as well. It wasn't a pleasant question, nor one I welcomed, and yet I recognized that these paintings reminded me of the elaborate patterns my aunts had created in their Deep South quilt-making, and whose level of artistic achievement had remained decidedly within the sphere of indigenous crafts. Would these aboriginal paintings be considered any different from my aunt's quilts, I wondered, if they were not 'aboriginal'?

No one can truly say what 'art' is, of course, but it is surely true that a primitive context has often been used to mask or romanticize ways of doing, feeling and thinking that are, after all, only primitive, or at least rudimentary. In the Southern town in which I grew up, a group of elderly white men used to sit about whittling pieces of wood into shapes that broadly represented human and animal forms. In the local lore, this was elevated to the status of high art. Indeed, had some creature from another planet read the local press, he or she would have thought that Rodin and Michelangelo daily occupied a park bench, carving works of timeless beauty. But really, it was just old men whittling. All condescension is, in the end, only a form of such inflation, a manner of thought by which rap lyrics become Shakespeare and graffiti is lifted to the status of fine art. There may be nothing deeply wrong in the offering of these blandishments, but a justly prideful people can only keep its pride by refusing to take them seriously.

Unfortunately, in Australia, I found both the offering and acceptance of condescension more or less the order of the day. In fact, condescension seemed pretty much all the immigrant whites of that huge country had to offer the continent's original inhabitants. A guide at Uluru, for example, belaboured the day with an elaborate and reverential discussion of aboriginal creation myths and 'dream stories', as if these tall tales had issued from some immemorial fount of wisdom. Some Australians even nail small plaques to the fronts of their houses by way of acknowledging the prior aboriginal ownership of properties the present 'owners' have no intention of giving back.

Such gestures reveal white Australians as a people fixed in a baffled liberalism, wholly at sea as to what to make of the aborigines or what might be done either for or about them. As reported in *In a Sunburned Country*, Bill Bryson had once heard someone darkly mutter that the aborigines 'all want hanging', but during my time in Alice Springs, or anywhere else in Australia for that matter, I heard nothing even remotely as unspeakable as that. What I saw and heard was a helpless perplexity that made it impossible to discuss what is, after all, an issue of race; in this case the failure of every attempt to 'integrate' the aboriginal population into the social and economic life of a country wholly dominated by immigrant whites. In fact, the most sweeping of these efforts, the forced education of aboriginal children, had failed so miserably that the Australian government had formally apologized for it in 2008.

Alice Springs had played a part in that doomed effort, as I learned later that day, when I happened into a bookstore there. A clerk approached, and during the ensuing discussion I mentioned that I was in the process of writing about 'dark tourism'.

'Ah,' the woman said, 'well, we have a pretty dark place here in Alice Springs.'

'Really?'

In a somewhat lowered voice, she said, 'The Barracks.'

She gave a few further details, the most salient of which

indicated that it was to this place that aboriginal children had been brought by their parents, then subsequently taken from them and sent to the sort of schools portrayed in the film *Rabbit-Proof Fence*, hence part of the last genuine effort at assimilation and in the face of whose failure even the most liberal of Australians now gave off a sense of helplessness and spiritual exhaustion that struck me as not entirely different from the trance-like states of the aborigines who sprawled across the grounds of the welfare centre, these two peoples, aboriginal and immigrant, now fixedly staring at each other, both seeking to answer a question neither knew how to pose, thus two peoples locked in a complex moral, social, racial, and economic dilemma whose solution neither could discover, so that the offering and acceptance of condescension and dependency had become the middle ground they now occupied and beside which – at least for the moment – there seemed to be no other.

Derry/Londonderry

When I was twelve years old, I had a job at a small clothing store in my hometown. Most of the work had to do with sweeping, washing windows, and the maddening task of untangling the bramble of clothes hangers that had accumulated during the course of a day and whose individual members gave every evidence of being both alive and ferociously determined to defeat any effort to untangle them. My workday ended with a walk to the post office where I mailed the store's orders, bills or other general correspondence. I lived in a small town in Alabama. It was 1958. And yet as I glanced up to see the American flag splendidly snapping in the wind at the entrance to the post office, I distinctly recall thinking that Old Glory was not *exactly* my flag. By then, the Civil War had been over for almost a hundred years, and God knows how many of my relatives had fought on the 'American' side in various conflicts since Appomattox. Still, one glimpse of that flag was sufficient to suggest that the formal dividing of a country, however briefly, invites lasting peril, a wound which, though it may no longer bleed, never truly heals.

In one of his many eloquent essays, the late Christopher Hitchens made the point that partition almost never works. One need only observe its spectacular failure in places as far-flung as Cyprus, India/Pakistan and the geographically filleted Middle East, not to mention the horrors of the Balkans and of Eritrea.

The bloody horns of human conflict are ethnicity and religion, and I am convinced that had American Southerners been of a different ethnic group or religion than their northern counterparts, then the war that ended in 1865 would still be going on by means of, to say the least, occasional acts of terror.

That Ireland remains somewhat in the grip of at least one of those twin devils became evident almost immediately upon arrival. Susan and I had landed in Dublin, where we'd arranged to rent a car in hope of making a full circle of the island, first heading south by way of Waterford, then west to Killarney, then straight north through Galway, and finally to Giant's Causeway at the northern tip of the island, a weirdly spectacular sight that Justine had earlier visited and said we absolutely should not miss. After that, the plan was to drive directly south again, back to Dublin. It was June 2007. Susan was now in her mid-fifties, and though we had travelled a great deal by then, it was this trip she had dreamed of all of her life. So much so, in fact, that the smile on her face when we touched down in Dublin was almost as radiant as the one she'd had upon seeing Justine for the first time. For that brief moment, I found it hard to imagine that

I would find 'darkness' in Ireland despite the fact that I was entertaining the notion of an essay on imprisonment (and thus wanted to see Kilmainham Gaol) as well as an essay on 'walls', and for that reason had planned a stop in Londonderry.

Once in Dublin, we made our way to the car rental office. Susan had already booked a car, and was by then showing some unease about driving on the opposite side of the road. American friends had told us of 'whacking off mirrors all over Ireland', and had warned us to be careful. We'd expected the same warning from the agent at the car rental, but it was of something far different and far darker that he warned us before handing over the keys.

'If you're going to Northern Ireland,' he said gravely, 'you'll need different insurance.'

'Why do we need different insurance to go into Northern Ireland?' Susan asked.

'Because we have nothing to do with the north,' the man said. *Nothing to do with the north?*

This was said by a man whose accent was no different to my ear from the one I would later hear at the Giant's Causeway, a spot within view, as it happened, of Scotland, which at that moment was not without its own pro-partition impulses.

For truth be told, we live in a world where the answer seems to be 'Break away', where the Basques want to leave Spain, an urge whose violence we'd personally experienced, ETA having set off several bombs while we lived in Madrid. But we'd also experienced less brutal forms of this need to separate. In Bruges,

283

for example, I'd been warned not to ask for directions in French if I expected to be helped, as the Flemish will not answer questions addressed to them in French. In Gijón, flyers had rained down upon us from the balconies overhead, demanding – in Spanish – for the designation of Asturian as the official language of the province.

And so Susan and I were accustomed to encountering the less extreme forms of 'partition' and thus, without further comment, we bought the additional insurance required of people who want 'something to do' with Northern Ireland.

Once on the road, Susan, as always, at the wheel, we made our way out of Dublin, stopped in Waterford, then headed for a lovely bed and breakfast Susan had booked in a town whose name, I confess, I have since forgotten. It was run by a young woman who was quick to tell us, like so many of the Irish do, of their many relatives in America, in this case a sister.

'My mother isn't well,' she said, 'and not long ago she came home from the doctor's office with a very slow pulse. I called my sister in Chicago, and she said that in America my mother would have been hospitalized immediately. But here, if you're old, they just send you home.'

During the course of a later conversation, I mentioned the odd fact that I'd had to pay extra to buy insurance if I intended to venture into Northern Ireland, along with the agent's comment about having 'nothing' to do with the north.

She shook her head resignedly. 'We are stuck with two countries inside one country,' she said.

And there it was, a line far less utterly arbitrary than those that had earlier carved 'nations' out of Africa and the Middle East, but no less a failure because it had simply turned warring parties within the boundaries of one country into two countries still more or less at war.

Anyone who visits Ireland, and who, like me, is almost immediately charmed by its people and its landscape, surely wants to believe that the Protestant–Catholic/north–south divide will one day be bridged, the long poison of Irish history finally drained. Certainly that was my hope as we continued our tour of the island. We danced in small villages and were mesmerized by the astounding physical beauty that greeted us at every turn. Like bedazzled tourists, we visited the Quiet Man Bridge outside Oughterard, and Susan kissed the stone at Blarney Castle, two large Irishmen firmly holding her legs as she lay on her back to do so. What people, I thought, the inhabitants of so magical a land, would not fight to the death to keep it as their own.

But that is precisely the problem, of course: Ireland has two peoples, one that claims the entire island, the other claiming only part of it, and that part taken to be not Ireland at all, but a province of the United Kingdom, as indissolubly linked to the motherland as, well, Kent or Oxfordshire or Stratford-upon-Avon. That part of Ireland, the north with which our rental agent would have nothing to do, was created by partition in 1920, and it will remain separate, according to the Belfast Agreement of 1998, until the population votes otherwise.

So will that be the end of Ireland's long Troubles, a surging

Catholic population in the north that will at last out-vote the Protestants, and thus, conceivably by referendum, unite the country once and for all?

Any such hope was somewhat dampened on the overcast afternoon we drove into Derry (as the Irish nationalists call it) or Londonderry (as the Unionists call it), two peoples inhabiting the same island, speaking the same language, but who, for all they have in common, cannot agree on the name of a town. Jonathan Swift (a Dublin born Anglo-Irishman) had lampooned just such comical absurdities in *Gulliver's Travels*, but when they are encountered in life, they are anything but funny. It is not for nothing, I suppose, that among artists, it is the satirists who most often go mad, as Swift did, or who most often kill themselves, as so many have.

I had come to Derry/Londonderry to see its walls. They are justly famous, and in fact, as any tourist brochure will tell you, they are the city's only true claim to fame. In fact, they are pretty much all that puts Derry/Londonderry on the tourist map. They rise to twenty-six feet in some places, and at some points they are thirty feet wide. They were completed in 1618, a fortification designed to protect the city from the Donegal raiders.

As walls, they are less beautiful than those of Avila, and more forbidding than those of York. They are grey, made of stone, and walking them presents the portrait of a divided city. From the battery, for example, it is possible to look down upon the site of 'Bloody Sunday', the January 1972 shooting by British paratroopers of twenty-six Irish civilians, fourteen of whom later died. Also known as the 'Bogside Massacre', the incident naturally became the iconic moment in Catholic Derry's history that the closing of the gates by the 'Apprentice Boys' represents in the Protestant history of Londonderry.

Susan and I walked the wall for a while, since there seemed little else to do in Derry/Londonderry. As a city, it is rather bleak, and under clouds or in rain, it would seem quite depressing. From the walls, you look down on a ragged landscape of squat buildings and brick terraced houses occasionally broken by a dark church spire. The palette is decidedly brown and grey. Doubtless the town has a vibrant nightlife, but in daylight, it looks terribly exhausted. Susan said that it was hard for her to imagine people dancing here, singing here, as they did in other parts of Ireland, though she was sure they did.

We descended the wall after a few minutes, and by chance stumbled upon the memorial hall of the Apprentice Boys of Derry. I'd not consulted a guide to the city, if there were one, and so I'd had no idea that this hall even existed. But the doors of the hall were painted bright red, and in that way quite eye-catching, so for a moment we stood on the corner, gazing up at the building's towers and turrets. It was an imposing structure but far from monumental and not particularly interesting in terms of architecture. We would not have lingered long, I'm sure, nor would we ever have ventured inside the building had one of its two bright red doors not suddenly swung open.

'Hello,' the man said as he stepped out of the building. He was middle-aged, but had a cane that he leaned into as he continued. 'This is the hall of the Apprentice Boys of Derry,' he said. 'Where are you from?'

'New York,' I told him.

'I'm a volunteer at the hall,' he said. 'Would you like to see it? We have a museum. There's no charge. We don't get many visitors.'

'Okay,' I said, and with that he ushered us into the hall as quickly as his limp allowed him.

'This hall is dedicated to the memory of the Apprentice Boys of Derry,' he said once the door closed behind us. Then, as we moved through the museum (which, as I later discovered by visiting its website, is 'committed to maintaining the spirit of liberty displayed by the Apprentice Boys in 1688 against oppression', and whose activities 'perpetuate that spirit of liberty, inherent to the Reformed Protestant faith'), he told of what he called the boys' 'heroic deeds'.

As it turned out, the story of the Apprentice Boys of Derry is a tale of Ireland at its most violent.

From the middle of April until the end of July 1689, Derry/Londonderry was under siege by James II, a former King of England and a Catholic, who had earlier been deposed by William of Orange, a Protestant. James had come to Ireland in an effort to regain his throne. In the course of that effort, he laid siege to Derry/Londonderry, a decidedly Protestant city, and it is here that the Apprentice Boys of Derry had committed an act of such renown that their names were still venerated and their memories kept alive by this very hall.

'Do I not have a right to defend my Protestant religion?' our guide asked as we stood before a perfectly forgettable painting. His voice was soft, even tender, and there was a certain plaintiveness in it, the sense of having his cause continually maligned by the powers that be. No one understands, he seemed to be saying, the depth of our fears.

It was a look that seemed to come from the distant time he'd only just described, a terror so fierce and consuming that the city mayor had disguised himself, and along with many others, had actually fled the city even before James's army reached it, a fear not simply that the city would fall, but that its inhabitants would be massacred, every man, woman and child.

It was in the face of this dread that thirteen boys, all of them apprentices, had fanned out along the walls of the city and closed all its gates, thus beginning the siege of Derry/Londonderry, as well as its most celebrated moment in Ireland's tortured history.

The story of what transpired in Derry/Londonderry during the 105 days before the siege was broken is one of enormous suffering whose endurance was fuelled by sheer terror of the besieging army. How else might a population of approximately twenty thousand have endured three and a half months of assault during which, as one contemporary account described it, 'the bombs played hotly with the city, with little intermission from setting of sun until morning'? Terror 'prevailed in all directions', and the 'shrieks of the women and children formed a terrific contrast with the thunder of the artillery and the crash of walls and houses thrown down by the shells'.

By the time the siege ended on 28 July 1689, half the population of Derry/Londonderry would be dead, most having succumbed to the most lethal elements of long-term siege, disease or starvation.

Even so, there was a celebration during which cannons were fired from atop the city walls and crowds jubilantly cheered the entrance of those who had broken the siege and whose leader, Major-General Kirke, was given the keys to the city, along with its civic sword and mace.

What these celebrants would have seen behind the windows and doors of Derry/Londonderry's bombarded houses, however, could not have been celebrated: a people dying of typhus and other diseases, 'swimming in dirt, faeces, urine and vomit', as one historian recorded it. Derry was 'free', but it was a sad and broken city.

Staring at the dark wall that had enclosed this misery, it struck me that one of the powers of such places is their kinship with others like them. In that sense, the walls of Derry/Londonderry reached out to other grim sieges, the terrors that must grip any people awaiting the breach of their city walls by an army lusting for revenge: to Leningrad's nine hundred days, Berlin as the Russians closed in upon it, to the sufferings of Masada and Nanking, a reach that had finally extended to the dark cellars where, on the very day I wrote of Derry/Londonderry, thousands of Syrians crouched in dread of Assad's assaulting troops.

We ended the tour after half an hour, the gentleman with

the cane clearly both surprised and appreciative that we'd taken it at all.

'We're not bad people,' he said and offered his hand.

'Most people aren't bad,' I said as I took it.

We continued our northern journey after that, visited Giant's Causeway, a spectacular sight that Justine was right in insisting that we see.

Two days later, we drove back to Dublin. It was 12 July, the day the Orangemen of every district hold their parades to commemorate the Battle of the Boyne, and thus the victory of the Protestant cause in Ireland. From Giant's Causeway in the north to the southern border of Northern Ireland, we were continually stopped as parading Orangemen with their bowlers and umbrellas marched through the towns and villages of the part of Ireland that is still theirs.

For all the determined spectacle of these parades, there seemed little doubt that with the Belfast Agreement now in force, the Catholic population would one day out-vote the Protestants of Northern Ireland, and thus bring about the political unification of the island. The greater question was whether an end to partition could ever heal the fear, distrust and outright hatred that had at one time made it seem the only answer to Ireland's deep division. Watching the Orangemen in their mock military stride, I had to conclude that in all likelihood it would not, and thus that one day, perhaps a hundred years after reunification, some little boy would stroll towards a post office over which flew a flag not quite his own in a country not quite his own, and that this would happen for the simple reason that the hearts of men remain partitioned even when their lands are not.

At that point, my mind returned to the hall of the Apprentice Boys, the man who'd suddenly appeared at the door, then later escorted us through the hall's small museum with the same modesty and sweetness I'd enjoyed throughout Ireland, whether Protestant or Catholic, north or south, and which had seemed near universal among this charming people. But even more than this, I recalled his limp, and the wince of pain that accompanied it, and these seemed now the perfect metaphor for this crippled island and the terrible truth that unlike healthy flesh, the wounds of partition rarely heal.

And yet?

Dark places always address man's many unfinished tasks, but not always darkly, and certainly not always with a forlorn sense of hopelessness. My proof of this is that not long after leaving Derry/Londonderry, I was thinking once again of how, as a boy, I'd felt a strange ambivalence towards the flag that flew over my local post office. Then my mind swept me forwards, and suddenly, it was eight or so years later, and I was a night student working my way through college in Atlanta. For a time, I'd worked as a floor salesman at Sears Roebuck. The year was 1967. I was twenty years old. One of my co-workers was a young woman of the same age, and we immediately hit it off. She was bright, ambitious, lovely, and from our talks I'd gathered that, like me, she was bent upon making a different life for herself. She had the most striking green eyes. She was kind and knowing, quick to laugh, quick to make me laugh, thus in every way the sort of girl I knew I was looking for . . . save that she was black.

I have no idea if she would have considered 'dating' me. Atlanta, though far more progressive than most other Southern cities at that time, remained more or less fixed in the region's racial customs. For that reason, she might have feared what any young black woman had plenty of reason to fear with regard to the matter of 'mixing' with whites.

But whether or not she would have gone out with me never came into play either for me or for her because I never asked her. She was everything I could have hoped for, but the notion of going out with her, of falling in love with her, of perhaps someday marrying her was one from which I remained entirely 'partitioned'. It was not that I thought myself in any way better than she was. Equality at any level was not the issue that separated us. The only wall that divided us, but which seemed to me as tall and thick as the one I would later see in Derry/Londonderry, was race, and at that point in my life, I believed it to be unbreachable without at the same time facing consequences I lacked the inclination, and probably the courage, to face. Better, I decided, that I go my way and she go hers.

Such would not be the case were I now that same young man. There is still plenty of prejudice, of course, and much needs to be done on both sides of the racial divide. And yet, for all that, I believe that the racial wall that had once made two well-matched young people turn away from any thought of making a future together is no longer either so tall nor so thick as to create an impossible divide.

And so, in the end, far from teaching the grim lesson I would have supposed the only one it had to teach, Derry/Londonderry, by eventually returning me to my Southern boyhood, reminded me that, indeed, things can change, that some walls do shrink, that some lines do grow less distinct, that some prejudices diminish, and that as a result, a unity that had once seemed unpalatable can become the daily bread of life.

It would be foolish of me to place too much hope on such a possibility, either for Derry/Londonderry, or for India/Pakistan, or for divided Cyprus, or any of the other of earth's many deep partitions. But equally, I believe that a small hope is a hope nonetheless, and that there is some historical evidence that we should hold to certain hopes regardless of how small they are, since, should we abandon them, as Dante so well knew, we would truly enter Hell.

Ground Zero

'And, of course, Ground Zero,' my editor said one evening over dinner in London.

Several months before, I'd been sitting in a similar restaurant, this time with Anthony Cheetham, then my British publisher, in Adelaide, Australia. Merely as a matter of conversation, I'd mentioned my lifelong interest in dark places, along with my feeling that the saddest places on earth had much to offer that was anything but dark. Anthony immediately mentioned the Memorial to the Missing at Thiepval in the valley of the Somme, how moved he'd been by the dawn memorial service he'd attended there.

'Over seventy-two thousand names are carved on that monument,' he said. 'And those are only the missing.'

To my surprise, others around the table began to relate their own experiences at various dark sites around the world. Many had experienced the same sense of edification that I'd felt when

I'd visited such places. One woman said, 'You know, in terms of what you get from them, they're not really sad at all.'

No one mentioned Ground Zero that night, so it had never occurred to me to include it in this book until my editor brought it up over dinner in London a year later. And yet, during the weeks and months following that first mention of Ground Zero as a 'dark place', the site itself, and what it meant to me, continually nudged itself back into my mind.

I was not in New York on the day of the attack, but when I returned to the city a few days later, I saw that it had changed in such strange ways that it was hardly recognizable. First, there was the immense hole that had been gouged out of the skyline. The Towers, so much taller than any of the surrounding buildings, had visually anchored lower Manhattan, and without them, you had the surreal sense that the southern end of the island had somehow become unmoored and floated out to sea. In place of the Towers, you saw only an opaque cloud that gave the impression, particularly at night, of a continually boiling steam.

'I had always thought of New York as permanent,' a friend said.

So had I.

So had everyone.

But looking south from the vantage point of Sixth Avenue, one saw nothing where something 'permanent', a fixed and iconic skyline, had once stood, and with the Towers' abrupt disappearance, you felt that other things had also vanished, boundaries that had been ours before, and behind which we had felt secure not only as residents of a fabled city, but also of a centuries-old civilization we'd considered, on all fronts, beyond serious challenge.

Beyond the emptiness at the end of the island, there were other changes that were similarly shocking.

Walking south from 42nd Street, you saw the slow militarization of your home. On Fifth Avenue, I watched soldiers in full combat gear waving over and instantly searching whatever vehicles they chose. On the West Side Highway, black-clad SWAT teams stood perched like gigantic crows atop the *Intrepid*. There were soldiers in the bus and subway stations, soldiers in the great terminals, soldiers in the parks and outside the landmark buildings. Everywhere, everywhere, there were guns. Even in the air. Walking down Seventh Avenue one morning, I heard the piercing shriek of what was certainly an F-16 fighter, and noticed, to my great surprise, that the people on the street did not look into the upper reaches of the sky in search of this plane, but towards what for New Yorkers is tree-level, the taller buildings of the city. For us, planes were no longer expected to be seen only in the distantly cocooning blue.

For a time, Ground Zero itself remained unapproachable by any but official personnel, and yet, like a tumour, it spread over the city. There was the dust, of course, grey-to-beige and very fine, that coated awnings and trees and park benches. It grew thicker the nearer you came to the fallen towers, but the September winds moved it steadily northward, almost into invisibility save that even when unseen it remained an acrid presence in your lungs. To live in New York now was to be continually assailed by this intensely bitter particulate. You breathed it in, felt its sting, and coughed it out.

The smell, sweet and mildly nauseating, was less widespread, though in the neighbourhoods nearest the attack, it lingered for many days. 'It's the bodies,' a reporter friend told me one evening as we sat on her deck of her apartment in Greenwich Village. 'We've confirmed that.'

Thus was lower Manhattan converted into a funeral pyre.

But it was the missing person flyers that proved the most ubiquitous of all reminders, usually with a picture and a name, a father, mother, brother, sister, lover, friend, the vast Unaccounted For. These postings were attached to every conceivable surface by every conceivable means. With glue, nails, brackets, thumbtacks, wire, plastic twisters, and tape of every description they were affixed to walls, windows, poles, the sides of buildings, almost any vertical structure. If you bought a newspaper, the little metal stand that contained it was covered with these flyers. If you went to mail a letter, the mail depository was covered. At Grand Central lines of poster board were erected upon which hundreds of these flyers were displayed. At Saint Vincent's Hospital, an entire outer wall was given over to this last best hope of love.

At Ground Zero itself, the overwhelming sense was less the enormity of the destruction than how ineffectively that enormity could be conveyed by television. I would look at the live coverage, watch the camera sweep the area, and marvel at how it miniaturized the actual expanse of Ground Zero. The attack dust cloud had been visible for a vertical distance of twenty miles, while the plume itself could be seen from outer space. The debris field covered sixteen acres and rose five storeys above ground. The fires were so intense they would continue to burn for sixty-nine days. In fourteen seconds, two hundred thousand tons of steel and almost eight hundred thousand tons of concrete had fallen to earth in the largest structural collapse in human history. Looking at all the toy-sized images of this massive destruction on television, I could think only: *It's not like that at all.*

Undoubtedly, then, the destruction of the Twin Towers was an unprecedented event that had in a single stroke taken the lives of people from ninety different countries, thus an international event whose consequences would resonate throughout the world and into the unknowable future.

And yet, in London that night, when my editor asked if I were considering Ground Zero for the book, I felt a certain hesitation. It had surely been one of the darkest places in my life, but was that enough?

No, I eventually decided, it was not.

For as a place of death and destruction, even mass death and wanton destruction, Ground Zero is a minor player. Two thousand nine hundred and seventy-six men, women and children had been murdered here, and each of these deaths had been a tragedy. But numbers do matter in such accountings, I thought, and horrific though the attack had been, on the scale of murder, Ground Zero could not compete with, say, the firebombing of Dresden, where conventional weapons had devastated an area of thirty-nine square kilometres and incinerated approximately 25,000 people, almost all of whom had been civilians. And what of Hiroshima with its 140,000 dead, or Nagasaki with its 80,000?

But for all that, something about Ground Zero drew me back to it again and again. It was a dark gravity I couldn't quite explain, though it did seem to me that the tragedy of the place went well beyond my personal attachment to New York, or even to America. Both my country and my city had suffered a blow, but it was one each of them had rather quickly absorbed and would incontestably survive. Something deeper had been struck, however, but what this other thing was continued to elude me until one afternoon, when I again recalled what my friend had said earlier: *I had always thought of New York as permanent.*

I was standing at Ground Zero when this recollection came, peering through the storm fence that had long ago been erected around what was now a vast construction site. I gazed upwards, into an emptiness I'd seen many times before, and suddenly realized why my sadness at the very thought of Ground Zero had always been so unexpectedly deep, and that the reason for this was that the darkness that had struck New York on September 11 was a darkness that had not come from some newly emerged geopolitical threat, but from the distant past. It was an ancient creature from a primitive lagoon, one who, should it ever actually bestride the world, would extinguish every light that had been lit since the dawning of modernity.

One wishes to think that the sort of barbarism that knows no boundary can be sustained only for a time. Hitler's Thousand-Year Reich did not endure a decade, and there was a phantasmagorical quality to Japanese military arrogance that made the horrors of Nanking unlikely to spread across the face of the globe. Stalinism had made a longer strut across the stage, but as history proved, its downfall had long been waiting in the wings. For that reason, it was reasonable to see these excursions into madness as little more than brief episodes in the long continuum of life on earth. The forces that had lifted these psychopathic regimes to power had generated the forces that brought them down, and in this welcome counterpoint, history seemed to provide evidence that the spectacularly insane had a limited shelf life.

Then, on a clear September morning, two planes were hurled towards Manhattan like stones from a primordial pit.

It was in this that the darkness of Ground Zero lay for me, that a struggle usually carried out on a small scale had ballooned into a history-transforming movement, the comforts of reason and secularism now once again imperilled by the old menace of religious fanaticism.

On that thought, I recalled a place that could hardly have been farther away or more different from the beehive density of lower Manhattan, and which, by my even thinking of it, suggested one of the great powers of dark places, that they inform each other and at last establish a network, as it were, in the heart and mind, a reservoir of impressions and experiences from which you may continually draw.

The place that came to mind was Uluru, formerly known

as Ayers Rock, a striking sandstone formation that rises three hundred and forty-eight metres above Australia's expansive central desert at a point approximately three hundred kilometres from Alice Springs. The mythical origins of Uluru are violent. One tells of warring serpents, another of warring tribes singing evil into mud, followed by a battle so violent in its action and so merciless in its toll that the earth itself rose up in grief, and in that stupendous rising became Uluru.

Because you approach it by way of a flat red desert, the great cliffs of Uluru rise before you long in advance of your actual arrival. It is pink or orange or red depending upon the sun, but in every sun it is massive.

Still, it wasn't the enormity of Uluru that I found most impressive, but the fact that it rests in an area of the earth that has seen practically no change for millions of years. There are no rivers here, and little rain, and the winds that occasionally sweep up the sands only bear them a little way before returning them again to identical terrain. For this geological reason, to observe sunrise over Uluru, as Susan, Justine and I did one morning, is to watch unfold a dawn almost identical to what, say, an Austrosaurus would have seen a hundred million years before.

At that sunrise, the light built slowly, so that the air brightened from a pale blue to a fierce clarity, at which time I could look out over a radically shaved-down landscape of red dirt and spinifex, with nothing to block the far horizon but the towering wall of Uluru. In part, it was the sheer intractable nature of this physical permanence that metaphorically came into play when I recalled how my friend had spoken of New York's lost permanence. For she'd been right. New York in this new age could no longer be considered permanent. Nor could Paris or London or Vienna or Madrid be thought permanent. Nor for that matter, Mecca, should the tables fiercely turn, and the sacred city of Islam be consumed by the same dust its most extreme adherents were raising in the West. This is true because something darker had proven itself far more permanent than any of these cities could ever with certainty claim to be, and it is this other permanence that has made Ground Zero so inestimably sad to me, a sadness that runs deeper than the number of the dead or the level of the destruction, and which has far less to do with the crumbled state of the fallen buildings than with the fallen state of man, a permanently fallen state mirrored not only in the changeless nature of Uluru, as I thought of it that day, but in the fact that by its own founding myth that great unchanging rock had been borne of evil, and in that way, rooted in mankind itself.

Something old and dark and deep lay at the heart of Ground Zero that was not reducible to the fanatical actions of a few men or the crazed ideology they had adopted. Ground Zero, located at the beating heart of modernity, had been struck by perhaps the most primitive aspect of human character, man's fierce dread of being alone, of having nothing higher to which he can appeal, nothing to magnify his smallness or attest to his significance in a universe from whose indifferent vastness he shrinks into a frightened crouch. The young men who'd brought these buildings down were Muslims, and as such, they represented the currently most driven and animated form of this ancient terror, but theirs was a fear far older than Islam, one that had doubtless been born in our caves when we were cold and in our bellies when we were hungry, and in our eyes when we looked into an infinitude that dwarfed us and upon whose blank, unfeeling space we imposed the image of ourselves. They were Muslims, followers of a young religion, but the terror of aloneness from which that religion, and all others, sprang was at one with the imperilled infancy of man.

It was the terrible evidence of our incapacity to accept our own metaphysical loneliness that Ground Zero came to represent for me in the dreadful way it exposed the trembling reed man remains, terrified by the spectre of his own solitude, and thus preternaturally vulnerable to whatever lifts him up, calls his weakness strength and his fear courage, and provides safe haven from the terror of accepting his own orphaned state.

A decade and a half has now passed since the attack, and because I live part of the year in New York City, I have watched over the years as the debris pile grew smaller and finally disappeared, watched the pit it left behind slowly fill with workmen and construction tools and supplies, watched as the foundation of a new building took shape and at last began to rise. But for all that, the gaping hole of Ground Zero will never be filled because it is but a small depression within a chasm whose fathomless depths still yawn beneath us, our failure to embrace the universal helplessness that should have been the gate by which we tenderly connected to each other as mutual orphans of the storm. But instead, we have gathered behind various walls of succouring delusion, and now rise to look over them only long enough to hurl slurs, insults, spears, rocks, bullets . . . planes.

Wieliczka

Wieliczka was recently listed as one of Kraków's five favourite attractions, the others being a pub tour, a trip to a paintball park, an afternoon of white-water rafting, and a visit to a shooting range where the visitor is assured that he or she will be allowed to fire a genuine Kalashnikov. Other websites tout Wieliczka as a 'fun trip' to a place visited by such luminaries as Goethe and Emperor Franz Josef, both of whom were 'suitably impressed' by this 'show-stopper' attraction. Various tour advertisements mention that Sarah Bernhardt, Copernicus and Bill Clinton also came to the mine, along with numerous 'crowned heads'. Clearly the value of a celebrity site is enhanced by the mention of previous celebrity visitors. The enthusiastic selling of Wieliczka has no doubt been energized by the overall regeneration of Kraków since the end of the Soviet domination of Poland. More than a million tourists now visit the mine each year. But in 1991, when we came here, it was a very dark place, and as such, was hardly heralded as a must-see attraction. As a matter of fact, as far as I can recall, it was advertised by nothing more elaborate than a small sign in the hotel lobby. The woman who sat at the table in front of the sign appeared to have little interest in giving out information concerning Wieliczka. She said nothing of its seven-hundred-year history, nor that it is generally considered to be Poland's first business enterprise. She was even unsure as to when the bus to Wieliczka actually departed, though when pressed, she finally checked the time, then pointed to the location from which it would depart. Suffice it to say that had I not already known more about the mine than she seemed willing or able to convey, I would not have gone there.

The bus that later took us to Wieliczka rattled through the city's bleak suburbs, passed a nuclear power plant that resembled nothing quite so much as a huge pile of tin cans, and finally came to a halt in front of a modest wooden building. This was the entrance to the mine, and it was exactly that, not a visitors' centre, or a place that sold souvenirs, save for a few trinkets carved from salt. Wieliczka had not been prettified for tourists. There was no tavern or fancy restaurant, as there is now. It was still a working mine and our guide had once been a miner. He was large and powerfully built, wore baggy pants and a very worn jacket whose lapel sported a small American flag.

'I love English,' he told me. 'My hope is that someday I go to America.'

I'd learned to be somewhat suspicious of statements of this kind. There was always the possibility that such amiable assertions were said in hopes of a bigger tip. But I also knew that at that moment in Polish history, with the Soviet Union slumping ever closer to collapse, America was quite well regarded by the reform forces then at work in Eastern Europe, if only according to the old and often erroneous notion that the enemy of my enemy is my friend. Still, I only smiled and wished him luck.

The descent into the mine was by a rickety wooden elevator that creaked and shuddered all the way down. There were about seven of us in the elevator and one of them, a young Italian woman, became unnerved, continually repeating, '*Mamma mia*,' and crossing herself.

Susan took her hand and whispered something to her that immediately calmed her down.

There was a considerable amount of light when we reached the bottom of the shaft, and once out of the elevator, our confinement was far less severe. By then our guide had noticed that Justine did not seem in the least frightened by the descent. 'You are brave girl,' he said. 'You will like tour.' And it was very much a tour, carefully guided, with no wandering about. There were things to be seen in the caverns of Wieliczka and along the nearly two-kilometre walk that would lead us through them. The sights had been carefully selected and the route had been carefully mapped, so that after a time I began to feel as if I were drifting in a little boat attached to steel rails, as one might proceed through a carnival haunted house or tunnel of love.

Wieliczka, however, was no midway attraction. For nine centuries, through two hundred kilometres of passageways and in the dugout space of 2,040 caverns, the work of mining salt had relentlessly gone forward. It was a labour whose arduousness and conditions no tour could possibly convey, but the curious thing about Wieliczka was that the miners themselves appeared to have had little interest in conveying it. Of all the scores of carvings that rose everywhere around us as we made our way deeper into the mine, I saw not one that suggested the actual function of the mine nor gave much indication concerning the lives of those who'd toiled here. Some sort of history of the mine, complete with such figures, has evidently since been added, but on the day I came to Wieliczka, I saw no such representations, no salt miners with picks digging out blocks of salt, nor tossing those blocks into wheelbarrows, nor bearing this treasure away. From what I could tell, the carvings of Wieliczka dealt only with escape. 'It's all salt,' the guide told us. 'Take your finger and touch the wall and taste.' Everyone did, and sure enough, the taste was salt. 'Everything you see here is made of salt,' the guide said.

And what you see at Wieliczka is indisputably spectacular, room after room of figures and reliefs. From the thirteenth century onwards the miners of Wieliczka had laboured to create a curious underground world. Throughout most of that period Catholicism had predominated and in response to its pervasive world view, Wieliczka became a grey-walled cathedral. There are carvings of the Nativity and carvings of the Last Supper and countless carvings having to do with the iconography of both Old and New Testaments, the flight from Egypt and the flight from Bethlehem. Communism had had a different world view, of course, and once it took control of the mine, the miners had been encouraged to explore other themes. Their response, at least judging by the salt sculptures they carved during this period, was to fall into fantasy. While grey-eyed Stalinism reigned above, below, in these unlit chambers, the miners of Wieliczka carved spectacularly whimsical figures: fairies and gnomes and all manner of fantastical creatures. As a result, these parts of the mine looked less like a church and more like the playroom of a young child.

Indeed, a sense of childlike escapism, even fairytale whimsy, runs throughout Wieliczka, so that visitors increasingly reacted to the mine as if they were attending a kindergarten art show. As we moved from chamber to chamber, I noticed that the people in our group often paused to release the sort of sighs usually heard from those gathered in front of the Christmas windows at Macy's or after a very young child has made a particularly cute remark. It is the sigh one offers to the harmlessly adorable, an homage paid to that which charms, but does not awe.

And yet there is something awesome about Wieliczka. In part it is the recognition of just how old the mine is, and of the vast number of men who must have laboured here over the last nine centuries. Their number cannot be calculated, though it must have been in the many thousands, and their labour had to have been arduous, to say the least, given the fact that as late as 1850 a visitor described 'half-naked' miners working in chambers where the temperature was a chilly fifteen degrees Celsius.

In the flickering of scores of Bengal lights, they were hacking blocks of sparkly grey salt out of the chamber floor while other workers, presumably less skilled, loaded these same blocks into wheelbarrows and bore them to the surface.

The curious thing – perhaps the true mystery of Wieliczka – is that when the work day ended, rather than return immediately to fresh air and daylight, some of these same miners put down their picks and took up the sculpting tools with which they then carved those statues of St Francis and Joseph that one of the mine's nineteenth-century visitors described as already melting away in the mine's humid upper chambers. In fact, the admittedly impressive array of figures that pop up around every corner of Wieliczka are simply those that remain intact, while countless others perished long ago. To carve in salt is not to carve for the ages, and yet carve they did, these miners, assiduously and determinedly, and evidently – since no mention was ever made regarding their being paid for this added labour – for the love it. And there was certainly plenty of love on view at Wieliczka; a love of God, of faith, of fantasy, and at last a love of grandeur that is spectacularly on display in the mine's most famous chamber. St Kinga's Chapel is the true masterwork of Wieliczka. It began when a massive block of green salt was excavated, leaving an enormous chamber, fifty-four metres long and twelve metres high. This gigantic room is now a full-blown Catholic chapel, complete with altar, sculptures, reliefs, and even several impossibly grand chandeliers, all made entirely of salt. It is as if the miners who perfected this chamber were intent upon creating an underground Versailles, a palace hall rendered in the gloomy colour of unprocessed salt. If the Underworld had an antechamber, I thought, it would surely look like this. Others in our party were equally impressed, a fact evidenced by sighs of genuine awe.

For a time, I stared about, truly speechless at the sight, and struggling quite futilely to take it in. The chandeliers were blazing, and the light that came from them flickered in all the surrounding walls. This created a vaguely mirror-ball effect, not bright and dazzling, but with its millions of tiny winks, somehow stranger and more startling.

Then, suddenly, the chandeliers went out and a gasp went up, and the guide spoke.

'This,' he said, 'is perfect darkness.'

And so it was, at least physically, for we were now just over a hundred metres below the surface of the earth, a chamber into which no light could possibly penetrate. In that blackness, I expected to hear another burst of '*Mamma mias*', but heard only a few murmurs of conversation, then a sigh, this one of relief and accompanied by a few nervous giggles, when the lights were turned back on.

For the next few minutes I wandered rather aimlessly about the chapel, looking at its many carvings, peering up at the flaming chandeliers, noting the many figures that adorned the room. It was easy to see why various celebrities had been 'suitably impressed', and I know that had we then been immediately ushered back to our elevator and lifted to the surface, I would have left the mine with that sense of having seen something marvellous and which had completely captivated me so that I'd utterly forgotten that it was the mine's 'darkness' that had drawn me to it, thinking to gain some sense of the hundreds of years of hard labour that had created and sustained it, all of which, as it turned out, had been quite successfully camouflaged behind tableau after salt tableau of gnomes and fairies, Catholic saints and figures of Polish myth. But Wieliczka had one more surprise.

From the wonder of St Kinga's Chapel, we were now escorted past yet more whimsical statues, and into a large chamber that was unexpectedly stripped of any adornment. The ceiling of the room was quite high, and below it, I saw what seemed an ascending wall of wooden bunks.

'Is this where the miners slept?' I asked our guide.

'Just the Jews,' the guide answered. 'The Germans brought them into the mine to build aircraft.'

So they'd been slaves, these Jews, and like the countless horses who'd been lowered into this labyrinth to pull lorries piled high with blocks of salt, they'd surely had little chance of seeing the sun again.

Or so I found out later, for none of our group asked any questions and the guide added nothing more. In fact, he seemed in no mood to linger in this bleakest of Wieliczka's many chambers, the only one in which whimsy or religious iconography did not reign. Thus, only minutes later we were all back in the elevator and creakily ascending towards the entrance to the mine.

On that brief upward journey, it seemed to me likely that

during all the Holocaust, none could have felt more abandoned, more wholly beyond rescue or more entirely cut off from the world than the Jews who'd been lowered into this mine. Imprisoned in its dark two-hundred-mile-long labyrinth, they had worked to assemble aircraft engines for planes they surely must have hoped would crash on take-off. They must also have harboured the hope that they would someday be liberated, though only two saved themselves by hiding in Wieliczka's maze of tunnels as the Russian army closed in upon the mine. All the others were taken directly to Auschwitz. But it was not only the tragic fate of the Jews who'd been imprisoned here that later made Wieliczka seem one of the saddest places on earth to me. Rather, it was also the effort to render this part of the mine's history, the slave labour that had been practised here, as little more than an afterthought, an episode to be recounted quickly, in passing, or perhaps not at all, as if any longer exposure to it would poison the visitor's cheerful experience of the mine. Wieliczka, after all, was supposed to be about faith, or whimsy, or art practised for the love of it. But the fact is, many of the sculptures and reliefs we'd all just observed with wonder and delight had been carved during a time when those very artisans of salt had to have passed the dark chambers where the Jews slept and toiled. What must have been on these sculptors' minds as they simply moved on to the other chambers where they busied themselves carving elves and gnomes? Were the extravagant Polish myths their work celebrated in any way called into question by their proximity to this suffering? As they trudged past those enslaved Jews, had any one of them recalled that St Kinga, for whom Wieliczka's great chapel is named, was made saintly by her noble defence of the undefended? To have raised that issue in the chamber we'd just departed would not have been to call the Polish people to account, or even a single one of the miners who toiled here alongside the imprisoned Jews. To raise such an issue in such a place is never to point the finger of accusation. It is simply to acknowledge the tragic irony of life in such a way that broadens our understanding of life itself. To speak with an open heart of this irony would not diminish the spectacular works that adorn Wieliczka, but would, instead, add something grave and complicated to our appreciation of both the work and those who did it, that element of darkness that, like salt, serves to season life.

Choeung Ek/Tuol Sleng

Flying over Cambodia, it is hard not to expect a landscape pitted with bomb craters. After all, during its 'secret' air campaign – one whose curious code name was 'Operation Menu' – the United States dropped more than 500,000 tons of bombs on this small, mostly rural country, thus almost three times as much ordnance as was dropped upon Japan during all of World War II. But this show of overwhelming force was not enough either to turn the tide of the Vietnam War, nor to prevent the Khmer Rouge, Cambodia's indigenous revolutionary army, from ousting Lon Nol's government, nor from capturing Phnom Penh, which it did on 12 April 1975.

Upon their initial entry into the city, the cadres of the Khmer Rouge were welcomed with enthusiastic cheers by crowds of people, many wearing *kramas,* the chequered scarf that is a traditional Cambodian signal of friendship. The journalist Jon Swain recalled seeing a smiling monk in his orange robes riding in a jeep alongside a Khmer Rouge soldier, as well as soldiers of both sides riding together on half-tracks. It is hard to say just how much of this photogenic glee was genuine. Certainly there was no love lost between Lon Nol and the Cambodian people. Even so, it is hard to imagine that there were not a great many people in Phnom Penh that day who had profound misgivings about the triumph of the Khmer Rouge, particularly those who had worked for Lon Nol's famously corrupt administration, or for the Americans, whose incompetent puppet he surely was.

Upon arrival in Phnom Penh something far different from its fall seems unimaginable, the fact that almost immediately the Khmer Rouge leadership decided that this sprawling capital city should be entirely evacuated. And by this, the Khmer leaders meant entirely – every man, woman and child. Riding only the short distance from the airport to my hotel was enough to reveal a teeming, bustling city of over a million and a half people. The notion of evacuating such a population in a matter of days is even more daunting when you add the fact that on 17 April, when the evacuation order was carried out, the city's population, long swollen with refugees from the bombed and embattled countryside, was perhaps as much as twice what it was in February of 2015, when I came here.

Prior to the evacuation, not one accommodation had been made to receive this surging river of humanity. On that April morning, the people of Phnom Penh were simply ordered from their homes and herded out of the capital. The road I took from the airport is one of the roads down which the people of

Phnom Penh made their way from their abandoned homes to Choeung Ek, the first and foremost of what would come to be known as the 'killing fields'. The horrors of that short journey have been well documented both by Cambodian survivors of the march and by the few Western journalists who witnessed it. What they saw was a ragged tide of human beings whose varied conditions and consequent agonies were simply not considered by their new masters. No exceptions were made. All the city's hospitals were emptied, along with orphanages, prisons and asylums. Everyone was forced onto the streets, often with as little as ten minutes to assemble whatever belongings they could carry. The young French missionary, François Ponchaud, remembered seeing a man who had neither hands nor feet 'writhing along the ground like a severed worm'. People were pushed in hospital beds, tubes dangling from their arms. The old were pushed in wheelchairs or carried on the backs of their relatives. Mothers and fathers stumbled forwards, laden with children too young to walk, all of them headed down a road that would bear them to the swampy lagoon that closes in upon Choeung Ek, and eventually, for most of them (one in eight of all Cambodians alive on that day) to death. Swain called it 'the greatest caravan of misery' he had ever seen.

The architect of this catastrophe was a man who, according to one biographer, wore the same smile you see carved on the faces of the gods at Angkor Wat. Later, when I went to Angkor Wat and compared those smiles to Pol Pot's, I couldn't have agreed more. They are assured smiles, entirely self-confident, smiles that suggest a certainty with regard to life that no human being can rightfully claim. In that way, their smiles, and his, are scary.

And with good reason, because it was precisely Pol Pot's certainty that made the evacuation of Phnom Penh, the killing fields at Choeung Ek, and the torture chamber at Tuol Sleng not only possible, but inevitable. Doubters do not burn people at the stake. That role in human history is reserved for true believers only, and few in human life have so fully believed in the absolute truth of their own ideas as Pol Pot did in his.

Following those ideas, he began Cambodian history all over again, at what he called 'Year Zero'. Money was abolished (the Cambodian National Bank was later blown up), as were religion, marriage, family relations and the health and education systems – these last two abolitions for the most part accomplished by killing all the doctors, teachers, professors and anyone who wore glasses. As a consequence, education predictably became dogma and family became cadre. Edmund Burke once wrote that the French Revolution's aim was to rip down 'all the decency drapery of life'. Pol Pot's aim was to rip down every room in which that drapery hung. He even wished to abolish names, taking a new one for himself: Brother Number One.

Under the Khmer Rouge, Cambodia became, as one historian has called it, 'a savage utopia', a country that perfectly realized George Orwell's image of life under totalitarianism as a boot eternally stamping on a human face.

There are few places where that boot came down harder than at Choeung Ek.

It lies only seventeen kilometres outside Phnom Penh. I went there by tuk-tuk, a common mode of transportation in Cambodian cities and which is essentially a motorized rickshaw. In a tuk-tuk, you remain at street level and ride in the open air, exposed to the sounds and smells of Cambodia, as well as the still unhealed wounds inflicted upon its people. These are visible not only in the terrible poverty through which you pass on the way to Choeung Ek, but by the ubiquitous picture menus necessary for a people still locked in the illiteracy imposed by the annihilation of its teachers and its schools. In the wake of those ravages, vast numbers of Cambodians cannot read or write the language they speak. As one Cambodian friend told me, 'We are struggling to reach a level our neighbours Thailand and Vietnam reached long ago.'

The route from Phnom Penh to Choeung Ek passes through a landscape of underdevelopment. Few houses have walls and almost none have plumbing. The lagoon this tide of terrified human beings passed on that April day is a fetid swamp whose waters are unfit to drink. The towns en route are little more than agglomerations of shanties. There is nothing quaint or charming about any of this. All you see is grinding poverty until you reach the white stupa that is the central memorial of Choeung Ek.

It is essentially an ossuary, but far more stark than any you would see in the West. Unlike the ossuary at Verdun, which has the feel of a national cathedral and strives to memorialize French sacrifice, the stupa at Choeung Ek is a simple tower of skulls, some five thousand of them, each with a dot whose colour coding indicates the manner of death, whether this unique human being, capable of experiencing the entire range of human feeling, every joy and every terror, was killed by an iron rod, a bullet, a wooden stick, a crowbar, or by 'chemical treatment'.

The skulls were found in the mass graves that surround the stupa. Almost nine thousand bodies were unearthed here, most political prisoners of one kind or another, and for whose 'crimes' their children were also killed. The place where the smallest of these children were executed is the darkest place at Choeung Ek. It is called 'The Children's Tree', and it is here that infants or toddlers were taken by their feet and swung against the trunk of a tree that is now hung with multicoloured cloth friendship bracelets in memory of them, and which, because of their great number, clothe the tree in an eerie rainbow. There is no more moving place at Choeung Ek than here, no place where the terror of ideological purity is more starkly expressed. For the Khmer Rouge cadres who bashed in these tiny skulls were young them-selves, members of that teenaged army of 'phantoms enveloped in darkness' that the Cambodian students who'd been studying abroad encountered upon returning to their country.

It was these 'automatons from another planet' who also pro-vided the guards and torturers of Tuol Sleng, which, along with Choeung Ek, occupies the reeking bottom of the nearly bottom-less savagery imposed upon Cambodia by Pol Pot's unassailable ideological puritanism.

In terms of physical structure, Choeung Ek and Tuol Sleng could not be more different. Choeung Ek remains an open field, the nearer suburbs of Phnom Penh clearly visible in the distance. Tuol Sleng, which fittingly means 'Hill of Poisonous Trees' in Khmer, is situated in the heart of the capital, only a few blocks from the palace. Choeung Ek was equipped with only the most tumbledown of structures. Tuol Sleng, on the other hand, had once been a fully functioning high school. Choeung Ek's outrages were committed in the open air, witnessed by hundreds of people. The cruelties at Tuol Sleng were carried out in the middle of an all but empty city, often in the dead of night, and witnessed only by the perpetrators and those they so brutally tormented.

The feel of Tuol Sleng is of a highly compact Auschwitz. The acreage is slight, with only a broad courtyard separating a tight rectangle of three-storey buildings. But despite its modest size, Tuol Sleng's sense of concentrated evil is extraordinarily intense. Perhaps it is its compactness that generates this overwhelming sense of life reduced to stink and blisters. At Auschwitz suffering is diffused over a very large space and offers a continuing echo of anguish. At Tuol Sleng, the air sizzles with immediate and excruciating physical pain. Auschwitz was a death factory whose product was extermination. Tuol Sleng was an interrogation centre whose function was to extract confessions. For those not immediately taken to the gas chambers, the soundtrack of Auschwitz was the Teutonic bark of cruel commands and the grunt of forced labour. The music of Tuol Sleng, at all times, was a scream.

For the most part Tuol Sleng remains as it was the day it was discovered by the Vietnamese combat photographer who noticed the great stink that wafted from its gate. He subsequently entered the grounds, and the pictures of the rotting corpses he found that day are still on view here. Other rooms display photographs of some of the thousands of men, women and children who passed through that same gate. These pictures are poignant, as are all such photographs, but what gives Tuol Sleng its unforgettable reality is the stark nature of the iron beds to which the prisoners were manacled, the metal ammunition buckets which were their only toilets, the instruments of torture that still lie, more or less helter-skelter, within the torture rooms, and the stifling sense of accumulated filth, all the blood, urine, vomit, spit and faeces that still stain the rooms' tile floors and remain splattered against its walls. Most such places are to one degree or another sanitized before they are opened to the public. Tuol Sleng barely seems to have been mopped up.

And so it will remain on display for all to see, the great reeking mess of ideological purity.

Pol Pot's ideological extremity is not the only one to be found at Tuol Sleng, however. On one of the ground floors, almost an entire room is devoted to an aggrieved *J'accuse* against those in the West who turned a blind eye to the outrages of the Khmer Rouge. Chief among those accused of this gross malfeasance was Jan Myrdal, who with three other members of the Swedish-Kampuchean Friendship Association, arrived in Phnom Penh on 12 August 1978, at the very time when Pol Pot's oppression was reaching what one historian has called its 'terrifying crescendo'. In one of Tuol Sleng's haunted rooms, much is made of the statements later penned by the members of this delegation, all of them in praise of Pol Pot and his revolution. Reading these statements is a disheartening experience. Even so, the lesson is clear: an idealist is one who wears blinkers; an ideologue is one who is blind.

Only fourteen people are said to have survived the agony of Tuol Sleng. On the day I visited it, one of them happened to be there. His name is Bou Meng, and he was sitting under a canopy in the courtyard, behind a table, selling his book about his experience at Tuol Sleng. His life was spared because he was a painter. He was put to work painting portraits of Pol Pot and other high Khmer Rouge leaders, always from photographs. He is a small man, and he appeared rather frail.

I picked up his book. It was a very slender volume. Buying it seemed the least I could do.

A young woman stood beside Bou Meng. She smiled and told me the price.

I gave her the money and she immediately handed a copy of the book to Bou Meng, who signed it.

'You want picture with him?' the woman asked as she handed me the book.

She was asking if I wanted to pose for a photograph with Bou Meng, who was now smiling at me very kindly.

Having one's picture taken with actors, authors, politicians and celebrities of all types is perfectly acceptable, of course, and such people are often judged by how accommodating they are at such occasions.

But Bou Meng?

He was not one whose works had made him 'famous'. His achievement had been survival, pure and simple, though he'd certainly joined a brotherhood of very few in having escaped from Tuol Sleng alive. More to the point of the moment, he had endured a level of physical pain and mental anguish I could not imagine. His wife had been murdered. His life had been uprooted. He would forever bear the mark of Pol Pot on his body and in his heart and mind. I could not help but consider to what degree, in the misguided bombing of Cambodia, my own country had helped create the conditions that had ultimately resulted in the horrors of Tuol Sleng, and thereby contributed to the wounds of this frail old man.

My country, the one to which I would return unscathed.

Dark places teach that there are certain situations and complexities in the consideration of which the moral compass can never reach true north. History's dark magnetic field is spread too wide beneath these events, too deep, extending outwards in too complicated a pattern. To have bought Bou Meng's book seemed at that moment incontestably right, or at least morally neutral. But to ask him to rise, to place himself at my side, perhaps even allow me to drape my arm over his small shoulders, to have him smile as his assistant took a picture?

'No,' I said, with a small, respectful bow to Bou Meng, 'but thank you.'

For it seemed to me that the limelight of his suffering was not one I should share.

Snapshot: Tangiers

I could not have been more surprised when, while watching a documentary on the 21 September 2013 terrorist attack on the Westgate shopping mall in Nairobi, Kenya, I suddenly returned to a particular afternoon in Tangiers some twenty years earlier. In that video, made up of footage taken from surveillance cameras stationed in various places throughout the mall, one sees women repeatedly risk their lives to protect their children. They curl their bodies around them, rush them to places where they may be safe, press them into corners and stand over them as if their all too vulnerable flesh could protect their cowering children from the annihilating spray of a Kalashnikov. What the surveillance cameras inside the Westgate mall revealed was that not one child was abandoned, not one left to fend for itself. For the mothers of Nairobi, panic was not an option, nor was the notion of leaving their children in order to protect themselves considered for a nanosecond. Theirs was a courage truly undaunted.

Nearly twenty years before I watched that documentary, with Justine's term at the American School of Madrid having just come to an end, we had decided that it was time for us to see more of southern Spain. We had been living in the country for quite some time, and had, from our base in Madrid, explored most of Western Europe. But other than visiting Granada to the south, Segovia to the north and Zaragoza and Barcelona to the north-east, we had seen little of the country whose language we could now use sufficiently to get by, and for whose generous, welcoming and immensely friendly people we had come to feel a very great affection.

And so down through arid Jerez and bleak Extremadura we journeyed, and from there towards the 'white towns' of the Mediterranean coast, where we paused at Cádiz, ancient enough to have been known by the Phoenicians, before heading to Gibraltar, where Susan and Justine, with their customary delight in almost any animal, fed the monkeys beloved by Winston Churchill.

Northern Africa is clearly visible from the southern coast of Spain. In fact, it is a mere fly-over for the birds of both continents. It is a nearness that makes itself felt as far north as Madrid, where cloudless skies are sometimes made milk-white by the high-lifted sands of the Sahara. But nowhere does Africa look so near, poised so at the ends of your fingertips, than at Tarifa, the little fishing town that stares out over the sea, towards Morocco's capital of Tangiers.

We never returned to Tarifa, but some thirty years ago,

when we came there for the first time, it was a quiet sea-coast town that seemed in all respects contented, slow-moving, immemorially without urgency, and wholly indifferent to the notion that it needed to change in any way. The beaches held no condominiums or beachfront hotels and I saw only battered, unpainted fishing boats either on or off the shore. In photographs I've lately seen, Tarifa looks like the beach resort it has since become, with cafés beside the sea and jet skiers in it. Jan Morris was once asked what he found most wanting about modern London. His answer was that he missed most the time when it had been, as he frankly put it, 'an English city'. I have little doubt that should I return to Tarifa, I would miss the fact that it had once been a very Spanish coastal town, and would never be such again. Places, like people, it seems, cannot go home again.

On the day we sailed out of Tarifa, however, it was still a village of that older Spain Hemingway would have had no trouble recognizing; a safe, steadfastly European harbour from which we were headed towards a country so alien to our experience that Susan would soon be called upon to prove herself as she never had before, and whose actions on that day would powerfully return to me a full twenty years later when I sat, stunned with admiration, for the mothers of Nairobi.

The crossing by ferry was uneventful, with a courteous crew who seemed as kindly as Morocco's King Hassan II in his portrait that hung at the front of the ferry, and whose amiable features confidently suggested that all were happy in his kingdom.

But as the ferry neared the harbour, something odd happened. All passengers were asked to surrender their passports. Those who did not, the captain of the ferry announced, would have to remain on board.

'So we either give them our passports or we bake in this boat?' Susan asked irritably.

'That seems to be the case.'

'For how long?'

'The foreseeable future, evidently.'

We surrendered our passports, of course, and a few minutes later boarded the bus that would take us into the unknowable labyrinth, or so it seemed to us, of Tangiers.

Throughout the tour, our guide repeatedly insisted that Tangiers was 'an international city', which, save for its reputation for multinational spying and smuggling, it hardly was, at least at that time. Rather, it looked for the most part like a much larger version of a relatively sleepy, north African town.

We almost never booked tours, but Tangiers had struck us as a place sufficiently outside our wheelhouse that we truly needed both guidance and protection. We were adventurous travellers, as Susan often pointed out, but not foolhardy ones.

The tour bus in which we took our seats that afternoon was clean and cool, with large sightseer windows. From those windows we saw the blur of Tangiers sweep by, the walls, the streets, the kasbah, along with the occasional prison where common criminals as well as the country's growing number of political prisoners were kept.

For most of that day all went well, so that, as the tour made its final stop (a 'bazaar' which was actually just a large emporium that sold various 'local' products at absurdly high prices), we'd expected to return to Spain after a pleasant and uneventful day trip from Tarifa.

But that was not to be.

For the tour had arranged that the bus that would return us to the ferry was parked a considerable distance from the emporium, one that had to be traversed on foot, and through the densely packed mob of vendors, hawkers, and all manner of procurers who awaited us at a door that promptly closed the instant we stepped out of it.

It was a truly frightening scene, literally scores of men screaming and madly gesticulating and waving whatever wares they were hawking, all of them, a true mob, pressing in upon us as we elbowed our way towards the distant bus.

I recall a hawk-faced man shouting, 'You want girl?' When I said, 'For God's sake, I'm with my family,' he shrugged and said, 'You want boy?'

It was perhaps at that instant that I realized just how terrifyingly alien and unreal this situation was, and with that realization, glanced behind me, both hoping and expecting to find Susan and Justine close by.

But they were not.

The mob had gotten between us, so that it was only through that roiling crowd of yelling men that I could see Susan pressing forwards, urging Justine ahead of her, until – and I saw this –

one of the men crowded in upon them reached out, touched Justine's hair, then mouthed something that sent Susan into an absolute fury.

'You asshole!' she cried. 'You fucking asshole!'

I had seen Susan angry from time to time, of course, but this was a rage like none I had ever seen before or would ever see again.

'This is a little girl,' she screamed. 'Get the fuck away from her!' She glared at the man, who seemed suddenly quite aware that he had unleashed an unfathomably horrendous force. 'What kind of man are you?' she demanded.

For a moment she simply glared at him while the other men looked on, utterly shocked, as I could tell. They did not seem ever to have encountered such a woman, or seen such ferocity in female eyes. Here was a mother who would stop at nothing to protect her daughter or avenge anything done to her. Here was a woman who would cry havoc and let slip the dogs of war, and I do believe that when those men looked into Susan's eyes, heard those curses in her American accent, imagined, with whatever exaggerated idea, the force she could bring down upon their heads, they saw not only Susan's fearful ire, but the Sixth Fleet in their harbour.

In any event, no further attempt was made to touch Justine, and so we proceeded onto the bus, and without further incident boarded it. Justine was crying with terror, but Susan was entirely dry-eyed. There was no hint of fear and certainly no hint of regret for her frightening outburst. Her gaze and posture showed nothing save the awesome power of the same maternal care I saw in the women of Nairobi nearly twenty years later, and which we who make up the other half of humankind must treasure and revere above all other forms of physical and spiritual courage . . . or cease to call ourselves men.

Martha's Vineyard

'The passing away of ineffective things,' H.G. Wells once wrote, '. . . is the essence of tragedy . . . The life that has schemed and struggled and committed itself, the life that has played and lost, comes at last to the pitiless judgment of time, and is slowly and remorselessly annihilated. This is the saddest chapter of biological science – the tragedy of Extinction.'

Sad indeed, but also very common. For the biological history of the earth is a chronicle of both immensely slow and startlingly rapid disappearances, the former having to do with changes in climate, sea levels, outbreaks of disease or the encroachment of invasive species, the latter with the sudden impact of asteroids.

These changes, and their accompanying extinctions, have been both numerous and extensive. It is hard to imagine any part of the planet that has not known a creature that it knows no more.

Even so, only one place on earth, Martha's Vineyard, Massachusetts, so carefully recorded such a disappearance that it is possible to locate within only a few square miles where this last of its kind met the worst of all possible fates. And so it seemed to me that if biological extinction truly was, as Wells wrote, 'the saddest chapter of biological science', then surely there would be no sadder place on earth with regard to that tragedy than Martha's Vineyard, where the final days of a specific species had been recorded with such melancholy attention to detail.

Susan was supposed to have gone with me to Martha's Vineyard that day, but a week or so before, she'd suddenly felt a pain in her back, one that, despite a round of physical therapy, had not been relieved.

'You go,' she told me that morning, when she made the final decision. 'Besides, I've been there before.'

Martha's Vineyard is an island off Cape Cod. It is only a short ferry ride from Hyannis to Oak's Bluff, one of the island's principal towns. I'd had a book signing scheduled at a local bookstore that morning, after which I'd planned to walk around a bit, think about the essay I would write about the place, perhaps stumble upon some aspect of this visit that would put everything into perspective, all that I'd read about extinction, particularly the one that had occurred here in 1932.

Its Latin name was *Tympanuchus cupido cupido*, but it was commonly known as the heath hen. In adulthood it was around seventeen inches long from the end of its beak to the tip of its tail. It weighed about two pounds, heavy for its length, a plump bird, though according to those who'd tried it, not particularly good eating. Even so it was so relentlessly hunted, both by

334

humans and by other predators, that by 1870 – some say much earlier – none was left on the mainland.

Three hundred still remained on Martha's Vineyard at that time, but over the next two decades that number steadily declined, so that perhaps as few as seventy were all that remained on the island by the end of the century. This was sufficiently alarming for the government to act. Thus, in 1908 a 5,100-acre heath hen reserve was created in land that is now a state park. The hope was that this measure would save the heath hen from extinction, and for a time it seemed to work. Within a few years its population on Martha's Vineyard had soared to over two thousand.

This was delightful news because by then the heath hen had become something of a tourist attraction.

And why not, since the heath hen was quite a performer, particularly during mating season, when the males spread the pinnates atop their heads so that they fanned out like rabbit ears. Thus crowned, they pranced about, dragging their tails behind them like feathered capes. During this part of the show, the sacks on either side of the neck inflated to the size and colour of a small orange, while at the same time producing a sound one observer described as resembling a puff of wind blown across the top of a bottle. No sound at all was made as the sacks deflated, but that didn't bother the heath hen, who proceeded to dance without accompaniment, stamping its feet one after another, before repeating this repertoire all over again, spreading its pinnates, inflating its sacks, then tooting so loudly, it could be heard – according to reports – from a mile away. Nor did this Elvis do only one show before leaving the building. In the case of the tireless heath hen, the spectacle went on from dawn to dusk.

Given these charms, it was not surprising that once the heath hen was seen truly to be in grave danger of extinction, every effort was made – for the first time in American history with regard to a bird – to save it.

But as with mankind, there is also a tide in the affairs of birds, and after 1910, that tide began to go decidedly against the heath hen, and as is also common in such matters, it came in successive waves.

The first of them was fire. In May of 1916, a disastrous conflagration swept the very area of Martha's Vineyard that had been set aside as the heath hen's preserve. Added to this tragedy was the fact that the fire occurred at a time when the birds were nesting. For that reason, the females, whom nature had made protective to the point of suicide, remained in their nests, shielding their young, and so along with their unborn, they were consumed by the flames. The males fled. From that time on, the ratio of males to females among the heath hens on Martha's Vineyard was grossly unbalanced, and unlikely ever to be righted.

With this fire, the heath hen's descent towards extinction began in earnest despite every effort of the Massachusetts Fish and Game Commission. Those efforts were sincere, varied and desperate. Corn was planted in the preserve, along with sunflowers and clover in hope of supplying the remaining heath hens with a ready supply of food. An attempt was also made to concentrate the birds so that their condition could be more closely monitored. A game commissioner took up residence in the preserve to oversee the commission's efforts and to discourage poaching.

Despite these efforts, yet more powerful forces gathered like a dark army against the heath hen's small encampment. Their great rarity made them a target for collectors who paid local hunters to kill or capture 'specimens'. Their popularity, particularly as a result of the mating ritual, attracted more people to Martha's Vineyard and some of these visitors, known locally as the 'summer people', were given kittens to kill mice in their summer residences. With the approach of autumn, when the summer people returned to their winter homes, these kittens, by then cats, were left to their own devices and quickly became the feral predatory prowlers of the heath hen's preserve. To this was added another lethal element, this one related once again to the great courage of the female heath hen who, at the approach of a motor car, would lift into the air and flutter crazily in order to distract the driver from a brood at that very moment huddled in one of the muddy road's deep ruts. Unfortunately, it was this same distraction that prevented the driver from seeing the brood and thus from running over it.

And, of course, there were more fires, many set by farmers clearing land for their crops of blueberries.

By 1927, it was estimated that only thirty or so heath hens were left on Martha's Vineyard. Worse still, the female population, so disastrously diminished by fire, and their own maternal nature, had been reduced to perhaps only two. These spare numbers continued to decrease so that only half a dozen or so remained by the end of that same year. None of that number was female, and so the death knell began to toll.

Finally, only a single, solitary male remained on the Vineyard. Someone dubbed him 'Booming Ben' because it is said that he tirelessly and very loudly and with ceaseless hope continued the tooting of his kind, the frantic dancing, the inflating and deflating of his orange sacks, the spreading of his pinnates, his crown of feathers. On 1 April 1931, he was trapped and a band, number 407,880, was placed on his left leg. A second band, this one numbered A-634-024 was placed on his right leg. Then he was released.

Booming Ben was last seen on 11 March 1932 – early in the breeding season. He boomed and danced and glanced towards heaven for the miracle of a mate.

But none came. At the end of the breeding season, he left the lekking ground so many had honourably done so much to protect. He was never seen again.

Even so, hope remained until the vanishing of the heath hen was made official by the publication of its obituary in the *Vineyard Gazette* on 21 April 1933.

Somewhere on the great plain of Martha's Vineyard, death and the heath hen have met. One day, just as usual, there was a bird called the heath hen, and the next day there was none. How he came to his end no human being can know.

But the death of wild birds is a violent death. The eye becomes dimmed, the beat of the wings lags ever so little, the star of fortune blinks for a fraction of a second – it is enough. An enemy strikes and death has come. Somewhere on the great plain, under the black twigs of a scrub oak, swift death and the heath hen have met.

When I returned to Cape Cod that evening I felt sad at the loss of the heath hen, though not without knowing that countless other species had become extinct both before and after. The tragedy of its loss was only a small part of that greater tragedy which, according to Wells, was the ineluctable fate of 'ineffective' things.

But how much deeper the loss, as I was soon to ask myself, of effective things.

Only a week or so after my return from Martha's Vineyard it became clear that Susan's back pain was getting no better. She reported this to her doctor, who ordered an MRI. A few days later, the doctor asked Susan to come into her office so that they could discuss the results of the test.

Those results were terribly disturbing. Susan's breast cancer of over ten years before had returned. It had invaded multiple sites. It was in her lungs. It was in her liver. Worst of all, it was sprinkled up and down her spine, and it was this that had caused the pain in her back.

I called a medically influential friend in New York City, and Susan was immediately given an evaluative consultation at Dana

Farber in Boston. At Dana Farber, Susan's doctor was quite optimistic. She prescribed letrozole, a hormonal treatment. Susan and I left this first meeting very much relieved, since we had been given every indication that Susan might live quite well for a long time, and, of course, during those coming years, we could hope for some breakthrough in the treatment of metastatic breast cancer.

But it was not to be. The letrozole proved ineffective. Susan's cancer grew. She was taken off letrozole and put on an oral chemo known as xeloda. Although she avoided the worst of this drug's side effects, she lost her appetite, became terribly fatigued, and began to lose her wit, her lively spirit, her facility with words, every element of the extraordinary intelligence and knowingness that had defined her.

'I hate this,' she said to me one night.

All I could answer was, 'I know.'

We managed to survive a terrible winter on Cape Cod, followed by a spring and summer during which Susan's mental and physical suffering only increased. She who had travelled the world, who had trudged through jungles and mounted the Acropolis, who had hazarded the Cliffs of Moher and looked down upon the Seto Inland Sea from the Misen heights of Miyajima, now moved forwards only with my help or with a walker, or, increasingly, in a wheelchair. She who had edited books and papers and jokingly but pointedly corrected the grammar of just about everyone she knew found it nearly impossible to find ordinary words, to put a sentence together, to finish a thought.

'I am no longer me,' she said.

'You will always be you,' I assured her.

And so she remained, very much fiercely Susan, fighting all the way, continuing her treatments long after I privately had given up on them and enquired of her doctor if they might be stopped, a possibility Susan's doctor cautiously suggested to Susan herself. 'There comes a time,' she said, 'when the treatment may be doing more harm than the disease.'

But Susan did not want to stop fighting, and so the treatments were continued through the following spring and summer.

By then Justine had come home several times to be of help.

'This is terrible,' she told me at one point.

'Yes, it is,' I said. 'But the treatment has to continue until your mother stops it.'

She nodded resignedly. 'I know.'

As the end of summer approached, Justine made it clear that she would not allow us to remain alone on Cape Cod for another winter. We were to come to Los Angeles, where she now lived with Sean, her companion in life. We would stay with them until the end came. Because we knew that Susan's true joy was travel, we told her that we would rent a Winnebago and visit the Badlands, Monument Valley, the Grand Canyon, the Painted Desert, Mount Rushmore, all places Susan and I had intended to visit in the autumn of our lives when we no longer had the stamina required by our earlier pursuits.

With this hope in mind, we arrived in early November. Susan's care had been transferred to a doctor at UCLA, who immediately took her off xeloda, and instead prescribed a different drug, faslodex, administered by injection once a month. She also ordered a new round of CTs and MRIs.

A week later, Justine told Susan that she was pregnant. Susan cried, happy for our daughter, but no doubt suspecting, though she never said so, that she would never see her first grandchild.

Over the next two weeks, her condition rapidly declined. Her mental processes markedly deteriorated. She could no longer read or even watch television. She stopped eating, and rarely seemed entirely conscious.

Two days before we were to have another consultation at UCLA, her doctor called. She had reviewed the results of the latest tests. They were very grim. Susan's cancer had spread in all its previous sites, and, in addition, had now invaded her ribcage and penetrated her brain.

'What do we do now?' I asked.

There were two options: radiation to the brain or the withdrawal of all treatment.

I talked with Justine. We made the decision to withdraw treatment. Then we held each other and cried. I called the doctor, who ordered in-home hospice care. 'You and your daughter have made the most loving decision possible,' she said.

Susan died at 11.04 a.m. on 17 December 2014, just eight days after her sixty-second birthday. I called the crematorium, then Justine and I washed Susan's body and dressed her neatly in the sombre colors she preferred.

Two hours later men from the crematorium arrived, and Susan was taken from us – our last glimpse was of her silver hair.

The California official who'd been sent to catalogue and destroy the unused drugs looked up from her work to see Justine and me weeping in each other's arms. 'This house has so much love,' she said.

And indeed it did.

An hour later, Justine and I sent out the following message to Susan's many friends around the world:

Dear Friends:

It is with a tragic sense of loss that we report the death this morning of Susan Terner, my dear wife, and the beloved mother of our daughter, Justine.

Susan wished to be cremated, and so she will be. She also wished that there be no memorial service, and so there won't be.

Even so, Justine and I would ask that you remember Susan fondly as one who danced on table tops in Paris, Madrid and New York City; who belted songs and directed actors on the stages of Cape Cod; who put every conceivable thing in a plastic bag; who never saw a hammock or a cat she didn't love; who staunchly held to her non-belief through all her pain and anguish; who edited manuscripts so superbly her method is taught in master classes; who incessantly corrected everyone's grammar, and once told a doctor to stop touching the bottom of his shoes; whose true vocation, as I often reminded her, would have been to be the Third Grade Teacher of the World; who loved to eat almost anything forbidden by Judaism, but couldn't resist belly lox, whitefish or full-sour pickles; whose favorite song was 'Send in the Clowns'; who used 'asshole' as a term of endearment; whose crap detector always functioned at 100% efficiency; who suffered fools not at all; who loved travel more than anything, and who, as a consequence, lived to kiss the Blarney Stone, see sunrise at Uluru and Ingrid Bergman on a London Stage and the light show in Hong Kong, who lived to be charged by an elephant in Ghana, take a boat to the Devil's Throat in Argentina, see a bullfight in Spain, stand silently before the ghostly dome in Hiroshima; who lived to weep at Auschwitz, the American Cemetery at Meuse-Argonne and in the slaughtered village of Oradour-sur-Glane; who defended her daughter against a frightening mob in Tangiers and an old woman against a bully in Macy's on one memorably courageous afternoon; who lived to leave behind a husband and a daughter who loved her as few people have ever been loved, and who feel quite certain that all who knew and loved Susan will agree that we shall never see her like again.

By the following April, I was back on Cape Cod, trying to complete this book.

I had often planned for the last dark place to be Martha's Vineyard, its poignant tale of the heath hen's fate. But any memories of my earlier trip to the island had long ago faded into the sixteen-month fog of Susan's illness. I would have to go back.

And so, towards the middle of May, I boarded a ferry and headed once again for Martha's Vineyard.

This time I ferried out to the island by way of Woods Hole, a much shorter crossing. Two old friends, Janine and Richard Perry, came with me, perhaps feeling that I should not make this trip alone.

Within a few hours, we'd found the area where the heath hen reserve had been located and which now held two memorials to its extinction, one a large statue of the bird itself, the other a plaque embedded in a large stone, at the base of which people had left small reminders in the form of plastic birds of various colours.

In past visits, Susan and I had stayed the night on Martha's Vineyard, but without her, I had no reason to stay. And so we all took the afternoon ferry back to Woods Hole. By twilight, I was back in the house Susan and I had for so many years shared on Cape Cod.

That night, I began my essay on the heath hen's extinction. Over the next few days I wrote the pages that you have just read, then faced that inevitable final paragraph, the one during which, in earlier essays, I had sometimes found some small light in whatever dark place Susan and I had come to see.

Now alone in the house, I could find no such light when it came to the heath hen. Had Susan lived, we would have talked about the visit to Martha's Vineyard over subsequent dinners or while having that evening glass of wine on the deck. But those talks were no more. Indeed, it seemed to me that with her death, much of life's shine, along with the soft music of a long companionship, had vanished like the heath hen. Like that fabled bird, Susan was gone. She had been one of a kind. And now she was extinct.

Thinking of all that, I found that I disagreed with the eminent H.G. Wells. For it seemed to me that it was not the passing away of ineffective 'things' that was life's greatest tragedy. It was the passing away of awesomely effective human beings, those whose lives become a texture in the lives of others, and in that way, hold back the ever-encroaching darkness that is natural to life. This was the only conclusion I could reach by way of Martha's Vineyard, and it added no cuddly warmth to the extinction that had been the heath hen's fate, as surely as it was Susan's. For the melancholy truth is this: there are limits to how much a dark place can relieve and restore you when the dark place is your own, when you have reached the tragic shore within you, and learned that here, at least for now, there is no light. There is only the necessity to go on.

Which is what I did over the next weeks and months, simply reading, thinking, listening to music, enjoying the fellowship of friends, talking with Justine, expecting no further word from any one of the many dark places I had visited with Susan, until that place suddenly announced itself to me so vividly and in a voice so fully audible, I half thought I'd actually heard Susan speak in that direct and commanding voice of hers:

Remember what you learned in Place de Grève.

Snapshot: Place de Grève

What I'd learned in Place de Grève was the simple value of knowing. Thousands of people stroll across the plaza every day without experiencing the pity that overwhelmed Victor Hugo each time he traversed it. The difference between the two is that Victor Hugo was one of those who knew its history quite well. I, on the other hand, had learned that history very late, and only after having passed through it many times.

In fact, anyone who has been to Paris has almost certainly been through Place de Grève, for it is the plaza that sweeps out before the city's striking Hôtel de Ville. It rests on the right bank of the Seine, near the Pompidou Centre, so that it is hard to miss it even if you are on your way, as most people are when they pass through it, to somewhere else.

Place de Grève is much used by Parisians. It is often filled with makeshift shops, and at my most recent visit, a brightly coloured carousel occupied one of its spacious corners. It is a well-travelled route from the banks of the Seine, from which it got its name (*grève* means 'strand') into the busy streets of one of the busier parts of Paris. At Place de Grève, people are often in a hurry. In the morning they scurry over the cobblestones to get to their jobs in nearby shops and offices. At the end of their work day, they no less hurriedly reverse course. As in every such place, there are those who lounge, tourists taking a rest, retirees taking the air, but the general atmosphere is of a plaza through which people pass rather than in which they linger. That is certainly how I had many times moved through it, and would have continued to walk it had I not learned a little of what Hugo knew, a smidgen of what he knew, really, but enough for me to stop, think a moment, then say to myself, 'Oh, it was here.'

Here, where on 1 March 1757 a public execution occurred that was arguably the most hideous in human history, an act Thomas Paine believed specifically designed to banish tenderness from the human heart and at which sight, Thomas Carlyle wrote, the stars themselves must surely have wept.

But long before that dreadful spectacle, Place de Grève had been a central site of tortures. It was here Parisians gathered for a midsummer festival whose cruel oddity Sir George Frazier briefly described in *The Golden Bough*:

> In the midsummer fires formerly kindled on the Place de Grève at Paris it was the custom to burn a basket, barrel, or sack full of live cats, which was hung from a tall mast in the midst of the bonfire.

This public celebration, Frazier goes on to tell us, was often attended by the kings of France, whose prerogative it was to light the bonfire. Louis XIV had done just that, wearing a crown of roses, and after which he had treated his subjects to a rousing, royal dance.

The zoosadism associated with the burning of cats at Place de Grève is certainly deplorable, but it was the cruel agonies that had been inflicted upon a singularly unfortunate human being that forever changed my appreciation – and I do mean appreciation – for it.

They'd been torments so precisely orchestrated, and attended with such cheering exuberance, they'd not escaped artistic notice. For example, at a site called art.com, where it is possible to buy *Starry Night* and *The Great Wave off Kanagawa*, connoisseurs of public execution can also find posters that depict the hanging of Anne du Bourg at Place de Grève in 1559 and the death by guillotine of Georges Cadoudal in 1804. The celebrated poisoner Antoine Desrues had also died here, along with François Ravaillac, the regicide, who was scalded and flayed before being drawn and quartered.

The death that had chilled Paine's heart, however, was that of Robert-François Damiens, a method of execution that had been arrived at by means of a nationwide contest, the winner being that Frenchman who could devise the most hideous of means. History does not record the winner of that contest, but the contents of his entry had become quite clear by the time the sun set over Paris on 28 March 1757.

349

On that morning, forty-two-year-old Robert-François Damiens was taken in a cart, wearing nothing but a shirt, and holding a torch made of candle wax, to Place de Grève, where a scaffold had been erected for the benefit of the viewing public. Charles Manselet reported huge crowds in Rue de la Tannerie, huge crowds at Rue de l'Epine and at Rue de Mouton, along with a massive throng on Place de Grève itself.

Just how many people in that throng were actually able to see Damiens is unclear, but chroniclers made the point that the crowd was huge, spilling out of the plaza and into its adjoining streets. The nearer seats were purchased, and it is said that people came from all over Europe to attend the event. 'For this was a festival,' as the Marquis de Sade is made to say in Peter Weiss's play, 'beside which our modern festivals must pale.'

Nor was the marquis the only famous Frenchman to observe Damiens' torment.

Casanova watched from a nearby balcony.

For the next few hours – and it was hours – Damiens was put through a series of tortures. First his right hand, the one that had held the knife with which he'd attempted to kill Louis XV, was burnt with sulphur. Then the fleshy parts of his body, his thighs, arms and chest, were slit open, the skin pulled back with hot pincers. After that, his other wounds were also doused with sulphur, but also with a mixture of molten lead, boiling oil, burning resin, wax.

Damiens still lived, and from all accounts, though he cried

out, he did not curse his torturers, and according to witnesses, he would sometimes struggle to lift his head and view his wounds, then drift back and await those that were to follow.

As the tortures continued, Damiens weakened, but did not fail. His screams became moans, but his eyes remained open and he often, and with complete lucidity, asked for a mercy he did not receive.

Lying on his back during pauses in his agony – for even torturers (in this case, there were six) must take a break, make preparations, mix the wax and resin, heat the irons – he would have been able to see much of what anyone crossing Place de Grève today would also see, though the terraces of the buildings would have been crowded with spectators.

Damien's final agony was a horribly bungled attempt to draw and quarter him. Chains were attached to his arms and legs, but the horses brought in to pull those chains were unaccustomed to complicity in torture, so that they had to be brutally whipped in order to drive them forward. Even so, they baulked, so that two other horses were added, whipped, and whipped again, but still they could not manage to pull Damien's limbs from his torso. This process alone took over an hour, and through it all Damiens remained entirely conscious, though witnesses claimed that by then his hair was white.

In the only act of mercy granted Damiens that day, it was at last decided that the muscles and tendons of his arms and legs should be sawed through. This would allow the horses to do their job. It worked. First one leg, then another, then one arm, then the other, and with each lost limb, a roar went up from the crowd.

Through all of this, Damiens remained alive, but he no longer pleaded for mercy or cried out in pain. Rather, he once again sought to glimpse what had been done to his body, but now with a look that struck observers as one of simple curiosity. Damiens had reached that moment when shock at last had numbed him, so that following that final glance, his head lolled backward and at last he died.

'Such was the end of that poor unfortunate who it may well be believed suffered the greatest tortures that a human being has ever been called upon to endure,' wrote the Duke de Croy, whose detailed description of Damiens' ordeal is the most often quoted in any account of what occurred on Place de Grève that day.

And such also was now my experience of Place de Grève, an experience that carried with it one of the vital lessons of knowing not only the charm of a place, but its darker history. For there was an enormous difference between visiting this plaza before I knew that history, and particularly with reference to the suffering of Damiens, and the times when I had come here bereft of that knowledge.

And 'bereft' is the right word, for it connotes something valuable you have been denied, and carries with it a sense of bereavement, the grief that accompanies loss. The fact is, for all the many times I had visited Place de Grève, noticed its pace, its small charms, its central location, I had failed to know its darkness, and for that reason, I had felt nothing memorable or of particular note during any of those earlier visits. Place de Grève might have been Saint-Germain-des-Prés or Place des Vosges or any other equally charming part of Paris. It was like a passing acquaintance, someone to whom I spoke casually and who replied casually, but with whom I had never had a serious conversation.

But with Damiens' execution, Place de Grève had opened to me in the same way that the modest little Busento had opened to Justine so many years before, so that, like her, I knew that this place would remain with me always and that though I might visit it many times in the future, it would be with a far greater and richer appreciation of it, with indifference replaced by reverence, forever after remembering that March day in 1757 when the very air around me would have trembled with Damiens' cries.

Remember what you learned in Place de Grève. Such had been Susan's good counsel, and by hearing it and heeding it, I felt myself regain my footing. The dark places we had shared were as valuable to us as the bright shining days we had known in Madrid, in Provence, in Donegal and West Africa, in Australia and on Cape Cod, and, yes, even at Disneyland in Orlando, Florida.

In the comforting wake of that understanding, I recalled the uncomprehending look I'd noticed on people's faces when I'd first begun to write this book. They'd seemed to think it the most depressing of efforts. It would drain all joy from travel, they said, and seemed to think me a professional depressive bent upon making others as depressed as myself.

But Place de Grève, both in remembering it and later when I visited it again, now without Susan, confirmed my original point, that the homage we pay to dark places ennobles and enriches us. Visiting them does not drain light from either life or travel, but it does drain triviality from both, and by that means lends something immemorial to our own brief lives. To avoid such places is to avoid the deepest experiences of humanity, to turn away from its many injustices and its long travail, that part of our legacy that is textured by our loss. To turn away from Place de Grève is to sanitize our collective memory, to hide it behind a drapery of pleasing illusion, to shave our experience with so radical a blade that we are left half believing that all our streets and houses, all our canyons, beaches, fields, all our forests and ravines are essentially the same. It is the spiritual and intellectual equivalent of listening only to Christmas music.

I was thinking of all this some months after Susan's death when I remembered what had probably been the last conversation I'd had with her on the subject of this book. Years of travel still lay ahead, we'd thought, for we had not yet discovered that she was deathly ill, that there would be no more journeying together, that our world was soon to shrink to a sickroom bristling with pills and creams and all the other many aids and appliances that come into use as a human life slowly gutters out.

On that day in late spring, as we'd strolled through a wooded area of Cape Cod, I'd brought up the subject of how this book should end. We'd talked about the places we'd been. Should it end with Auschwitz? Should the last place be Kalaupapa?

Or should I aim for a softer landing, perhaps the 'snapshot' of Cosenza, or that edifying little episode in Granada? I once again suggested Martha's Vineyard, but Susan wasn't persuaded.

'Where, then?' I asked.

She considered the question, but as I could tell, no particular site made an obvious bid to come last.

It didn't matter, I thought, besides, there were places yet to visit, miles to go before we slept.

'I guess it will reveal itself in time,' I said confidently and fully expected to go on to another subject.

But Susan kept thinking, walking silently beside me until she suddenly stopped, then turned to me and said, 'I don't think you should end the book with any particular place you've been.'

When she saw that I didn't get her meaning, she added, 'I think you should end it by facing the darkest personal fact there is, that one day you won't be able to go to dark places any more.'

She meant death, of course, that darkness, total and eternal, that, according to her 'faith' and mine, awaits us all.

'So write about all the places you would go if you could make the case for darkness forever,' she added.

Then she smiled, clearly pleased at the startling rightness of the ending for *Tragic Shores* she had envisioned. 'An itinerary.'

And I thought, *Of course.*

The Case for Darkness: An Itinerary

London was the first place Susan and I visited. We were in our twenties. Justine had not yet been born. We stayed in a tiny room in Belgravia, and walked the streets of London in a swoon of joy. At some point I'd read a celebrated passage from Lord Macaulay's *History of England*. In that passage, he had designated a little chapel known as St Peter ad Vincula (St Peter in chains) as the saddest place on earth.

We knew it was in the Tower of London, and on our first morning in the city, we set off to find it.

A few minutes later we caught sight of it, a large, austere fortress that loomed over the Thames. It was flatly monochromatic, and although a few little flourishes had been chipped into the stonework, its severe grey walls suggested not just power, but besieged, perhaps even paranoid, power. Prisoners could be kept within its walls, certainly. But other forces, rival armies, rebellious subjects and the like could also be kept outside them.

In that way, the Tower seemed to question the value of the very thing it protected, and by doing so, it made power and the people who both wield and covet it seem prisoners of their own designs.

Unfortunately, this first visit to the Tower failed even to suggest the power we would later find in dark places. There were Beefeaters in their bright-coloured attire, ravens prancing obliviously on the green, vendors hawking T-shirts, banners, plastic swords, and everywhere, the noise and bustle of crowds eager to see the Crown Jewels or the Royal Armouries. The atmosphere was jovial, nearly carnival, the footpaths crowded, and everywhere, everywhere, children scurrying about, crawling over this, jumping from that, the Tower, in that sense, imaginatively transformed into a stone-faced whirligig.

'They've reduced it to an attraction,' Susan said.

Reduced was the right word. And so, yes, we were disappointed by the playground atmosphere. But we'd been far too young and unschooled in the enduring rewards of dark places to let that reduction keep us from enjoying the sheer thrill of a first trip abroad together. Besides, there is delight simply in watching other people delight, and the people at the Tower were clearly having fun. And so we continued to walk about the Tower's grounds, and as we did so, that initial disappointment fell away, and we accepted the Tower for what it was, rather than some notion of what we'd hoped it to be.

Even so, Lord Macaulay had felt something darkly powerful here, and so we made it our business to locate the specific place he'd designated as the saddest spot on earth.

The Royal Chapel was modest, with relatively little to catch the eye of the people who twined among the dead, looking for the most famous among them. Here and there, a discovery was made, and someone would cry out, 'Here's So and So.' Heads would turn and a rustle of feet would carry a little knot of tourists over to where the famous one lay. For a moment, they would peer down at this celebrity gravesite, their faces either blank or vaguely perplexed, as if unable to decide exactly how they should act in the presence, if it can be called that, of a famous person who happened to be dead.

We remained in St Peter's longer than most of these other visitors, but after a time, it was clear that the chapel was not having a similar effect on us to the one it had had on Lord Macaulay, and so we strolled back out onto the Tower Green.

It was then I noticed a large wooden block. It was along one of the pathways that led to the Chapel. People milled around the block, though none stayed for too long, so that within a few seconds we'd inched our way near enough to get a good look at it.

It was only two or three feet high, brown in colour, and completely without adornment. But there were various chop marks on the block, some very deep, and thus evidence enough that on certain occasions the blade had come down with the shuddering force of execution.

I had no idea how many people might have lost their heads on this particular block, but I suddenly thought of Lady Jane Grey, perhaps because her age, only sixteen, made her death more poignant to me. In any event, I found myself imagining the last minutes of this poor girl's life. On the scaffold, she'd been confused as to how things were to be done and asked the executioner if her head was to be taken off as she knelt. He'd replied, 'No, Madam,' so she'd endeavoured to find the block in order to lay her head upon it. But she'd been blindfolded and so, uncertain of where the block was, she'd finally asked, 'What shall I do? Where is it?'

What shall I do? Meaning: *What shall I do* so as to carry out this grim ceremony as graciously as possible? She'd asked this question like a child seeking to determine which utensil to use with which course. She had asked it because during the last dwindling moments of her life this no doubt terrified young girl had sought to comport herself according to the formal rules of the occasion: in this case, the social graces of the scaffold. She had all her life been taught, above all, to be polite, to be well mannered, to behave correctly, a lesson – as the final seconds of her life so hauntingly attest – she had learned very well indeed.

At that moment, thinking of this young girl's last question, something of what Macaulay had called 'whatever is darkest in human nature and in human destiny' suddenly became a part of my experience in the Tower. But it had come to me *despite* the Tower, rather than because of it, for the Tower had summoned nothing, and during the coming years it would become even less capable of summoning the gravity of its own history.

Years later, when Susan and I visited the Tower again, and for what would be the last time, we saw that it had been stripped of everything but commercial enterprise. Tickets were now dispensed at extravagantly high prices from ultramodern glass booths. There were five different gift shops: the Jewel House Shop which specialized in jewellery 'inspired' by the Crown Jewels, the Medieval Palace Shop with offerings no doubt equally inspired by the Middle Ages, the Beefeater Shop whose wares were not difficult to imagine, the White Tower Shop, located in what had once been the Tower's all too busy torture chambers, and the flagship Tower Shop, a multi-level emporium whose many display cases contained an dizzyingly ahistorical collection of wares, everything from bottles of 'Ration Book Plum Wine' to photographs of Winston Churchill cradling a sub-machine gun.

Worst still, the wooden block that had brought Lady Jane Grey's death so vividly to mind all those many years before had been replaced by as bizarre a memorial to public execution as I have ever seen: a circle of glass about the size of a large coffee table with a crystal pillow at its centre, as if the executed had been brought here for an afternoon nap. As such, it was about as moving as a Las Vegas ice sculpture.

In fact, only the words that adorned the base of this memorial gave any sense of what had happened here, and they proved so forgettable that I instantly forgot them, turned and headed back through the milling crowd, past the shops and finally beyond the walls of the Tower.

Fortunately, by then we'd discovered that a great many dark places did not share the Tower's failure to move those who visit them. We'd also discovered that during the course of a single lifetime, one can barely touch what Alexander Pope rightly called 'the sad variety of woe'. Even so, we'd remained convinced that we should try and fully believed that in the years that lay ahead, we would continue our odd quest. Perhaps in old age, when we were 'full of sleep and nodding by the fire', we might even begin to ponder which among the many dark places we'd visited had actually been the saddest place on earth.

But that was not to be, and so, following Susan's advice with regard to how this book should end, I have come to ask myself not which dark place was darkest of them all, but to consider how many tragic shores yet remain to be visited and revered, a list that could stretch out into eternity if eternity were mine.

But it is not.

So here.

I would go to Prince William Sound, where the *Exxon Valdez* spewed millions of gallons of oil into a breathtakingly beautiful and delicate natural habitat.

I would go to Schloss Hartheim, the seventeenth-century Austrian castle that had provided refuge for the mentally disabled for half a century before it was taken over by the Nazis and converted into the worst of the country's six 'Aktion T4' centres, and after which some thirty thousand mental 'defectives' were 'euthanized'.

I would go to Chernobyl.

I would go to the site of the Alexandria Library, which burned down four times, conflagrations that cumulatively resulted in the loss of 95 per cent of the literature of antiquity.

I would go to the Yellow River, whose 1931 flood was perhaps the greatest natural disaster of all time.

I would go to Lake Issyk-Kul, in eastern Kyrgyzstan, where many historians believe the Great Plague began.

I would go to Magadan, the gateway to the Gulag, and to Nazino, where in May 1933, six thousand people were summarily deposited without food or shelter and whose subsequent ordeal renamed the place where it was endured: Cannibal Island.

I would go to Goa, Democratic Republic of Congo, where, following the Rwandan genocide, the most ambitious humanitarian relief effort of all time devolved into the greatest 'hijacking' – the word used by *Médecins Sans Frontières* in its condemnation of it – of that same humanitarian aide in human history.

I would go to Dachau, Sachsenhausen, Ravensbrück, Treblinka and Babi Yar.

I would go to Kayaköy, the formally Greek town from which all Greeks were driven in 1922 at the end of Greco-Turkish War, and which remains a ghost town monument to their suffering.

I would go to Gallipoli.

I would go to Bhopal, India, where, on the night of 2–3 December 1984, a leak of poison gas at the Union Carbide chemical plant killed 3,787 people whose only crime was to fall asleep.

I would go to Drancy, a short ride outside Paris, where the Jews of that fabled city where held in horrible conditions before being sent on to Auschwitz.

I would go to Masada.

I would go to Bamiyan in the Hazarajat region of Afghanistan, where the great Buddhas were destroyed in March of 2001, statues so magisterial in size that the process took several weeks, because, as the Taliban leader in charge of this demolition declared, 'This work of destruction is not as simple as people might think.' Indeed.

I would go to Shaanxi, China, where, in a single quake, nearly a million lives were lost.

I would go to Stari Most, the old bridge in Mostar, Bosnia, that had stood for 427 years before Croat forces wantonly destroyed it on 9 November 1993.

I would go to Culloden, where the Highland Scots were slaughtered.

I would go to Sand Creek, where, on 29 November 1864, a 700-man force of the Colorado Militia massacred all the inhabitants of an entirely peaceful Cheyenne-Arapaho village, two-thirds of the dead having been women and children.

I would go to Wounded Knee.

I would go to Hama, Syria, where over a period of twenty-seven days, in February 1982, the Syrian Army massacred perhaps as many as forty thousand men women and children in what one historian has called 'the single deadliest act by any Arab government against its own people in the modern Middle East'.

I would go to Andersonville.

I would go to Nicosia, Cyprus, the last world capital to be formally divided by ethnicity, in this case by a Green Line that physically divides the Greek and Turkish parts of the city.

I would go to Koh Kra, in the Gulf of Thailand, where in

December of 1979 hundreds of Vietnamese 'boat people' were taken to be killed, raped and sold into sexual slavery by Thai pirates. A small plaque on the beach commemorates this enormous loss.

I would go to Amritsar.

And what of famine? A cursory internet review reveals that Medieval Britain was struck by famine ninety-five times. France was struck at least seventy-five times. Between 109 BC and 1911 AD, China was ravaged by 1,828 famines. The toll of famine is awesome. In 1097, a famine in Palestine killed half a million people. Between 1601 and 1603 one third of Russians starved. In France, in 1693–4, the toll was two million. The following year, one fifth of Estonians died of hunger. The year after that, famine claimed a hundred thousand Swedes and one third of the population of Finland. It should be added that these numbers, along with those of the modern period, pale beside the twentieth-century famines of China (estimates run from twenty to forty-three million) and the old Soviet Union (around fifteen million). Where might one go in order to pay due homage to so dark and widespread a fate? I confess that I do not know.

But were I not physically or financially able to visit these dark places, I would remind myself that there are other tragic shores, many of which lie much closer to home. Recently a friend of mine wrote:

I was only there once. I walked through the double entry on a stifling hot August day. I remember that the day was like many of those summer days in Southern Illinois. It was a day without shadows where it was so hot the light from the sun was white and bleached the color out of everything. The dark lobby was chilled. Not from air conditioning, but from lifelessness. Ugly stained yellow shades blocked out light from the tall, ornate turn-of-the-century windows. The lobby was empty except for old mattresses stacked up along one wall and a half-dead bat flapping its wings on the floor in front of me. I turned around, walked out, went to my car and cried. There was a three-year-old child stuck in that horrible building (along with a lot of other children) and I didn't have the will, courage, what have you, to cross that dark lobby, climb its grand staircase and do an intake, perhaps giving a bit of hope to that child's future. I quit the job in a matter of days after the incident. I have traveled extensively, known a lot of people, been a lot of places, but the LeClede Hotel stands out as the saddest place on earth to me.

Nothing happened there of a historical nature. It was just a welfare hotel, but to my friend, it had all the aspects of the saddest place on earth.

In short, there are many dark places with cases to be made, and whether far or near, each is waiting with a gift, the very least and most rudimentary of which is the knowledge that in the face of devastating loss, each of us must find a reason, however personal, to go on, if for no more compelling reason than, by the anguished, mourning millions, those destined to survive their own tragic shores have done exactly that.

Selected Bibliography

Abelard, Peter, *The Story of My Misfortunes*, Dover Publications, 2005.

Applebaum, Anne, *Gulag: A History*, Anchor Books, 2004.

Arnold, Catharine, *Bedlam: London and Its Mad*, Simon and Schuster, 2008.

Bataille, George, *The Trial of Gilles de Rais*, Amok Books, 2004.

Bess, Michael, *Choices Under Fire: Moral Dimensions of World War II*, Knopf, 2006.

Bollinger, Martin J., *Stalin's Slave Ships: Kolyma, the Gulag Fleet, and the Role of the West*, Naval Institute Press, 2003.

Brinkley, Joel, *Cambodia's Curse*, Public Affairs, 2012.

Burge, James, *Heloise & Abelard*, Harper, 2003.

Buttimer, Anne, *Geography and the Human Spirit*, John Hopkins University Press, 1993.

Chandler, David, *Voices from S-21, Terror and History in Pol Pot's Prison*, University of California Press, 1999.

Chang, Jung and Jon Halliday, *Mao: The Unknown Story*, Knopf, 2005.

Charles, H. Robert, *The Last Man Out: Surviving the Burma-Thailand Death Railway, A Memoir*, Zenith Press, 2006.

Clendinnen, Inga, *Reading the Holocaust*, Text Publishing, 1998.

Cokinos, Christopher, *Hope is the Thing with Feathers, a Personal Chronicle of Vanished Birds*, Penguin, 2009.

Colmache, G.A., *Under Spell of Dark Powers; or, the Gates of Machecoul*, Ward, Loc & Company.

Conquest, Robert, *Harvest of Sorrow: Soviet Collectivization and the Terror-Famine*, Oxford University Press, 1986.

Cruvellier, Thierry, *The Master of Confessions*, Ecco, 2015.

Davis, Wade, *Into the Silence: The Great War, Mallory and the Conquest of Everest*, Vintage, 2012.

Daws, Gavan, *Holy Man, Father Damien of Molokai*, University of Hawaii Press, 1973.

Day, A. Grove and Carl Stroven, *A Hawaiian Reader, Volume I*, Mutual Publishing, 1959.

Dower, John W., *Cultures of War: Pearl Harbor, Hiroshima, 9-11, Iraq*, Norton, 2010.

Dyer, Geoff, *The Missing of the Somme*, Vintage Books, 1994.

Ehle, John, *Trail of Tears: The Rise and Fall of the Cherokee Nation*, Anchor Books, 1988.

Erwin, Douglas, *Extinction*, Princeton University Press, 2006.

Farmer, Sarah, *Martyred Village: Commemorating the 1944 Massacre at Oradour-sur-Glane*, University of California Press, 1999.

Feitlowitz, Marguerite, *A Lexicon of Terror: Argentina and the Legacies of Torture*, Oxford University Press, 1998.

Foucault, Michel, *Discipline & Punishment, The Birth of the Prison*, Vintage Books, 1995.

Fromkin, David, *A Peace to End All Peace*, Avon, 1989.

Fussell, Paul, *The Great War and Modern Memory*, Oxford, 1975.

George, Don, ed., *Tales from Nowhere*, Lonely Planet Publications, London, 2006.

Gilson, Etienne, *Heloise and Abelard*, Henry Regnery Company, 1951.

Ginzburg, Evgenia, *Into the Whirlwind*, Harvill Press, 1967.

Gottesman, Evan, *Cambodia After the Khmer Rouge*, Yale University Press, 2002.

Graves, Robert, *Goodbye to All That*, Anchor Books, 1998.

Guéhenno, Jean, *Diary of the Dark Years, 1940–1944*, Oxford University Press, 2014.

Hachiya, Michihiko, *Hiroshima Diary*, University of North Carolina Press, 1955.

Hajari, Nisid, *Midnight's Furies: The Deadly Legacy of India's Partition*, Houghton Mifflin Harcourt, June, 2015.

Hallam, Tony, *Catastrophes and Lesser Calamities: The Causes of Mass Extinctions*, Oxford, 2004.

Hanson, Neil, *Unknown Soldiers: The Story of the Missing of the First World War*, Vintage Books, 2007.

Harris, Ruth, *Lourdes: Body and Spirit in the Secular Age*, Viking, 1999.

369

Hart, William, *Evil: A Primer: A History of a Bad Idea from Beelzebub to Bin Laden*, Thomas Dunne Books, 2004.

Hartley, Aidan, *The Zanzibar Chest: A Story of Life, Love and Death in Foreign Lands,* Riverhead Books, 2003.

Hébras, Robert, *Oradour-sur-Glane: The Tragedy Hour by Hour*, Les Chemins de la Mémoire.

Hedges, Chris, *War Is a Force that Gives Us Meaning*, Anchor Books, 2003.

Hersey, John, *Hiroshima*.

Hitchens, Christopher, *Arguably*.

Holmes, Richard, *Acts of War: The Behaviour of Men in Battle*, Cassell, 1985.

Horne, Alistair, *The Price of Glory, Verdun, 1916*, 1962.

Horne, Alistair, *Seven Ages of Paris*, Vintage, 2004.

Hough, Henry Beetle, 'The Heath Hen's Journey to Extinction', 1792–1933, Dukes County Historical Society, 1933.

Hunt, Tom, *Cliffs of Despair: A Journey to Suicide's Edge*, Random House, 2008.

Gebler, Carlo, *The Siege of Derry*, Abacus, 2005.

Gilbert, Martin, *The Somme, Heroism and Horror in the First World War*, Henry Holt and Company, 2006.

Gimlette, John, *At The Tomb of the Inflatable Pig: Travels through Paraguay*, Alfred E. Knopf, 2004.

Glover, Jonathan, *Humanity: A Moral History of the Twentieth Century*, Yale University Press, 2001.

Jahoda, Gloria, *The Trail of Tears, The Story of the American Indian Removals, 1813–1855*, Holt, Rinehart and Winston, 1975.

Johnson, Steven, *The Ghost Map: The Story of London's Most Terrifying Epidemic, and How It Changed Science, Cities, and the Modern World*, Riverhead Books, 2006.

Joiner, Thomas, *Why People Die By Suicide*, Harvard University Press, 2005.

Joiner, Thomas, *Myths about Suicide*, Harvard University Press, 2010.

Keegan, John, *The Face of Battle*, Viking Press, 1976.

Kelly, John, *The Great Mortality: An Intimate History of the Black Death, The Most Devastating Plague of all Time*, Harper Perennial, 2005.

Keniston, Allen, 'The Last Years of the Heath Hen', Duke's County Historical Society.

Kurlansky, Mark, *Salt: A World History*, Walker Publishing Company, 2002.

Larkin, Emma, *Finding George Orwell in Burma*, Penguin Books, 2004.

Lengel, Edward G., *To Conquer Hell: The Meuse-Argonne, 1918, The Epic Battle That Ended the First World War*, Henry Holt and Company, 2008.

Liebow, Averill A., *Encounter with Disaster: A Medical Diary of Hiroshima, 1945*, Norton, 1970.

Lindqvist, Sven, *Exterminate all the Bastards: One Man's Odyssey into the Heart of Darkness and the Origins of European Genocide*, The New Press, 1992.

Levi, Primo, *The Drowned and the Saved*, Vintage Books, 1989.

Lewis, Paul H., *Guerrillas and Generals: The 'Dirty War' in Argentina*, Praeger, 2002.

Logevall, Fredrik, *Embers of War: The Fall of an Empire and the Making of America's Vietnam*, Random House, 2014.

London, Jack, 'The Lepers of Molokai'.

Maury, Richard, *The Saga of Cimba: A Journey from Nova Scotia to the South Seas*, Narrative Press, 2001.

Mendelsohn, Daniel, *The Lost: A Search for Six of Six Million*, Harper Collins, 2006.

Montefiore, Simon Sebag, *Jerusalem: The Biography*, Knopf, 2011.

Moorehead, Caroline, *A Train in Winter: A Story of Resistance, Friendship and Survival in Auschwitz*, Harper Perennial, 2012.

Moorhouse, Geoffrey, *Hell's Foundations: A Social History of the Town of Bury in the Aftermath of the Gallipoli Campaign*, Henry Holt and Company, 1992.

Morris, Jan, *Journeys*, Oxford University Press, 1884.

Morrow, Lance, *Evil: An Investigation*, Perseus Books, 2003.

Nalaielua, Henry and Sally-Jo Bowman, *No Footprints in the Sand, A Memoir of Kalaupapa*, Watermark Publishing, 2006.

Némirovsky, Irène, *Suite Française*, Vintage, 2007.

Nicolson, Adam, *Why Homer Matters*, Picador, 2015.

O'Shea, Stephen, *Back to the Front: An Accidental Historian Walks the Trenches of World War I*, Walker and Company, 1996.

Pellegrino, Charles, *The Last Train from Hiroshima*, Henry Holt, 2010.

Pollard, Justine and Howard Reid, *The Rise and Fall of Alexandria: Birthplace of the Modern World*, Penguin Books, 2006.

Ponchaud, François, *Cambodia: Year Zero*, Holt, Rinehart and Winston, New York, 1977.

Radice, Betty, Ed., *The Letters of Abelard and Heloise*, Penguin Books, 1974.

Raup, David M., *Extinction: Bad Genes or Bad Luck*, W.W. Norton, 1991.

Rosenbaum, Ron, *Explaining Hitler*, Harper Perennial, 1999.

Scarry, Elaine, *The Body in Pain: The Making and Unmaking of the World*, Oxford University Press, 1985.

Schneidman, Edwin S., *The Suicidal Mind*, Oxford, 1996.

Sloan, Bill, *The Ultimate Battle: Okinawa 1945*, Simon and Schuster, 2007.

Seiden, Richard H., 'Where Are They Now? A Follow-up Study of Suicide Attempters from the Golden Gate Bridge.'

Stamp, Gavin, *The Memorial to the Missing of the Somme*, Profile Books, London, 2006.

Strangio, Sebastian, *Hun Sen's Cambodia*, Yale University Press, 2014.

Swain, Jon, *River of Time*, Berkeley, 1999.

Theroux, Paul, *Dark Star Safari: Overland from Cairo to Cape Town*, Houghton Mifflin, 2003.

Tritle, Lawrence A., *From Melos to My Lai: War and Survival*, Routledge Press, 2000.

Tully, John, *A Short History of Cambodia: from Empire to Survival*, Allen & Unwin, Crow's Nest, Australia, 2005.

Vizetelly, Ernest Alfred, *Bluebeard*, Chatto and Windus, London.

Walker, Stephen, *Shockwave: Countdown to Hiroshima*, Harper Perennial, 2005.

Walvin, James, *The Zong: A Massacre, the Law & the End of Slavery*, Yale University Press, 2011.

Watson, Lyall, *Dark Nature: A Natural History of Evil*, Harper Perennial, 1996.

Weatherford, Jack, *Genghis Khan and the Making of the Modern World*, Three Rivers Press, 2004.

Wilson, A.N., *London: A History*, Modern Library, 2006.

Wilson, Thomas, *Blue-Beard: A Contribution to History and Folk-lore*, Benjamin Blom, Inc., 1971.

Wright, Lawrence, *The Looming Tower, Al-Qaeda and the Road to 9/11*, Knopf, 2006.

Wright, Robert, *Nonzero: The Logic of Human Destiny*, Vintage, 2001.

Acknowledgements:

In the autumn of one's life, it is good to look back and remember those who have most added hope and beauty to the living of it. My list would be too long to publish here, but I do wish to thank my mother, Mickie Cook, for giving me everything a great mother should give a son, freedom and self-confidence, along with all the basic necessities of life. Thanks, Mom.

As a friend, I could not ask for better than Otto Penzler, not only a fabulous companion, but a tireless supporter of my work through the years. Thanks, Otto.

In Australia: One night in Adelaide, Anthony Cheetham was the first to give his full support to this book. Thank you, Anthony.

In London, Jane Wood, at Quercus, is all that could be asked for in an editor. Her support for *Tragic Shores* never wavered. Thank you, Jane.

In Paris, Marie-Caroline Aubert has given her all to bring my work to her fellow countrymen. Thank you. Marie-Caroline.

Every life confronts crises, and I have weathered mine with the help of many wonderful friends. You know who you are. Thank you from the bottom of my heart.